D0641142

$26.95
B/PINKEL
Pinkel, Gary
The 100-yard journey

9/17

BRUMBACK LIBRARY
215 WEST MAIN STREET
VAN WERT, OHIO 45891

The 100-Yard Journey

A Life in Coaching and Battling for the Win

The 100-Yard Journey

A Life in Coaching and Battling for the Win

Gary Pinkel
with Dave Matter

TRIUMPH
BOOKS

B PINKEL

Copyright © 2017 by Gary Pinkel and Dave Matter

No part of this publication may be reproduced, stored in a retrieval system, or transmitted in any form by any means, electronic, mechanical, photocopying, or otherwise, without the prior written permission of the publisher, Triumph Books LLC, 814 North Franklin Street, Chicago, Illinois 60610.

Library of Congress Cataloging-in-Publication Data available upon request

This book is available in quantity at special discounts for your group or organization. For further information, contact:

Triumph Books LLC
814 North Franklin Street
Chicago, Illinois 60610
www.triumphbooks.com

Printed in U.S.A.

ISBN: 978-1-62937-465-9

Design by Sue Knopf

Photos courtesy of the author unless otherwise indicated

Contents

Foreword *by Nick Saban* vii

Introduction. xi

1 Akron: My Ohio Roots 1

2 Kent State: My Alma Mater 21

3 Seattle: Winning & Learning in Washington. . . .39

4 Toledo: Head Coach, Day One. 61

5 Mizzou: Building a Winning Culture 89

6 Mizzou: Competing for Championships 121

7 Mizzou: Reload & Redeem 153

8 Mizzou: Welcome to the SEC. 177

9 2015: Season of Change. 209

10 Retirement: A New Direction 235

Appendix 249

Acknowledgments. 253

Foreword

My friendship with Gary Pinkel began when we were teammates on the Kent State University Golden Flashes football team in the early 1970s. Gary was a great friend in college, and we have remained steadfast and loyal friends throughout our coaching careers. The first thing that stood out when I met Gary was the class and presence he exuded, albeit in a very unassuming way. He was actually a year behind me; however, from the get-go, he demonstrated a leadership quality that set him apart from all of the other guys on the team. Gary was a very talented tight end, yet he worked harder than any player on the roster and, without meaning to, set a standard for our team that we all tried to emulate. Even though I was older, I regarded Gary as someone I could look up to. He was what I wanted to be. Though composed off the field, Gary was a tough, competitive, fearless player on the field and made our team better every time he stepped foot on the turf. Gary was part of the 1972 Mid-American Conference championship team, the one and only for Kent State University, an accomplishment we are both very proud to have achieved under the direction of another one and only, Coach Don James.

It would take volumes to recap the highs (championship season), the lows (Kent State shooting), and everything in between that we shared, however, some of my favorite "Pinkel Stories" stem from our days as graduate assistants. After the conclusion of my playing days in 1972, Coach James asked me to stay on as a graduate assistant. Gary, Jack Lambert, and our team went on to lead the Golden Flashes to a 9–2 record, and, following the 1973 season, Gary was offered a graduate assistant position by Coach James. The GA's role in today's world of football is a walk in the park compared to the time, work, and effort we invested in breaking down film for coaches to evaluate. Nowadays, GAs simply press a button on their computer, a software program breaks down the film, and voila—the cut-ups are on the screen. Gary and I used to have to take turns driving to Pittsburgh every Saturday night after our games just to get the film developed! One of us would make the drive while the other slept. The "sleeper" would then pull an all-nighter breaking down the film into offense, defense, and special teams so each specific set of film was ready for the coaches to view upon arrival to the office early the next morning. We had to do the same thing in the offseason, too—cutting up the plays; placing (and a lot of splicing!); recording each play, down, and distance; and then putting it all on a reel. We're talking celluloid tape here, folks. Brittle, delicate, forever-jamming celluloid tape! Trust me—Gary and I performed many 11th-hour miracles that I'm certain no one in coaching today would even dream of doing! The hours logged and the output of work was incredible; when I think about it today, I'm not sure how we packed it all in! Gary always had a tremendous work ethic, which served him well and, I believe, was paramount to his success at Toledo and Missouri.

Obviously Coach James was a tremendous influence in terms of his organization and philosophy. He cared about us as players and maximized our potential on the field. However, he put a greater emphasis on our personal development, the importance of getting a degree, and our evolution post-KSU. Gary followed that protocol as a player; however, it was during our time as graduate assistants that his real prowess and skill to develop a program and be a good coach became quite evident. He continued to perfect his craft as an assistant coach and coordinator at several stops until 1991, when he took over for me as head coach at the University of Toledo, and was presented yet another challenge in 2001 when he landed the head coaching gig at the University of Missouri. Gary had a brilliant career with the UT Rockets and an equally successful tenure with the Missouri Tigers. In fact, he still owns the record at both schools for all-time wins. There are a lot of similarities between the programs we've built over the years. However, I have no doubt that the successes we have achieved stem from our days under the tutelage and mentorship of Coach Don James.

Gary's story is one everyone should know and illustrates how perseverance, hard work, and dedication can lead to tremendous success while impacting so many student-athletes both on and off the football field. The real takeaway from this book is that Gary accomplished all of these milestones with the utmost class, character, and integrity. As you read this book, I know you will appreciate the message Gary has to deliver while he recounts the trials and tribulations of a truly outstanding college coaching career.

—Nick Saban

Introduction

I NEVER THOUGHT THIS DAY WOULD COME. Coaches don't retire. They get fired. For the first time, the end of my coaching career was in sight. I was leaving on my terms.

It was Monday, November 16, 2015. Our Missouri football team was coming off an emotional win over BYU with two games left in what would be my final season.

I remember walking through the back service entrance of Mizzou Arena as if I were sneaking into a men's basketball game. But this day was different. I've experienced many press conferences that were difficult, emotional, celebratory, and even frustrating. This one seemed like all of the above. Three days earlier, I had announced during an emotional team meeting my plans to retire at the end of the season and revealed that I had been diagnosed with lymphoma in the spring, just days after my 63rd birthday. This was my first chance to speak at length about my decision. Gathered in a small room off the court were my family members, my wife, daughter, son-in-law, and grandkids. I felt a mixture of relief and loss and hope, but fortunately I was surrounded by their support and love.

The commotion from the Mizzou Arena floor was getting louder and soon it would be time to take our place for the press conference. Like little soldiers, my team of family members took the field wearing their best game faces for what would be the hardest, most emotional play of my career. Our season wasn't over, but that day felt like my chance to close a chapter on a 15-year run that delivered more triumphant wins than crushing losses and more historical milestone moments than I ever could have imagined when I came to Mizzou after the 2000 season and inherited a program with two winning seasons in 17 years.

I saw it all in those 15 years at Mizzou. We took the program to heights unseen in decades: 10 bowl games over 12 seasons, five division championships, and four conference championship games in eight years. We maneuvered through conference realignment. We encountered challenges that aren't included in any coach's manual. What happens when one of your players dies during a workout? What happens when one of your players says he's gay? What happens when your players stage a boycott in the middle of the season to save a person's life? Through it all, we turned the University of Missouri into a nationally respected football program that won games, graduated players, and produced young men who became successful professionals in all walks of life and, most importantly, good husbands and fathers.

When I decided to retire, I didn't have a plan for how I'd approach the rest of my life. I certainly didn't think about publishing a book. This project started to take shape in the fall of 2016, then rapidly developed into the story of my life and career in football.

These pages start in Akron, Ohio, where my life began, and tell the story of my family, my parents, and my siblings, who inspired me as I discovered football, first as a game and then a profession. My story takes you through coaching stops at Kent State, Bowling Green, and Washington, where I'd earn my doctorate in coaching from my mentor Don James, whose philosophies would shape the program I'd later bring to Toledo and, eventually, Mizzou.

Coach James' program became my program when I became a head coach. One of Coach James' traditions that I adopted was his

Thursday speeches. Every week during the season, Coach James would pick a theme and deliver a speech to the team on Thursday before practice, just as we entered the last 48-hour stretch to game day. I did the same each week at Toledo and Mizzou, and I saved every speech from my 25 years as a head coach. Between chapters in this book, you will find excerpts of my speeches from some of our signature games.

We didn't capture a national championship at Missouri, but we took hold of a down-and-out program and accomplished what few people thought was possible, building Mizzou into a sustained winner on a national scale. "You can't win at Missouri," I was told when I took the job in 2000. Well, we did—and so much more.

The
100-Yard
Journey

A Life in Coaching
and Battling for the Win

1

Akron: My Ohio Roots

MY CAREER IN FOOTBALL HAS TAKEN ME ALL OVER THE COUNTRY, but I've been lucky to have only called a few places home. The first was Akron, Ohio.

In the early 20th century, Akron became known as the "Rubber Capital of the World," as the tire industry's four major manufacturers set up their headquarters in the northeast Ohio city along the Little Cuyahoga River. Rubber brought my parents there in 1952.

The Pinkel side of the family came to America from Usingen, Germany, and my father, George Pinkel, grew up during the Great Depression in Buffalo, New York. I never met his father—he left my grandmother, Margaret, before I was born—but my dad would later say the best thing his father ever did was sign for him to join the Navy when he dropped out of high school. My dad was stationed in Guam for the final stages of World War II, and when his tour ended, he moved back home where he married my mother, Gay Robbins, an acquaintance and Buffalo native. (Among the countless things my mom gave me was my middle name, Robin, from her maiden name.

She thought it would toughen me up, I like to joke. A boy named Sue? No, a boy named Robin.)

The war was over, but my dad wanted to continue his service, so he joined the Marine reserves when the Korean War broke out. He had just started a family, so he was able to serve stateside at Parris Island. Their first child, my sister Kathy, was born in 1949.

By then, my dad started looking for a new career path. George Pinkel had so many skills. He learned drafting in high school. He had the hands of an artist and could write in calligraphy. He also had an incredible curiosity when it came to technology. He built TVs and radios from scratch. He could take anything apart and put it back together. In other words, he was everything I am not. There are days I struggle to manage the remote control or the apps on my iPhone.

My dad used all those skills on his base in Guam, but once the war ended, he was ready for a job in the civilian world. At the time, my mom's mother, Alice, whom we called Nana, wrote letters to some companies on my dad's behalf. The tire and automobile industries were booming in the post-war economy. One of those companies she contacted was General Tire, one of the four tire titans in Akron. Nana came through, and my dad landed a job in the sales division. We were off to Akron. I say "we" because the Buffalo family of three was about to become the Akron party of four. My mom was pregnant during the move to Ohio. I'd join the Pinkels on April 27, 1952.

• • •

We settled into a neighborhood called Firestone Park—it's all about tires in Akron—where we lived for four years until we moved to a nearby part of town, Castle Homes, a new neighborhood in the southern part of Summit County. We moved into a new home at 1102 Winston Street, a one-story, three-bedroom house that sat on the corner of a tree-lined suburb, just a few blocks from the Ohio and Eerie Canal. I would call that house home until I moved to college. In 1958, our family got bigger when my brother Greg came along.

Most people in the neighborhood worked for one of the tire companies. We lived a typical middle-class American experience. Our neighborhood was friendly and safe. We played in our yards and parks with our friends and rarely thought about locking the doors at night. I'd often say we lived in "la la land" and had a far more idyllic childhood than many of my players experienced before they had the chance to play college football.

Years later, when I would have players over to my house for what we called crossover dinners, I'd tell them, "I'm going to be honest, guys. I came from a much better situation than a lot of you. My mom and dad loved me. I knew they loved me. They cared for me and my sister and brother. It was a really, really good home environment."

It was important for me to recognize how blessed we were as kids—and just as important to realize not everyone came from such a fortunate background.

One summer my parents splurged and bought a $50 family membership to the local neighborhood beach club where we could entertain ourselves all day. We'd swim in the lake, play volleyball, play bocce, throw horseshoes, and deal hands of euchre for hours. Some days our parents would drop us off at the club. Other days, Greg would hop in a wagon and Kathy and I would take turns pulling him down the street, the three of us off to spend a summer day without a care in the world.

By the time Kathy was in high school and I was in junior high, our mom went back to school and enrolled in a yearlong program to become a licensed practical nurse. My mom always wanted to become a nurse, and once we were old enough to take care of ourselves she had the chance to pursue her dream. With my dad at work and mom at school—she'd later work at a local hospital, then a doctor's office close to home—we were left to fend for ourselves during those days of summer.

But it was good for our family. My mom was able to add some income to the household—before that, my dad had a second job in the evenings, working a few nights a week at a local hardware store —but it also gave Kathy, Greg, and me some sense of independence. We grew close as kids. I looked up to my big sister—and so much more years later when our family changed forever.

• • •

It was my parents who first taught me the value of hard work. When I was about eight years old I wanted to buy a boat. The canal was about 50 yards from my house, just down the street. My buddy had a seven-foot long flat boat that he'd play with in the canal. I wanted that boat. I wanted it bad. He said he'd sell it to me for $10. I was $10 short.

"Mom, can I have 10 bucks for a boat?"

"You want a boat," she said, "then go get a job."

A job? I was eight!

But here's one of the great and many lessons my mom taught me. While I pouted about not having the 10 bucks to buy the boat, she worked out an arrangement with the neighbors across the street. They agreed to pay me to do their yard work. I had to clean out their shrubs and perform other jobs around the yard. The neighbors paid me $10 for the work. That boat was mine.

I have no idea whatever happened to that boat, but those are the stories you remember that shape your childhood. My other friends' parents probably would have just handed them the cash. That's not how the Pinkels operated. We had to work to earn.

Around eighth grade, my parents gave me an allowance every two weeks. It wasn't much, but it was all about developing a work ethic. In high school, I started working at Young's Hotel and Restaurant, an Akron landmark out on Manchester Road. It was a local treasure that first opened as a tavern in the 1850s. It had a big blue sign out front: Delicious Chicken, Tasty Tender Steaks. For years, I bussed tables, washed dishes, and handled any handyman task they asked me to do. I'd work three nights a week, every week, December through July, from the end of football season in the winter to the start of preseason camp in late summer.

I also worked during summers in college, unlike today's players, who stay on campus and spend the summer preparing for the season and taking classes to advance their degrees. Not for me in the 1970s. I came home from Kent State each summer and managed a variety of jobs. One summer, I ran a jackhammer for a bridge crew. I installed cable TV to houses around Akron—until I drilled a hole where there wasn't supposed to be a hole and was kindly reassigned by the cable company. One year I drove a Coca-Cola truck and made deliveries to businesses all over Akron. I knew my route forward and backward, but one day I had a stop at a local bank. It was the end of the day, so I was hauling less cargo than I had in the morning. I came across an overhang at the bank that I figured I would have no trouble clearing. Oops. The truck was sitting higher with its lighter load and, sure enough, I scraped the roof of the truck pretty good against the bank. When I got back to the office, my secret was out. "Gary, I heard you ran into a bank?" That was my last summer delivering soda.

Another summer I worked for an electric company and put together motors on an assembly line. All day long, whizzing and whirring one piece of machinery into another. Hour after hour, day after day. I had great admiration for the people doing those jobs, but I thought I'd go crazy.

My summer jobs taught me plenty about the value of hard work, responsibility, self-sufficiency, and teamwork. But they also motivated me to chase my dreams. I saw adults working those hard jobs on the bridge crew, on the assembly line, on the delivery routes.

The one conclusion I had coming out of high school was I would find a career that made me happy.

• • •

In our home, church was important for our family. My dad was raised Catholic and my mom was Presbyterian, but my dad agreed that we'd worship at a Presbyterian church, Firestone Park Presbyterian. (Years later, my parents would divorce and remarry, my mom to a Catholic and my dad to a Presbyterian.) We went to church all the time, whether I wanted to or not. God was important in our lives and so was prayer. As I grew up, I usually kept my faith private. It wasn't something I displayed outwardly. I'm not one of the Righteous Brothers, but certainly faith and prayer were important to me, because of my parents. Without my commitment to the Good Lord I think my life would have been significantly different, in a negative way. I have been blessed.

Politics weren't a big deal in our home, though my mom favored Republicans yet my dad was a Democrat. She and some friends in the neighborhood campaigned for Richard Nixon when he ran for president, but I don't remember there being much discussion around the dinner table. There wasn't much discussion about the Vietnam War around the house either—or it just wasn't on my radar yet. My dad was a law-and-order guy because of his military background. He respected the rule of law as the backbone of our society.

But my parents always talked about virtues. The golden rule, "Do unto others as you would have them do unto you," was a big thing with my mom. It wasn't once a month or once every couple months you heard this from her. It was all the time, especially if one of us got into trouble for something. I don't know how many times I heard, "Gary, if you don't have anything nice to say, keep your mouth shut." I heard that one a thousand times. When she got mad at me, that was her adjusted golden rule.

"Respect all people all the time," she would tell us. "No matter what color they are. White, black, rich, poor, fat, skinny, whatever. You respect all people."

When I was about eight years old, I was over at a friend's house. Some of the neighbor kids had been using the N-word. Well, that was not something you said or heard in my house. This was 1960. Society was going through all kinds of changes at the time and for decades to come. One of my neighbors heard me use the N-word and it got back to my parents.

I got home that day and my mom asked me if what she heard was true. At that point, I knew I was in trouble. I told her, "Yes, I did. Some of my friends were saying it, so I said it, too."

I didn't get any sympathy points for being honest. She took me right into the bathroom and got a washcloth and a bar of soap. She lathered that thing up until the suds were bubbling off the fabric. She stuck it into my mouth and turned it and turned it and turned it—almost until I threw up. She got right up in my face. "You don't ever, ever say that word again. Words like that will never come out of your mouth again. We respect everyone and you will, too, for the rest of your life."

I didn't get in a lot of trouble growing up, but that was a moment that stuck with me forever. That's how my parents brought us up. You never followed the crowd. You never let people talk you into doing something you know is wrong. My mom would always say, "You bring your friends up to your level. You don't go down to theirs." When I got older and went away to college, I probably wasn't very fun because I never forgot what my mom taught me.

This one stuck with me, too, from my mom: "If you're around a bunch of friends and they're talking about someone who isn't there, guess who they're talking about when you're not around? You." For me, that was profound. There's a lot of gossip in college coaching, but my mom knew better long before I started my career.

My dad's influence was also profound, and I'd share this with my players: "You're going to have many, many friends, but you're going to be fortunate if you can count your really, really good friends on one hand." I always come back to that message. For me, trust is so important, in life and coaching. Knowing who you can trust and who you can't trust is a message that rang true several times during my coaching career.

• • •

From what I remember growing up, my mom never participated in sports. My dad ran track in high school, but otherwise he wasn't a star athlete. But as long as I can remember I was interested in sports—and my parents always encouraged me to pursue what interested me. I played little league baseball at a young age as a pitcher and center fielder. When I was eight, I joined my first pee-wee football team. We played at Hamlin Field in Akron, where my dad helped build the broadcast booth and set up all the speakers at the field. My thigh pads drooped down to my knees and my knee pads hit around my shins. My mom played the role of equipment manager as efficiently as she ran our house. She would buy us jeans and tell us to roll them up so in two years they'd fit. Same thing with football pants. She'd buy them large enough to account for my growth. "They'll fit eventually," she'd tell me.

Football in that region of northeast Ohio was ingrained in the culture. So many great coaches came from the state of Ohio. Bo Schembechler was from nearby Baberton. Ara Parseghian was from Akron. Woody Hayes came from Clifton. Don Shula, Paul Brown, Don James, Chuck Noll. They were all from Ohio. We also had Bob Stoops, Les Miles, Urban Meyer, and Jim Harbaugh. The state had the Cleveland Browns and later the Cincinnati Bengals and eight Division I college teams. We loved our football in Ohio. In 1963, the Pro Football Hall of Fame opened in Canton, just 20 miles away from our house in Akron.

I loved the sport, especially the team aspect and camaraderie that developed within the team. When we weren't in pads playing on the field, we were in the backyards around our neighborhood playing football for hours and hours. I was usually the quarterback.

I dabbled in other sports, including baseball and basketball. During one baseball season, I came home and told my mom I was going to quit. I was probably 11. She looked at me straight in the face and said, "You're not quitting. You don't start something and not finish. After the season if you don't want to play next year, that's okay. But quitting isn't an option." That was such a great lesson to learn.

I played a little basketball, too, but I had to work so much during the school year that by the time I got to high school, football was my only sport.

Every summer my dad would take me to a couple Cleveland Indians games. In the fall, we'd catch a few Cleveland Browns games. Some summers we'd make the 45-minute drive to Hiram College where the Browns held their training camp every year. One year, I'll never forget. I must have been in middle school, and my dad and I were the only fans on the field after the Browns' practice. Here comes Jim Brown, the legendary running back. We said hello and the great Jim Brown put his hand on my shoulder as he walked by. *The* Jim Brown! I knew all the players on the team. Milt Plum at quarterback, Gary Collins at wide receiver. I was touched with football fever, and my passion for the sport would grow with frequent father and son visits to Canton to visit the Hall of Fame. Years later I'd have another amazing experience at a Browns game that strengthened my love for the game.

Back then, dads were the disciplinarians of the house and usually worked the long hours. The moms kept the house in order, though my dad always helped with the laundry and the ironing, which was probably unique for that generation. My dad and I were close, but during that era, feelings weren't always communicated.

But over time, something changed, and about five years before he died in 2010, my dad started telling me he loved me. On the phone he would say it. In person he'd say it. I'd pull the phone away from my ear and stare at it, like, "Where the heck is this coming from?" But it was a profound moment in my life to learn and feel my dad's love.

I tell my three kids I love them, much more so in the last 10 years, but back when I was a kid, I didn't hear my dad say that out loud. Our relationship really developed later in his life, and that was important to me.

My dad was never one to pat me on the back. He was happy for my success in football, but the sun didn't rise and shine because I was a good player.

In 1973, I played my final college football game at Kent State, a home game against Central Michigan. We won the game 28–7. Back at my apartment after the game, I was in my bedroom changing clothes when my dad walked into my room. He just wrapped his arms around me and sobbed and sobbed. This went on for five minutes. He said, "Thank you, Gary. I'm so proud of you. Just so proud of you." I was blown away. He was never like that, but it was such a personal, touching moment for me. My mother and I had a very special relationship. She was about tough love. She was about preparing me for life after high school. She was demanding! She always held me accountable for my actions. Most importantly, she loved me and communicated that to me daily. I loved her so much. What a wonderful mother I had.

Years later, I recruited a quarterback out of Texas, Chase Daniel, who helped take our program to new heights at Missouri. In his bathroom and bedroom at his parents' home in Southlake, Texas, he had all these positive sayings posted all over the walls.

He saw those messages every day and it's how he lived his life. My parents didn't plaster their wisdom all over our home on Winston Street, but their virtues and lessons had the same result. They raised us a certain way, and we became the adults they helped shape.

• • •

When I was around the age of nine and when my older sister was about 12, she started having trouble walking. I wasn't paying much attention at the time and really hadn't noticed that my parents had become concerned. When my sister got to high school she wanted to join the cheerleading team but her body just wouldn't cooperate. She didn't have the coordination. When Kathy was 14, doctors diagnosed her with a rare neurological disorder. Her symptoms persisted and became progressively worse. As time went on she lost her ability to walk. But it never stifled her spirit. She fought so hard to get from place to place but never complained about her challenges.

The more her condition deteriorated, the more protective I became. I was her guardian, at least in my eyes. People would stare at her when she struggled to walk and it would make my blood boil. I would stare people down when they looked at her. How dare you stare at my sister? She's fighting like hell just to move her body. Don't you dare stare at her. It made me angry.

Nothing pissed me off more than when I saw people park in handicap spots who didn't need it. Twice I almost fought someone over disrespecting the sign and the law. One time when I was in college I saw a guy park in a handicapped spot. No sticker, no tag, clearly no disability. He got out of his car. I approached him and said, "Hey, pal, move it." He said, "I'm not moving it."

"My sister can't walk," I told him, firmly. "She could drive here and need that spot." Other times I had to cool my temper when I saw such disrespect.

Years later at Mizzou, I had a couple players park illegally in handicap spots. The word got out pretty quick among the players. It's safe to say it didn't happen again. All through my life I've felt an overwhelming compassion for people with disabilities.

After high school Kathy enrolled at Kent State and later transferred to Wright State, a school in the suburbs of Dayton. At 19 she started using a cane in college. Later at Wright State, she moved to a wheelchair. She resisted for years and dreaded the day she had to use the chair. It was a small campus with just a few buildings, but they were connected by underground tunnels, which made it more conducive for wheelchairs. The wheelchair brought her great relief. Suddenly she was able to get around so much easier. In the tunnels, she could zip around from class to class with much less trouble than trying to walk through campus.

At Wright State she met a guy, Greg Grinch. He was from Columbus and had gone to Ohio State out of high school but then enlisted in the Marines during the Vietnam War. After he served his tour of duty, he came back to Ohio and enrolled at Wright State. He got to know my sister and one day she asked him if he liked football. Of course he did. He was from Ohio. She invited him to my spring game at Kent State. It was their first date—the first of many. He is an incredible guy.

• • •

Just like Kathy, I attended Kenmore High School, the public school in our district. By then, football was my game. I had mostly played quarterback throughout pee-wee football, but around junior high I moved to receiver. Why? I could catch better than I could throw. That was about the extent of my skills.

Our head coach was Dick Fortner, who a few years earlier had come from Stow High School in Akron where he won a championship and coached Larry Csonka, the future Hall of Fame fullback for the Miami Dolphins. But in 1963 he came to Kenmore, a program that hadn't produced a winning record in more than a decade. His friends probably told him he was nuts for taking the job—just like my friends told me when I took the coaching job at Missouri.

Coach Fortner was upfront and honest with his players. You could sense he genuinely cared about us. He was also demanding. But you could talk to him like an adult. He wasn't a dictator. He was in his mid-30s when I got to Kenmore, so he was young enough that he could relate to his players but experienced enough that he earned our respect.

My senior year, 1969, he pulled off one of the greatest coaching moves I've ever witnessed. We were getting ready to play Garfield High, our archrival. They were undefeated and loaded with talent. They had Larry Poole, a running back I'd later play with in college who'd play several years in the NFL; Dave Brown, who'd become an All-American cornerback at Michigan and play for two decades in the NFL; Renard and Bernard Harmon, twin brothers, both running backs, who'd also play at Kent State. That year, Garfield had 10 players on the All-City Team. We had two, myself and our quarterback, Eric Schoch. Earlier in the year, Garfield had trounced us 34–0. In nine regular-season games they allowed only 14 points—and scored 298.

That fall, we recovered, made it into the playoffs, and clinched a spot in the city championship game, the Turkey Day Game, played every year on Thanksgiving morning at the Rubber Bowl in Akron. Garfield had kicked our butt the year before and earlier in the year. The combined score in those games was 76–6.

But Coach Fortner knew our team. He believed in us, maybe when nobody else in the city of Akron had any faith we could win the game. He knew he had to do something to make us believe the same. That week before the game, he had all of us over to his house. He lived just outside of Akron. We come over for dinner and then he turned on his 16-millimeter projector. We started watching footage of our last game against Garfield. By the time we were done, every player in that room was convinced Garfield didn't beat us. We lost the game because of our mistakes. We were a better team than we played that day—and the film didn't lie. Coach Fortner was a genius when it came to motivation. He made us believe we could win. It wasn't going to be about Xs and Os. It was all about confidence. My buddies and I walked out of there convinced we were going to win the game—because it wasn't about Garfield. It was about us playing our best game. This was a lesson I learned and used in coaching for years to come. We didn't have to worry about all their star players. This was about us, the Kenmore Cardinals. In the week leading up to the game, Coach Fortner put signs in storefront windows up and down Kenmore Boulevard that said, AVERAGE PLAYERS WIN THE BIG GAME.

He was right. We won 21–12. We were city champions, just like he made us believe.

Seeing the impact Coach Fortner had on me and my teammates, I started thinking about my future. Being a high school football coach was tempting and might be fun. I didn't put much thought into it at the time. But I would.

• • •

If I look back on my early years in football and try to trace the steps that led me to coaching, there was a pivotal moment that came a year before we won the championship at Kenmore. My dad took me to the 1968 NFL championship game in Cleveland. The Browns were playing the Colts, and the winner would go to the Super Bowl. It was a few days after Christmas, and my dad got tickets at the last minute. We made the drive to Cleveland and we were walking into the stadium early in the first quarter. A limousine pulls up outside Municipal Stadium and out steps this man wearing a big fur coat and Russian fur hat. I stopped dead in my tracks.

"Dad, Dad, that's Vince Lombardi." I was in absolute awe. He had stepped down from coaching the Packers the previous season but still served as the team's general manager. We're standing right in front of him. Next thing I know, the great Vince Lombardi walks over and introduces himself. Vince Lombardi is talking to me? He puts his arm around my back and starts walking with us to the stadium gates. He asked if I played football. He asked me about my goals. I told him my dream was to play college football and maybe play in the NFL someday. He told me I had to do well in school before anything else. Then he patted me on the back and said, "Good luck, son."

Consciously, at the time, I wasn't thinking about a coaching career that day just because I had met the greatest coach in the world. But that moment and Vince Lombardi's words always resonated with me. To reflect back on that day, and think that down the road I'd get into coaching and have some success, man, it's pretty cool.

• • •

I played well enough my junior and senior years that college recruiters started to pay attention. All the Mid-American Conference schools were interested in me. I visited Miami (Ohio) and thought about playing there. Iowa State out of the Big Eight wanted to sign me. I talked to Michigan and Ohio State, too, but I wasn't really on their radar—and probably rightfully so. I knew I could play at the next level, but I didn't necessarily have the elite size and speed those schools wanted for a receiver.

My decision came down to Miami and Kent State. Both schools offered me a full scholarship. Miami, in Oxford, Ohio, was about three and a half hours away. Kent was 20 miles from my house, just a short trip on Highway 76.

I didn't have that urge to go to school far away. When I was a kid, I was always a homebody. When I'd be out playing with my buddies until 11 at night, they'd stay up and sleep outside in a tent. I'd go home and sleep in my bed. I liked the comfort of home. That held true throughout my coaching career.

Bo Schembechler had just left Miami to take over at Michigan, and the new Miami coach was Bill Mallory. Kent had me concerned because the team hadn't been winning a lot. But they had a fairly new coach, too, in Dave Puddington. In the end, I accepted the scholarship offer from Kent.

• • •

The country was still at war in Vietnam when I was in high school. I turned 18 in the spring of my senior year, so I wasn't eligible for the first draft lottery that took place. There were more lotteries in later years, and I was eligible in 1971. You were assigned a random lottery number 1 through 365 based on your birthday. My number was 124. Fortunately, the highest number called that year was 95. Had I been born on April 26 instead of April 27, my number would have been 45—and I would have been drafted into the military and likely sent to Vietnam. Who knows what direction my life would have taken.

On May 4, 1970, the nation's perspective on the war changed for a lot of people. It was a Monday. I was two weeks away from my graduation from Kenmore. Then, after the summer, I would be off to Kent State. For lunch that day I went to Dairy Queen with my girlfriend. We were in my car eating our sandwiches when a news report started crackling on the radio. There was a shooting at Kent State. Anti-war protesters had been gunned down. The Ohio National Guard had shot into a crowd of protestors on the school's campus. Yes, the shooting had occurred at the college I had just agreed to attend in the fall.

I went back to Kenmore for an afternoon college composition course. News reports had started to come out from Kent. During class, our teacher picked up a piece of chalk and wrote on the board: "National Guard 4, Students 0."

Four protesters had been shot and killed during the rally. That day, my teacher said Kent State would struggle to recover from this for at least 10 years. I looked at the guy like, "Come on. This is a tragedy, but we'll overcome this." Every class we had the rest of the day, that's all we talked about, just trying to sort out why it all happened.

Naturally, people asked me if I would change my plans to attend Kent. I had just signed my national letter of intent, and now, Kent's campus was the stage for the biggest story in the country. Maybe it was time to reconsider my future.

Toledo vs. Purdue

September 6, 1997

Toledo, Ohio

In the season opener of my seventh season at Toledo, the Big Ten team visited the Glass Bowl and I made sure my team understood nobody gave us a chance to win. In the speech, I read excerpts from recent interviews with Purdue coach Joe Tiller and several players. None of them mentioned their upcoming game at Toledo.

Team Meeting
Thursday, September 4, 3:30 PM

"Does this sound like a team or coach that respects you? There is none. If that doesn't piss you off, you shouldn't be on this team. I'm tired of it! There comes a time in your life where you stand up and say, 'That's it!' We must decide that we will change Purdue's attitude. If we want respect, we kick their ass!"

Final: Toledo 36, Purdue 22

The Boilermakers knew who we were by game's end. The only way to gain respect in games like this is to win—and wins like this are a tradition in the Mid-American Conference. Behind first-year starters at quarterback and tailback, we scored on our first three drives and compiled 280 yards by halftime.

2

Kent State: My Alma Mater

I HAD GIVEN KENT STATE MY WORD, and even after the May 4 shootings, I wasn't worried about attending school there in the fall. Campus had shut down for the rest of the spring and then reopened in the summer. The shootings opened a lot of people's minds about the direction of the country and the support for the Vietnam War, but in my world, I still wanted to play football at my nearby school.

There were always reminders on campus about what took place that spring day. You'd occasionally see a burning flag on campus. On the one-year anniversary of the shootings, I vividly remember sitting in a friend's dorm room watching the National Guard marching around campus. Tensions were high and some people worried there'd be more violence. It was a difficult time on campus. I remember one day walking past the main administration building to get on a bus and there were two guys standing next to the flagpole. I suspected they were going to take it down and possibly burn it. "You guys aren't really going to do that, are you?" I said to them. They just kind of looked at me. I just said, "That's not the right thing to do." They walked away. There were so many different opinions on campus about politics and the war and current events, but I was always just a rule-of-law person. I probably got that from my dad and the influence of his military background. I disagreed with a lot of things, but what's right is right and what's wrong is wrong. My dad fought for that flag and our country.

My freshman year, the students designed T-shirts to show our unity on campus. We all wore those shirts on the one-year anniversary.

The university faced a lot of criticism. Enrollment plunged drastically. As a student body and community we really needed something positive to happen on campus, something the students could rally around, bring people together and help the healing process from the May 4 tragedy.

Nobody figured football would be the solution, at least temporarily.

But first, a coaching change. The NCAA didn't allow freshmen to be eligible to play in games until 1972, so my first year in the football program was essentially a redshirt year. I moved from receiver to tight end and spent most of my time on the scout team.

During my freshman year, Coach Puddington announced he was stepping down after eight games. We were 2–6 with two games to play. He was later quoted as saying part of the reason he left the job was "the prevailing contagious negativity on campus and the community."

"The fatalism around us," he also said, "and the current tendency to politicize every facet in life—even sports—has certainly affected the young men in our program." He finished out the season as we split our final two games, including a 10–8 loss to Miami. The May shootings had rocked our campus, and our coach didn't believe we could recover. We had a new athletic director named Mike Lude who would be responsible for hiring our next coach. Lude would become one of the most successful and respected ADs in the country in his time.

When I first got to Kent, I was so disappointed in the work ethic of the players. Back at Kenmore, we always had a relentless approach to the sport. Coach Fortner created that environment. But that wasn't the case at Kent, which I realized quickly. Maybe I was naïve my first year on campus. I never drank in high school or partied too much, so I was a pretty straight arrow. But all around me I saw a lack of commitment and focus from other players.

That all changed when the school hired Puddington's successor: Donald Earl James, a 38-year-old who had never been a college head coach.

Coach James was another football coach who hailed from the state of Ohio. He played at Massillon High School, a legendary program in a town by the same name just south of Akron. James played quarterback at the University of Miami, Florida, but when he came to Kent State, his coaching background was squarely on the defensive side of the ball. He had been a defensive assistant at Florida State, Michigan, and most recently Colorado, where he worked under head coach Eddie Crowder.

Considering the situation at Kent State, a campus still reeling from the 1970 shootings, Coach James had to be confident in how he was going to manage his program, especially when the outgoing coach made such strong statements about the negativity on campus. Years later in his autobiography, Coach James wrote that people told him he was crazy for taking the Kent State job. They called the place "the graveyard of coaches," he wrote. Coincidentally, Coach Fortner heard the same things about the Kenmore High job. We must have had similar friends because I heard the same things 30 years later.

Coach James wasn't a yeller, but he was serious and always intense, especially in those first few months. We knew at his first team meeting that Coach James meant business. It was like a combat situation. We were instantly going to set the bar much higher than it had been. I was so impressed with everything he stood for. Coach

James changed the culture from the day he arrived. His program was all about discipline, structure, and attention to detail. This would be the foundation for the football program that would define my career.

Our winter conditioning workouts were brutal. Players quit left and right. In our first spring under Coach James we had a teammate who quit in the middle of a particularly grueling practice. He just had enough. He had to walk about 125 yards from the field to the locker room. He started making that walk and peeled off his gear one piece at a time. First his helmet. Then his jersey. We watched him make that long, torturous walk off the field, and by the time he got to the locker room there was a trail of clothes behind him. As much as we laughed about that scene later, we understood not everyone was cut out for Coach James' style.

A couple times I wondered if I wanted to stick around and make all these sacrifices with no guarantees about playing time or the role I'd have on offense. Was I willing to invest everything it was going to take to play for this man? Like everyone else I would have to prove myself. Once Coach James settled in and his plans took root in the program, a remarkable story took place.

◆ ◆ ◆

My sophomore year, I earned the starting job at tight end—but it didn't last. I was demoted to the second unit for the last few games of the season. I was still immature as a competitor. At that level you need to have your mind right. After a brief spell of success, I had started to struggle. I wasn't mature enough to battle through some of these problems, and I wasn't sure how to earn back the starting job.

After the season, our offensive coordinator Dick Scesniak gave me a book called *Psycho-Cybernetics*. It was a best-selling self-help book written in 1960 by Maxwell Maltz, a plastic surgeon. It was all about the mental side of competition and changing your attitude to help achieve your goals. The book changed me and opened my eyes to the importance of mental toughness. It was all about self-control and learning how to think the right way. My attitude and my production climbed to new levels after I read that book.

We finished the 1971 season with a 41–6 loss at Toledo. We had lost the week before to Miami 30–0. It goes without saying we weren't happy with our season.

Coach James gathered us in the locker room after the Toledo game and pointed out to the field where their players were celebrating a perfect regular season. "If you guys want to ever win a championship here, that's what you have to become," he told us. "We can be the team celebrating next year, but we have to work our asses off to get there. If you want to win a championship, that's the team we have to look like."

I could hardly believe he was already thinking ahead to the next season, all but commanding us to watch Toledo players celebrating their special year. That visual aid was supposed to motivate us for the offseason. A lot of the guys embraced this mentality.

For those of us who stuck around and bought into Coach James' program, a special team took shape in 1972. At running back, we had three playmakers from Garfield High: my high school rival, Larry Poole, and Renard and Bernard Harmon. At quarterback, Larry Hayes broke his arm the first game of the season against Akron, so we turned things over to Daryl Hall, a converted tight end, and Greg Kokal, a freshman. It was the first season the NCAA allowed freshmen to play in games. At slot back, we had Gerald Tinker, who earlier that summer won a gold medal at the Munich Olympics on the 400-meter relay team. I came into my own that season and led the team with 34 catches for 477 yards and three touchdowns.

But our biggest star played on defense. John Harold Lambert came to Kent State in 1970, the same year as me, as an unheralded quarterback from Crestwood High School in Matua, Ohio, a town in northeast Ohio that's so small it's considered a village. Now it's known as the home of one of the great linebackers to ever play the game. He went by Jack.

Jack Lambert wasn't exactly destined for stardom. He came to Kent State on a partial football scholarship as a defensive end. He was 6'4" and lanky, not much more than 200 pounds. He'd wanted to play for Miami of Ohio, but they didn't think he was the right size. It would be their loss.

Going into the season, our middle linebacker was Bob Bender, a transfer from Buffalo. He was enormous, a hulking dude who had NFL stamped all over him. But in the middle of preseason camp, Bender quit. Just walked away. We thought maybe Coach James was going to lighten up for his second season so we wouldn't lose any more players. Not at all. He and his staff, "the James Gang" as they became known, only made practices more intense, more grueling. But they had to make a move on defense and needed a middle linebacker. Lambert was too gangly for the position, but they plugged him into the spot.

As for Bender, he vanished from Ohio and became a bodyguard for some English rock band. He'd spend years protecting Mick and Keith and the rest of the Rolling Stones.

As for Lambert, he was unique in so many ways. Taller and skinnier than the prototype middle linebacker, he quickly adapted to the position and became a tackling machine. He played the game with a rare intensity, unlike anyone I'd ever seen on the football field. He was easily the most competitive guy I'd ever call a teammate.

Jack would go on to become a nine-time Pro Bowler and six-time first-team All-Pro with the Pittsburgh Steelers as the centerpiece of the Steel Curtain defense. I had the fortune of playing with him again for a few weeks with the Steelers during the 1973 preseason. (He was a second-round draft pick; I was an undrafted free agent.)

During training camp in Latrobe, Pennsylvania, Jack and I usually walked together to meetings and practices, but one day I couldn't find him anywhere. Finally, I found him in the shower with three different nozzles beating water on his leg. He had bruised his thigh in practice doing the Oklahoma drill against rookie center Mike Webster.

"Jack, what are you doing? We've got to get to practice," I told him.

I didn't know if he was too hurt to practice. His leg looked pretty nasty. He looked me in the eye, water splashing everywhere, and made one thing clear.

"Jack Lambert never gets fucking hurt," he snarled.

I said, "Okay, buddy, I'll see you later." I was out of there. I told a couple trainers they might need to check on Jack, but I doubt he missed a practice.

Jack was famous for missing his front two teeth. When I got into coaching in the late 1970s, just as Jack was at the height of his playing career with the Steelers, I would joke with recruits that I was the guy who first knocked out his teeth. Over time, that line got lost on recruits and it was their dads who appreciated the humor.

One year older than me was a defensive back from West Virginia named Nick Saban. He suffered a serious ankle injury in the eighth game of the season against Northern Illinois and eventually got into coaching. Our paths would cross again.

♦ ♦ ♦

As for our team, we opened the 1972 season 1–3–1. So much for all that offseason motivation. After a narrow win at Bowling Green, we stood 2–3–1. That's when Coach James gathered us for a meeting and said the damnedest thing.

"Okay, we've got five games left," he told us. "We can win a championship if we win these games." We're all looking at each other like, "Seriously? We can win a championship?" This guy was crazy, right? Kent State had never won a conference championship. For the previous 20 years, Bowling Green, Miami (Ohio), and Toledo had taken turns winning the MAC championship—but never Kent State.

Going into the '72 season, we decided we'd stop watching movies on Friday nights before games and instead watch offensive and defensive film to prepare for what we'd face the next day. It was a young team, but we were hungry. We had a huge game at Miami. I played one of the best games of my career, but Lambert made the game-saving plays for us on defense with four straight tackles on the goal line to preserve a 21–10 win. Our team confidence soared with that win. For years Miami had been one of the elite teams in the MAC, but not that day. The next week we hosted Toledo for our regular-season finale. The MAC championship was at stake along with the league's only bowl berth, to the Tangerine Bowl in Orlando, Florida. Toledo had come into the season on a 35-game winning streak. They had dominated our six-team league and beaten Kent five times in a row, including that 41–6 bloodbath the year before.

But on this day, our stadium was full, and the energy was in the air. It was the largest home crowd in the history of Kent State football, with 20,715 at Dix Stadium.

The support from our student body had grown tremendously in the wake of the 1970 shootings. On our campus we had a lot of students who were part of the anti-establishment culture. Some people called them hippies. The guys wore their hair long. They had no interest in sports. But they rallied around our team, especially that year, especially that day when they showed up armed with tangerines, ready to pummel the field to celebrate if we won.

At that point we had won four of our last five games. And then we trounced Toledo 27–9. The fans swarmed the field as the clock ran out and toppled the goalposts. The whole campus and community celebrated the victory, even the hippies. I'll always be convinced that Coach James and our team had a significant impact on the healing process at Kent State. A little pride came back to the university. I was so honored to be part of that experience.

We were the unlikeliest of champions. We were only 6–4–1, the fourth-best overall record in the MAC, but we had the best conference record at 4–1. We were actually outscored by two points during the regular season, but it didn't matter. We were going to a bowl game, the school's first Division I bowl.

In 1968, the Tangerine Bowl in Orlando became affiliated with the Mid-American Conference and matched the MAC champion against the winner of the Southern Conference. Ohio and Toledo represented the MAC the first four years of the agreement. Then, in 1972, it was our turn. We played the University of Tampa, an independent team coached by Earle Bruce. Tampa would only field a team for two more seasons.

The Tangerine Bowl would later be known as the Florida Citrus Bowl, the Capital One Bowl and then, again, the Citrus Bowl. Coincidentally, this bowl was my first as a player and last as a coach in 2014.

But in 1972, Orlando was hardly the metropolis it is now. Walt Disney World had just opened in the fall of 1971. On Christmas Day a bunch of us went to Disney World, but we had to hitchhike from the team hotel. We had to pass about 25 miles of nothing but palm trees to get to the Magic Kingdom. Otherwise, there wasn't much to see.

As for the game itself, I got hurt in the first half after catching a few passes. It was the first time I didn't finish a game. We fell behind 21–0 and rallied to get within a field goal but came up short 21–18. For all of us it was a great experience, especially after all the struggles Kent had gone through for so many years. Tampa had two outstanding players who went on to have success in the NFL: Freddie Solomon, a wide receiver, and John Matuszak, the great Oakland Raiders defensive lineman, a guy who actually began his career at

Mizzou before he got kicked off the team. Matuszak was a wild man, and we knew it going into the game. He'd go on to star in a bunch of movies after his NFL career.

Our offensive guard, Rick Gembar, was going against Matuszak the entire game. Rick thought Matuszak was playing dirty and got really upset because he thought he went for his groin on one play. Rick tried to retaliate and hit Matuszak as hard as he could. That didn't go very well. Matuszak literally chased him off the field.

We came back the next year with a lot of talent. Jack Lambert, Eddie Woodard, and I served as captains and we started the year 7–1. (Jack became a pro football star, but Eddie Woodard made his own mark as a minister.) We dominated all of our MAC opponents— except one. Miami beat us 20–10 and cost us the conference championship. We were ranked No. 19 and Miami was No. 17. It was the first time two nationally ranked MAC teams met in the regular season—and two MAC teams wouldn't be ranked in the same week again for 30 years. I made the All-MAC team and earned honorable mention All-American honors.

My senior year was bittersweet. I had great personal success on the field and our team won nine games, the most in school history. But we fell short of a championship and a bowl game. That didn't erase all that we accomplished the previous season.

• • •

The summer before my senior year I married my college girlfriend, Vicki. Back home in Akron, my family was reliving a nightmare.

My brother Greg was six years younger than me. He absolutely loved sports and got to be a pretty good basketball player. When I was at Kent State, I'd go home and catch his games when I could. Around junior high he started to struggle with his coordination. He just seemed gangly and awkward. I tried to teach him some agility drills I had learned in football. My parents became concerned, but I tried to tell them there was nothing to worry about.

Later on during my senior year, my mom called with devastating news: doctors had diagnosed Greg with the same disease that afflicted my sister. I put my head on the table and cried for 20 minutes. Just sobbed. I was crushed for my brother. Deep down, I was afraid he would have more trouble with the disease than my sister—and he did. Kathy was different. She was so stubborn, so independent, almost to a fault. She learned to cope with the disease because she absolutely refused to let it hold her back. Don't tell Kathy she can't do something, because it's going to be a really short conversation. She never complained about anything, ever. Not once did I hear her say, "Why did this happen to me?"

I wasn't sure if my brother had the same resolve.

Meanwhile, here I am, the middle child, the college football player. I was perfectly healthy. Was I the chosen one? Why was I spared? I felt a tremendous amount of guilt. Mentally, I beat myself up. I had a lot of anger and issues that I had to work out internally over time.

My brother's diagnosis triggered my sister to learn more about her condition. At this point, Kathy had been living with her symptoms for almost 10 years. She had gotten married to her boyfriend Greg, and they started to think about having children. But clearly her condition was hereditary if our brother suffered the same symptoms. She visited the Cleveland Clinic to meet with doctors and undergo genetic testing. My brother would visit there, too. That's when doctors came up with a new diagnosis: hereditary spastic paraplegia, a rare genetic disorder that's defined by progressive weakness and stiffness of the leg muscles.

Their strain of HSP was caused by a recessive gene, meaning Kathy and my brother Greg both inherited the abnormal gene for that trait from both of my parents. Somehow, I didn't inherit the same gene from my mom and dad. If Kathy's husband Greg carried the same recessive gene, they would be at risk of passing it along to their children. On the other hand, the doctors told me and Vicki there was only a miniscule probability that we both carried the same gene. The doctors believed we were okay to have children.

It turned out so were Kathy and her husband. They would have two healthy boys, Andrew and Alex.

After his diagnosis, my brother Greg became involved with wheelchair basketball. I got a chance to see him play a few times. His team was good enough to win a championship. I was so proud of him.

I'd visit him all the time in Akron. He never lost his love for sports. One day he called me and said he'd discovered a basketball player better than Michael Jordan. Of course, I rolled my eyes. "Sure, Greg, what's his name?" I asked him.

"LeBron James," he told me. "He's an eighth grader here in Akron. He's going to be amazing." I guess he got that one right.

As the years passed, Greg's health didn't hold up. In 2005, he suffered a heart attack and died on January 30, one day before his 47th birthday. After the funeral, they gave me his trophy from his wheelchair basketball championship, which still sits in my office, every bit as important as the awards that came during my career.

When I got into coaching and had my own family, I constantly used my siblings as an example to my players and my kids. Don't tell me how tough things are. You want to see tough? Her name is Kathleen. That's my sister. She's tough.

And don't come to me whining about things. I told my players this because I wanted them to recognize they had no right to complain about anything. Get your stuff together, let's get a plan, and fix it. But don't whine and complain. Kathy had every reason in the world to complain about the hand she was dealt—and never once said a word.

I took on the role of Kathy's protector. She was my hero. She is my hero. I've always had so much respect for her. She never wanted your help for anything. "Stop, I'll get it," she's said countless times.

When I first got to Missouri, I started to second-guess my decision to take on such a big challenge. "What the hell are we doing here?" I asked myself at the time. "This is so much worse than I thought it would be." But then I'd catch myself. Don't complain. Don't whine.

I don't think I could have handled my siblings' disease. Whatever they had to fight through the symptoms and the pain and the disappointment I don't think I shared in the same supply. That's why I marvel at Kathy so much. Had the genes not skipped me, I'd like to think I could have lived with her strength and toughness, but she's a stronger person than me. Always has been.

When Drew and Alex were born, she'd cruise around in her wheelchair with them on her lap. "Kathy," I'd insist, "put a seatbelt on that baby." But those boys didn't know any different. They grew up with the wheelchair. And nobody tells Kathy no.

Later in life, two things struck me when I reflected on my brother and sister. One, my three kids being healthy was the most important thing that happened to me in my life. And two, my parents maintained a wonderful home considering the adversity thrown on their backs. They accepted my brother's and sister's condition and dealt with the challenges. My mom probably took on more of the burden, but my dad was very supportive and always there for us. I'm always sensitive to other families who have similar struggles.

Not long after Greg's diagnosis, my parents decided to get divorced. When Kathy's symptoms first surfaced, it put an incredible strain on their relationship. It could be overwhelming at times. Then time passes and the disorder returns, this time with my brother. The trauma of another diagnosis was too much for them to overcome. Both of my grandmothers were divorced from my grandfathers, back in a time when divorce was less common. Our biological grandfathers were never part of the family picture, but fortunately that didn't happen when my parents split up. My mom made sure their relationship remained friendly, even with each other's spouses when they both remarried.

When I got into coaching, they made a point to reunite for my games, my dad with my stepmom, Shirley, and my mom with my stepdad, Bill. Somehow, they made it work. Thanks to football, the games have always brought the family together.

• • •

Before I got into coaching, I gave the sport one last stab as a player. After my senior year, I was disappointed the NFL draft came and went and I wasn't selected. And that was back when the draft lasted 17 rounds, not seven like today. I signed a free agent contract with the Pittsburgh Steelers shortly after the franchise had chosen what might have been the greatest draft class ever assembled. Four of the Steelers' first five picks from that year have been enshrined in the Pro Football Hall of Fame: USC wide receiver Lynn Swann, Alabama A&M receiver John Stallworth, Wisconsin center Mike Webster and, my old teammate, Jack Lambert from Kent State. There was only one other player in the 17-round draft who'd become a Hall of Famer. The Steelers also signed an undrafted safety that year, Donnie Shell, who'd become a five-time Pro Bowler.

In training camp, one of my top competitors at the tight end position was Randy Grossman, an undrafted rookie from Temple. I wouldn't have been crushed if I didn't make the team, because by then I decided I wanted to launch a career in college coaching. Don James and I had talked about becoming a graduate assistant on the Kent State staff once my playing days were over.

After about four weeks of camp and a couple catches in the preseason, I left the team before they could cut me. I just assumed I wasn't in their plans for the season. Plus, I wanted to coach. I really enjoyed my brief time around Chuck Noll and all those star players, including Terry Bradshaw, Franco Harris, Rocky Bleier, plus all those outstanding rookies. Noll reminded me a lot of Coach James. No nonsense. No bullshit.

I left with no regrets. I had a passion to coach. I had a plan.

• • •

Nick Saban got hurt his senior year and he seemed really conflicted about his future. His dad ran a service station back in West Virginia, and for a while, Nick figured it was his duty to return home and work with his dad or open a car dealership.

Coach James had another idea. He encouraged Nick to try coaching. "You can always go back to selling cars," he told him. Who knows, Nick might not have pursued coaching if not for their conversation. Nick was part of the Kent State staff as a graduate assistant in 1973, my senior year.

After I left the Steelers, I returned to Kent State and joined Coach James' staff as a grad assistant alongside Nick Saban.

Saban and I had to monitor the study table and oversee all the freshmen on the team. One night, while the freshmen studied, Nick and I got to talking about our futures. He thought it was important to connect with an established coach and stick it out to help yourself land other opportunities. "You've got to find a good horse and ride it," he told me. We realized back then that coaches get fired a lot, and if you have a family they'll have to make sacrifices in such a volatile job market. I had to ask myself the same question Nick had tackled: "Do I want to coach?" At the time, I had given a lot of thought about being a high school coach. Coach Fortner had been such a positive influence on me in high school, I thought that was one job I could figure out. Then I started thinking about the college coaches I knew. On one hand, they were under fierce pressure to win and recruit. On the other hand, compared to high school coaches, the college coaches don't have to teach during the day. It all started coming into focus. You mean, they'll pay me to do something I absolutely love to do? This wasn't driving a Coke truck or installing cable TV. I decided

I wanted to be a college football coach, just as Nick decided, too. Nick took over as linebackers coach in 1975. As a grad assistant, I was taking classes toward a master's degree in school administration. If coaching didn't work out, I decided I wanted to work in education administration. Fortunately, I never got that chance.

Toledo vs. Penn State

September 2, 2000
State College, Pennsylvania

I didn't want to schedule a game at Penn State, but this became the signature game of my 10 years at Toledo.

Team Meeting
Thursday, August 31, 3:30 PM

"If you asked me what's the one word we could embrace to help achieve our goal, that one word is *accountability*. As individuals you are accountable to the team. Accountability means that your teammates can count on you. If you're accountable, you don't care if the game is home or away. You don't care if it's hot or cold outside. You don't care if you're in the lead or behind. If you're accountable, you have no excuses. If you're accountable, you get your job done for the team. You ask me, 'Coach, what can I do to get a ring?' Be 100 percent accountable to this 2000 team and a lot of good things will happen."

Final: Toledo 24, Penn State 6

The biggest win of my career to date set the stage for a 10–1 season. We controlled the line of scrimmage and outrushed Joe Paterno's Nittany Lions 245 yards to 30 and sacked their quarterback seven times. We led 17–0 at halftime and never looked back. "I'm a little numb right now because I haven't had a chance to relax," I told reporters after the game. "The whole time the clock was running down, I was focusing on not letting our guard down."

3

Seattle: Winning & Learning in Washington

AFTER THE 1974 SEASON, Coach James got an offer he couldn't refuse from the University of Washington and took over as the Huskies head coach. I was still on staff at Kent as a grad assistant, and the school promoted defensive coordinator Denny Fitzgerald to head coach. He had a rough first year and won only four games. After the season I sent Coach James a letter. I didn't care what he paid me. I just wanted to prove myself as a football coach. He wrote back and offered me a part-time job coaching tight ends. Done deal.

I hadn't finished my graduate degree at Kent, but we were off to Seattle.

I wasn't a full-time assistant coach, but the job had one perk: Coach James assigned me to recruit Hawaii. The older coaches on staff must have loved that. The rookie assistant fresh out of college gets the best recruiting gig on the staff. It was considered a part-time job, but Coach James treated my role as a full-time position. It was a lot of time and commitment but not much pay. That was okay. We made it work financially. I loved coaching so much, I didn't worry about anything but doing my job, no matter how many hours it required each day, each week. Years later my players would tell me they wanted to get into coaching, and I'd warn them, "If you want to have success in the coaching world, you have to be prepared for the time commitment." I'm not sure most kids realize what a grind this job becomes.

• • •

My first year on the Washington staff was the rare year the Huskies didn't make a bowl game. We were 6–5, third place in the Pacific 8 at 5–2 but back then the conference only secured one bowl bid. The champion went to the Rose Bowl. The rest stayed home.

Over the holidays I was back in Ohio and got a call from Denny Stoltz. He was the new head coach at Bowling Green. Before that he was the head coach at Michigan State. He wanted to talk about a job on his staff. I drove to visit with him and interviewed for a few hours. He offered me a job coaching wide receivers. The most he could offer me was a $5,000 salary. Keep in mind, this was 1977. Still, that wasn't very much money. Most assistant coaches back then were making closer to $17,000. He was almost apologetic that he was offering such a low figure. That was okay with me.

"I don't care how much you pay me," I told him. "I just want to coach. If you think I'm worth more later, you can pay me more."

I took the job for $5,000 a year, but I didn't have to wait long for that raise. During spring practices Coach Stoltz pulled me into his office to say he was going to double my salary. I guess I made a good first impression.

I really appreciated the chance to coach there, but it was frustrating for me because I was used to Coach James, his program, and his process. Denny was a great guy and a good coach, but I struggled to adjust to a different philosophy. I was used to such a detailed, structured environment. At Bowling Green, I'd show up for staff meetings early while the other assistants waited until Denny showed up. I was just stubborn. I had been so immersed in Coach James' system that it was difficult to work in a different setting.

I coached at Bowling Green for two years and both seasons ended with losing records. We just weren't very good yet, but we helped recruit the core of a team that would start winning more games and going to bowls under Denny in the 1980s.

One of the best days of my life came during my first season on the staff. Our first child, Erin, was born on Halloween. We had upcoming road games at Hawaii and Long Beach, California, so naturally I was worried about Erin's timing. We played at Central Michigan on a Saturday, and on Monday, my wife went into labor—for a long time. I was on edge to say the least. I wanted the doctors to help her. Then her doctor came in the room wearing a Popeye surgical mask. I about jumped over the bed and attacked the guy. He was just trying to keep things light so nobody panicked, but this late in the game I wasn't in the mood for Popeye to walk in the room. Erin was born later that night. What a gift. Erin and I grew very close over the years—she'd get two brothers, Geoff and Blake, along the way—and she grew up into a wonderful lady, a caring mother and, for me, a loyal and devoted friend.

• • •

After my second season at Bowling Green, our coaching staff went to the University of Tennessee in February to visit with the coaching staff there to share ideas on the principles of their offense. I got a call from my wife during the trip. She said Don James wanted to talk to me. She said, "Coach James doesn't call just to say hi." She knew something was up. She was right.

I called him back and Coach said, "Gary, Dick Scesniak is going to the New York Giants. I'm moving Bob Stull up to coordinator. I'm looking for a receivers coach. I've got 150 names and I've narrowed it down to five. You're one of the five. If I offer you the job right now, will you take it?"

Whoa.

I said, "Coach, I've got to go home and talk to my wife." We'd already lived in Seattle for a year, but we had just bought a house and Vicki was pregnant with our second child. I just needed to talk to her. I could tell he was a little bothered by that. He knew I knew everything about his program and the situation in Washington. It's not like I had to go home, look at the map, and figure out where Seattle was. So when I returned to Bowling Green, Vicki and I discussed the offer and I called him back the next day. I told him I'd take the job. He said, "Well, I was a little angry you didn't say yes right away."

Years later, Don's wife Carol revealed to me she told him when he got off the phone, "Isn't that the kind of person you want working for you? He wanted to talk to his wife first to make sure everything was okay." That settled him down a little bit, but he still wanted the answer immediately. Either way, he got me. We were headed back to Seattle.

• • •

Don James is the greatest coach in Washington Huskies history, but he wasn't necessarily the school's first choice when it needed a head coach in 1975. UW wanted Green Bay Packers coach Dan Devine, but the former Missouri coach instead accepted an offer at Notre Dame. Instead, James made his way to Seattle, and after going 11–11 his first two years, the breakthrough came in 1977, when the Huskies made the Rose Bowl. They finished 8–4, won the Pac-8, and beat Michigan in Pasadena. He got things built pretty fast. I think one of the reasons he hired me was I had just played for him. They were going through the transition process, but Coach James could look at his staff and say, "This guy played for me. He gets it. He already knows what we're all about." He didn't have to train me. I knew the structure of the program. I understood his standards, the discipline, all the details. The program at Washington was the same program he ran at Kent State. The budget was bigger and the uniforms were different. Otherwise, he was running the same operation. A lot of players would come to me with questions because I had just played in Coach James' program. His other assistants were older coaches, and they hadn't played under him like I had at Kent. Younger Husky players, especially, could relate to me. I believed so strongly in the program after what he pulled off at Kent State, so when I got back to Seattle, I was fully immersed in the system.

I just tried to be myself, but I had such respect for Coach James. That awe had to wear off a little bit. I knew the program inside out. He just plugged me into the system. Coach James wanted me to be honest with the players. I understood what made him tick and I could relay that to them.

When he would speak at coaches' clinics he would say, "I coach my coaches." That's his philosophy. He was the CEO of the company. He had a book called *The One-Minute Manager*, one of the foremost books at that time on management. It was all about being efficient and productive. In practice he took notes and shared his thoughts during staff meetings and critiqued the coaches on how they ran drills, the good and the bad. He wanted everyone in that meeting to learn from the experience. If there was something really personal he wanted to address about your coaching style, he'd bring you into his office alone. But that rarely happened.

The reason I loved his management style is you always knew where you stood. At Bowling Green, it was entirely different. I struggled without the constant evaluation. But under Coach James, you became a better coach because of his style. That's how he treated the people who worked for him. He very rarely raised his voice. Sometimes he did, but that happens to everyone in this business. That's how he made us better and how he made the program better. You're always learning. He never said, "We have staff evaluations coming up in six months, so we'll address this issue then." Why put it off for six months? Why let something linger that long? Under Coach James, you couldn't be afraid of confrontation. If you can't handle confrontation or criticism, you can't coach for him. But when he critiqued your performance, he was always professional and never threatening or personal. The structure and the standards didn't change from the days I played for him.

Years later, when I was a head coach, I'd attend conferences sponsored by the leaders at Nike. They always discussed goal-setting and talked about what they called "relentless evaluation." They're incredibly diligent when it comes to evaluating how they do business and how they make billion-dollar decisions. Hearing those business leaders talk about "relentless evaluation" always reminded me of working for Coach James. We analyzed absolutely everything we did. When spring practices were over, we evaluated how they went. When spring recruiting was over, we evaluated how we managed that part of the program. Winter conditioning ended, we evaluated. We were so oriented around the calendar. When spring ball came up a year later, we pulled out our notes from the previous year and adjusted the drills we talked about changing. None of this had anything to do with coaching football—but it had everything to do with management and how we coached football under Don James. He was very clear it was all about the process. Everyone wants to be good September 1. But what you do daily—from the coaches to the academic staff to the food service employees to the weight room staff to the players, matters. What are we doing every single day to run this organization as efficiently as possible?

Coach James had one big tradition that he carried on from Kent State to Washington—his Thursday talks. Every Wednesday during the season Coach James wrote out a speech longhand on yellow legal pads, then delivered them to the team the next day before practice. This was how he started the final 48 hours until kickoff.

He'd introduce a major theme each week. He wanted his players to visualize the steps it took to win on Saturday during those final 48 hours. I borrowed from this tradition when I became a head coach and, like James, saved every Thursday speech I gave during my 25 years as a head coach. After Coach James' death in 2013, one of our former players, Peter Tormey, published excerpts of those talks in a book called *The Thursday Speeches*.

As a young assistant working under Coach James, I took a lot of notes. I took notes on his Thursday talks. I'd keep a notebook for the entire season, starting in August camp. We'd have meetings every single day covering the entire program. A lot of details. A lot of notes. That's part of the whole process. Ultimately you're trying to get everyone on the train. Everybody. Both feet on. At some point the tracks are going to start shaking. A storm's going to test you. When a coach starts a program, some people are on, some people are off, and some people aren't even close to the tracks. You've got to get everybody on board. That's how you change culture, and I got to witness that process as a player under Coach James. When you get to see it all unfold through the eyes of a player, you see how it works. When I worked under him that first year at Washington in 1976, that's when players really embraced me because I had just played for him. I was only a year or two older than the seniors. I'd see players struggling and I'd pull them aside and tell them why he's making them go through hell. "There's a plan here," I'd tell them. I think that's why he wanted me there. I was a company man. The next year, that team went from 3–4 in the conference to 6–1 and reached the Rose Bowl.

My first year back on the staff we finished 9–3 and won the Sun Bowl, beating Texas, which was a landmark win for our program. We were even better the next two years, winning 19 games combined, both ending with conference titles and trips to the Rose Bowl, ending in a loss to Michigan and a win over Iowa, respectively. We won 10 games again in 1982 and beat Maryland in the Aloha Bowl. In 1983, it was back to the Aloha Bowl after an eight-win regular season. From 1977 to '84, we never finished lower than second place in the conference.

Coach James' background was on defense so he sat in on our defensive meetings for game planning. He played quarterback in college, so he understood offensive football. But he trusted our offensive staff. Bob Stull was our offensive coordinator and Ray Dorr coached the quarterbacks. Both had been on Coach James' staff at Kent State. Dorr coached three really good quarterbacks in Seattle: Warren Moon, Tom Flick, and Steve Pelluer. I learned a great amount from Dorr. I'd run my receiver meetings and then duck into the quarterback meetings and watch Ray train the quarterbacks. I'd try to absorb as much as I could. After the 1983 season—an 8–4 year with a loss to Penn State in the Aloha Bowl—Ray left the staff to become the head coach at Southern Illinois in Carbondale. Bob got a head-coaching job at Massachusetts. I loved those guys. They trained me for years. But Coach James knew, without me ever having to tell him that I wanted to coach quarterbacks.

I was hoping to get promoted. One day, Coach James called me into his office. He said, "Can you coach quarterbacks and be my offensive coordinator?" I wasn't about to say, "What do you think?" I told him I could do both jobs. He said, "Gary, that's hard to do, especially coaching that position. You'd be running the whole offense." But I had to be confident. I told him I could do it. He said, "I think you can, too." That was it. I got the job. He had to make a couple more hires, but like always, he went out and found some former graduate assistants, people who had worked for him in the past. That way they were already trained.

He could have gone out and hired a more experienced play-caller or someone already established with his own offense. But he was never concerned about how the media or the fans might perceive a staff hire. That was never important to Coach James.

I was pretty confident, but at times I asked myself, "What did I get myself into?" I'd never coached quarterbacks. I knew the reads, but the biggest thing was coaching the fundamentals of the position and all the drill work. I had my struggles early. I didn't always sleep at night, but you persevere through those times.

We didn't want to make all kinds of changes to the offense when I took over as coordinator. We had already experienced success in Coach James' preferred I-formation, power offense. Our defense, under coordinator Jim Lambright, was good enough to hold most opponents to a touchdown or two. My first year as coordinator, only one team scored more than 17 points against us. Washington State, our heated rival, scored 29 against us in the Apple Cup. Fortunately, we scored 38—and clinched a spot in the Orange Bowl, where we beat Barry Switzer's Oklahoma Sooners team on New Year's Day and finished No. 2 in the polls.

We were 11–1—the only loss came to Pac-10 champ Southern Cal in Los Angeles—but I remember that season as being a real challenge. We were very, very conservative on offense. I figured Coach James wanted to be conservative on offense, but it was probably to a fault. Hugh Millen became our top quarterback, but we were hardly a prolific passing team. We played great defense and protected the ball. Why change the offense if we're winning?

The next year we took a step back and won only seven games, though we beat Colorado in the Freedom Bowl. For the next few years we won enough games to keep our bowl streak going, but we slipped some in the Pac-10. In 1988, we went 6–5 and missed a bowl game for the first time in 10 years. The offense really struggled. We lost home games to UCLA and Arizona and had one-point losses to Southern Cal and Washington State. After the season, Coach James did something he'd never done as a head coach and fired an assistant, offensive line coach Dan Dorazio. Dan was a good coach, but Coach James felt like we needed a change offensively. At the time we were still running a two-back, I-formation offense, but offensive football in the college game had started to evolve elsewhere.

At the I-AA level, Dennis Erickson was having great success with the one-back offense, a system that would later help spark the rise of the spread. Erickson coached at Idaho and would later take the one-back offense to Washington State and Miami. His coordinator and close friend was an old colleague, Keith Gilbertson, who coached with me on the Washington staff as a grad assistant in 1976. Gilbertson was from the Seattle area and later replaced Erickson as the head coach at Idaho. In three years, Gilby won 28 games, each time making the I-AA playoffs. After his third season there, Coach James and I convinced Gilby to join us at Washington as offensive line coach. He had a great offensive mind and he helped reinvent our offense and installed a version of the one-back attack.

That's the beauty of Coach James. We needed something different, and that's why we brought in Gilby. He and I were good friends and we didn't worry about conflicts. I still called the plays, but he'd give me suggestions with things he saw. It was a great move on our part. A lot of coaches wouldn't bring in someone to make a move like that, but I suggested it. Coach James wanted to do it, too. It really worked out. Gilby told me years later he was a much better offensive coordinator than he was a head coach. I told him I was probably just the opposite. We had a good laugh over that.

In 1989, with our new offense installed, we set single-season school records for rushing and total offense and, more important, got back to a bowl game. We finished 8–4 and won six of our final seven games, including a Freedom Bowl victory over Florida. (The day after the game, Florida officially named its new head coach for the next season—a guy named Steve Spurrier.)

In 1990, we turned the offense over to a redshirt sophomore quarterback who had gotten a taste of playing time the year before. We recruited the gifted southpaw out of Southern California and he continued our string of passers who would make a living on Sundays. He was the best of the bunch: Mark Brunell.

• • •

Starting with Warren Moon in the late '70s, Coach James built an assembly line of great quarterbacks at Washington. Moon, of course, would become a Pro Football Hall of Famer. After Warren, Tom Flick guided the Huskies for a couple seasons then bounced around the NFL for a few more. Steve Pelluer would finish his career No. 2 all-time in passing yards at UW and was named the Pac-10's player of the year in 1983. He'd play several years in the NFL as a backup and starter in Dallas and Kansas City.

I took over as offensive coordinator and quarterbacks coach in 1984, when Hugh Millen emerged as our starter—as a walk-on junior college transfer. Hugh threw the tightest spiral I've ever seen. It was absolutely unbelievable. He was a big, tall walk-on. He was just a really talented thrower and he won some big games for us, including the 1985 Orange Bowl. He'd have a long career throwing passes in the NFL.

Next up was Chris Chandler, a really talented athlete from Everett, Washington. He was an especially good golfer. What he wasn't was a great practice player, at least not early in his career. One day we were meeting in our quarterback room and I told him he needed to start practicing better. "You know, Coach," he told me, "I'm just not a very good practice player. I'm a gamer."

Uh-oh.

As a coach, I had to learn how and when you say something so everyone gets the message the right way. I had to deliver a message to Chris, but not around the other quarterbacks. When the meeting broke up and everyone left the room, I kept Chris around. "First of all," I told him, "if you ever tell Coach James, 'I'm a gamer,' it's going to be a real quick meeting with him. If you don't start practicing well, you'll never, ever play a down for him. Ever. You can sit there and tell me you're not a good practice player, but guess what? You're never going to play if you don't do something about that."

I remember him giving me this look like, "You're actually serious?" I sure was. Chris would never play for Coach James with that mentality. But that conversation seemed to really change his attitude. He was a great kid and a really good athlete. He just needed to commit himself to the practice field. When he did, he became a great player. By the time he finished his college career in 1987, he'd thrown 32 touchdowns, second all-time at Washington. He'd have the longest NFL career of my Washington quarterbacks and play for seven franchises in 17 seasons. His best years came in Atlanta when he led the Falcons to the Super Bowl in 1998.

Cary Conklin came next. He was from Yakima on the west side of the Cascades. He was another big strong-armed kid, a lot like Hugh. Conklin wasn't the most consistent passer, but he was behind center in our bounce-back year in 1988 and led us back to the postseason. Cary had played some as a true freshman backup in 1986—the rare freshman quarterback to see the field for Coach James—but we planned to redshirt him in 1987 when Chandler was clearly our best option. But nine games into the season, Chris got hurt at Arizona. We told Cary at the beginning of the year, "If there was ever a time we needed you, we'd have to activate you and pull your redshirt." Well, we needed him to finish the Arizona game. It was just one game, but he made a statement to the team with his unselfishness. Chandler resumed his starting role to finish the season, though Cary replaced him in a crucial Apple Cup win over Washington State that preserved our consecutive bowl streak at nine.

Cary had to use his whole year of eligibility for that late stretch, but the amazing thing was he and his parents never said one word. That was their duty. They knew it. It was so different than the approach some kids and their families take in today's game. He played because that's what the team needed. He probably would have been a better player over time if we could have protected that year of eligibility, but he never questioned our decision. He became the starter in 1988 and took off under our new offense in 1989, setting a single-season school record for passing yards on our way to the Freedom Bowl.

That season, we gave a few snaps to Mark Brunell, our left-handed redshirt freshman from Santa Maria, California. In 1990, we turned the offense over to Brunell, now a sophomore. Mark and I became very close, but we had some rough moments together early. His first game as the starter, the home opener against San Jose State, was brutal. I was calling the plays and absolutely nothing worked. It was one of those days. The fans booed Mark at Husky Stadium. Yes, our fans. Husky fans can be hard on the quarterback, especially after a string of so many passers who ended up in the NFL. That day, he wasn't the most popular guy in Seattle. We were lucky to win by a field goal.

Then we went on the road to Purdue. He struggled as badly if not worse there. And this wasn't a very good Purdue team. They were in the middle of a stretch of 12 straight losing seasons. Coach James and I talked throughout the game on the headsets. Coach James' philosophy on quarterbacks was all based on control. If he felt like the quarterback was playing under control, he'd stick with him. But as soon as you see the kid's head isn't in the game, and he's hurting the team, helping the opponent, then it's time to play someone else.

Mark was playing pretty poorly. At halftime we decided we'd give him a couple more series and then make a decision. Early in the third quarter, Mark broke the huddle and lined up under the guard, Dean Kirkland, instead of Ed Cunningham, our center. Not good. When the quarterback slaps his hand under the center, it's routine for both players. But if you're a guard and never had a hand slapped under there, it's a different kind of feeling. On the film, you could see Dean nudge a little bit when Mark's hand gets under there. But Dean showed great discipline. He didn't pop up or make a scene. He just tried to wave Mark over to Ed at center.

At this point, a linebacker from Purdue got his attention and waved at Mark and motioned to the center. Finally, Mark shifted over, got behind Ed and took the snap. One problem. He ran the wrong way. The running back went one direction to take a handoff, and Mark went the other way. We ended up punting and Coach James decided Mark would get one more series before we'd have to decide. From there, he completed a few passes and made just enough plays to win the game.

In the press conference after the game, a reporter asked Mark about lining up behind the guard. He said, "When you're out on the field, all those big butts just look the same." I thought that was pretty cool. It takes some poise to make a mistake like that and then laugh about it after the game. Although at the time, I grabbed him and said, "You put me through hell out there and then you go up there and joke about it?" He had a big smile on his face.

A week later, we came home and hosted Southern Cal, coached by Larry Smith. Our goal at Washington was to have the best program among the four Pac-12 schools in the Northwest: UW, Washington State, Oregon, and Oregon State. Oregon was starting to become a serious rival in those days, but for us in Seattle, the benchmark was always the two Los Angeles teams, UCLA and USC. Coach James always reminded us that when we're on the road recruiting, we had to find players good enough to beat UCLA and USC. Our goal wasn't just to win some games. The goal was to beat those guys. If you want to win championships, you have to go through the Bruins and Trojans.

The 1988 recruiting class featured a few elite quarterback prospects from Southern California. USC went hard after two of the best: Todd Marinovich and Mark Brunell. Todd committed to the Trojans first, then Mark chose us, setting up a showdown in Seattle the third game of the season. USC was 3–0, ranked No. 5, and carried a 20-game Pac-10 winning streak into Husky Stadium. Marinovich already had a full year of starting experience on our guy, but it didn't matter that day. We started using Mark's speed on bootlegs and nakeds and his true talents came out. We not only won, we ambushed the Trojans 31–0.

I'd always tell our players, "When we're struggling, you never know when greatness is around the corner. You just never know." But it's happened throughout my career. That's why you persevere. Mark ended up being second-team All-Pac-10 and the MVP of the Rose Bowl that season. Who would have imagined that?

We slipped up the next week on the road against eventual national champion Colorado—a week later the Buffs used five downs to win at Missouri—but finished strong with six wins over the final seven weeks. We finished with 10 wins, smashed Washington State in the Apple Cup by 45 points, and beat Iowa in Pasadena. Washington finished the season Pac-10 champions and ranked No. 5. For the season, Mark threw for more than 1,700 yards and ran for another 400. Not bad for a guy who couldn't find his center in his first road game. And to think the home fans booed him in his first start of the season. Husky fans are awesome but can get a little spoiled sometimes.

Everyone's favorite player is the backup quarterback. Years later, our Mizzou coaches wanted Brad Smith to play his freshman year. They'd seen him in practice, so halfway through the season they wanted to play him. I just said, "We're not going to do this. We're not going to waste all this talent on half a season." I wasn't worried that he'd be so good that he'd come out early to enter the NFL draft.

But I just knew the personnel issues we had at the time, and it wasn't worth playing him. I learned how to make those tough decisions under Coach James. And when it comes to quarterbacks, those decisions are magnified so much more. It's a gut feeling.

Rock bottom for Mark was when he lined up under the guard, but I think it was a turning point. Somehow he worked through that mistake—and the rest is history. That kind of patience served us well over time, at Washington, at Toledo, and certainly at Missouri. You see a lot of coaches get rid of a quarterback at the first sign of struggles. We stuck with Mark that day at Purdue, because you never know when greatness is around the corner.

• • •

I coached some great quarterbacks at Washington, but the Huskies' best player in that era was a defensive lineman, a player I recruited to play for Coach James. Steve Emtman was from Cheney, Washington, a small town on the Eastern side of the state near Spokane. Steve was heavily recruited, but he really wasn't interested in a lot of places. He was just a real grounded guy who never got caught up in the recruiting process.

It came down to us and Washington State. He didn't want to visit other places. The more I got to know Steve, the more I realized he was wired differently than most kids. He was unusually intense. He had a great passion to be a great player, even as a high school recruit. When he came on his recruiting trip, he'd already had his official visit to Washington State. Pullman, Washington, was closer to his hometown. We had to have a unique sales pitch. He came to Seattle on a Sunday morning and spent all day with us. I wanted him to feel the enormity of Husky Stadium because it was so different than what he'd experience at Washington State. We had just had the stadium renovated with a new big deck. I walked him all the way to the top of the stadium and told him, "Imagine 73,000 people in here. This is why we've been to Rose Bowls. This is why we win championships."

The magnitude of that stadium is impressive. I never did that with any other recruit. I wanted to separate our program from the other guys. We couldn't let him look at Washington in the same light as our rivals. I thought he had a great visit. I took him to the airport and kidded around and said, "If at any time you want to be a Husky, even if you decide at three in the morning, you call me."

He kept his thoughts very private. We couldn't tell where he stood. At 2:00 AM, I got a phone call. I assumed it's one of my quarterbacks and it's something serious. I grabbed the phone. "Coach, it's Steve Emtman." I tried my best to sound awake, but years later he told me I sounded like I was half asleep, which of course I was. "I just want you to be the first to know I'm going to be a Washington Husky." Well, that woke me up. I started yelling and screaming in the middle of the night. I just thought this guy had something special. He was really good on film, but the more time you spent around him, you got a sense for his passion to be great. That's why he chose us over Washington State. He felt we were the program that could get him to where he wanted to go. I told him, "I would call Coach James right now, but it might be best we wait until about six in the morning if that's okay with you. But this is the best 2 AM call I've ever gotten."

We recruited Steve to play along the defensive line, but there was a push on the staff to play him on offense. We never told Steve that, but Coach James said we'd settle on a position once we got to preseason camp. Obviously we never made that move. I put Steve at the highest level of competitor of players I've coached or played with, right there with Jack Lambert, my teammate at Kent State, and Shane Ray, our All-American defensive end at Mizzou. There are other people in that conversation, but those three were at the top. In 1991, Steve went on to win the Outland Trophy and the Lombardi Award. He finished fourth in the Heisman voting and became the

No. 1 overall NFL draft pick in 1992. Injuries cut his career short, but that couldn't erase everything he did for the Huskies.

• • •

After we finished the 1990 season with the Rose Bowl victory, I interviewed for the head coaching job at Bowling Green. I had been an assistant coach there for two years. I was from Ohio, won a Mid-American Conference championship as a player at Kent State, and coached for 12 years under Don James, someone with a great legacy in that state and the conference. It must not have helped. The Bowling Green job went to Gary Blackney, a defensive assistant at Ohio State.

It wasn't the only vacant job in the MAC. I also interviewed at Kent State, my alma mater. The AD asked me what I planned to do differently. I said, "Well, my personality is different than Coach James, but what he did here works. What he's doing at Washington works. I'd build the same program here at Kent State." That wasn't the answer he was looking for. They wanted to get away from the Don James approach. I didn't understand why. All Coach James had done was deliver the school's first conference championship. They'd gone through six coaches since Don left for Washington. I didn't get the job. They turned down Nick Saban, too. They hired Pete Cordelli, one of Lou Holtz's assistant coaches at Notre Dame. Holtz had played at Kent State.

At the time, I remember my wife told some of her friends in Seattle, "Well, if you're worried about us moving away, the place where he went to school wouldn't hire him and the place he used to work wouldn't hire him. We're probably going to be here for a long time." Maybe she was right. But I always believed I'd end up at the right place at the right time, eventually.

Most of Coach James' assistants would get their chance to be a head coach somewhere. If any of them struggled or got fired in another job, I made the habit of asking them what didn't work. Most of them had tried to run their program their own way, not the way they learned under Coach James. There's nothing wrong with that at all. Most of them changed their recruiting evaluation system. That was okay, too. But I always told myself I'd stick to the program that proved to be a success…if I'd ever get that chance.

I loved Seattle. I loved the environment. It's a beautiful part of the country. In 1983, Coach James, myself, and some of the staff climbed Mt. Rainier, the highest mountain in the state, 14,409 feet above sea level. The climb was a great experience that taught us about perseverance, commitment, and the fragility of the future.

We were so connected to the area. It was such a special place for our family. Both of our sons were born in Seattle. First it was Geoff on September 9, 1979. It was really exciting to have a boy. We had just moved back to Washington, and to this day, Geoff still has a group of lifelong friends from our time in Seattle. Geoff played sports when he was young and became an exceptional golfer. Then Blake came along on February 26, 1983. Both boys have grown up to become devoted husbands and fathers. I'm so proud of all three of my kids.

My schedule was so consumed with coaching and recruiting that when it came to family, my time with the kids was about the quality of the moment not the quantity of moments. We spent a lot of time visiting the parks around Seattle. When Erin and Geoff were old enough I'd wake them up early and take them to parks in Bellevue or around Lake Washington. I'd jog while they rode their bikes. We'd usually sneak in a Slurpee or Dairy Queen Blizzard before heading back home. On days off we'd take the ferry to Whidbey Island for the day.

During the season I was usually out of the house before the kids got up for school and rarely home before they went to bed, but any chance I could steal some time away from work I'd cross the Evergreen Point Bridge and zip home. We lived close to the team facility for that very purpose. We could have had a nicer house farther away, but I wanted a quick drive home. The kids would come by the office on Monday nights when we'd have 90 minutes to get away for dinner. In the summers we'd go back to Ohio to visit family, but in the winter we were fortunate to have free family vacations 11 of our 12 years in Seattle: bowl games. Whether it was Los Angeles or Honolulu or El Paso, we could count on a December vacation almost every season.

I thought I was ready to run my own program, but I swung twice and missed both times that offseason. Another year at Washington wouldn't be the worst alternative. Brunell and Emtman would be back for another season, and the quarterback pipeline was stacked with Billy Joe Hobert and Damon Huard, both from Puyallup, Washington. I went into the offseason fully expecting to be back for another year with the Huskies.

An old teammate had another idea.

Mizzou vs. Nebraska

October 11, 2003

Columbia, Missouri

Nebraska had dominated this series for more than two decades and came into the ZOU ranked No. 10 in the national polls.

Team Meting
Thursday, October 9, 3:30 PM

"I've been waiting for this game for a long time, to beat Nebraska on national TV. What a great opportunity! How exciting is this? This game is very important to our program.

1. It's on national TV.

2. We're playing at the ZOU. Play great on offense, defense, and the kicking game, and the fans will go wild!

3. Show people around the country that Mizzou can beat the best.

4. Give back to Mizzou fans. There are a lot of doubters. That's okay. We will change that.

5. Earn respect! Nebraska has no respect for you. We can change that. They'll respect us kicking their ass!

6. Now I'm going to tell you how we are going to win this game. This is what I want from you—know the plan. I want instinctive play. No thinking, only reacting. I want you the most enthusiastic you have ever played as an individual and as a unit. Every play for four quarters! I want you to outcompete Nebraska for every play for four quarters. Play harder every play for four quarters. Hit harder every play for four quarters. Outfight them every play for four quarters. Finally, I want you to have fun and turn it loose!"

Final: Mizzou 41, Nebraska 24

Brad Smith and a timely defense led us to our first breakthrough win as a program and snapped a losing streak of 24 games to the Huskers. Smith was electric and accounted for 350 yards of offense, including a 47-yard touchdown catch on a trick play. We were aggressive all night and also threw a touchdown on a fake field goal as we outscored Nebraska 27–0 in the fourth quarter.

4

Toledo: Head Coach, Day One

THROUGHOUT MY FOOTBALL LIFE A PATTERN SEEMED TO DEVELOP. Kenmore High School wasn't supposed to be a place where you could win championships. But we won a championship. Kent State wasn't supposed to be a place where you could win championships. We won a championship. Coach James turned Washington into the class of the Pac-10 and won championships year after year.

Back in the Mid-American Conference, the University of Toledo won MAC championships in the 1960s, '70s, and '80s, including three straight undefeated seasons from 1969 to '71. The program won the MAC six times from 1967 to '84. But in the mid-1980s, the rest of the league began to catch up. Toledo hadn't upgraded its facilities for decades until a renovation began in 1989. In 1990, Toledo looked to the NFL to hire its next head coach and chose my old teammate, Nick Saban, who had been working under Jerry Glanville with the Houston Oilers. Saban bounced around several college programs after leaving Kent State but landed his first head-coaching job at Toledo. He was an instant hit and guided the Rockets to nine wins and a share of the conference title.

Meanwhile, back in Seattle, after coming off our Rose Bowl victory over Iowa, we knew we'd have another great team in 1991. It was the middle of February. National signing day had passed. Spring practices were still weeks away. After a day out skiing with Jeff Woodruff, our receivers coach, I stopped by the office to check my messages. Saban had called. That was a little unusual.

I called him back and he said, "Gary, don't tell anyone, but I'm going to work for Bill Belichick with the Cleveland Browns. I can't promise you the Toledo job; if you're interested, I can get you an interview. It's a good job." Saban and Belichick had coached together years earlier at the Naval Academy. Belichick wanted Nick to become his defensive coordinator in Cleveland. Nick couldn't resist that kind of offer.

It was well past the time of year when college head coaches moved around accepting new jobs. The timing was unique.

I had already lost out on the head-coaching jobs at Bowling Green and Kent State. Why not try for another? I flew to Ohio for the interview with athletic director Al Bohl. At the time, Nick's assistant coaches were already planning for the 1991 season. If I got the job, I didn't have to keep Nick's staff, but it was strongly implied that it would be a good idea. I figured if I agreed to keep the staff for one year the transition would be a lot easier for everyone involved. From there, I'd see where things led. The job was mine if I wanted it. And I did.

On my last day in Washington, I decided I had to visit Coach James' office one last time. I thanked him for all he'd done for me. We hugged. I wasn't sure what he'd have to say. Maybe, "Good luck." Maybe he'd have a list of things for me to remember when I'm running my own program. But he didn't say anything. I walked out of the office...and then slowly walked back in. I wanted him to say something.

"Do you have any advice for me?"

He sure did.

"Gary," he said, "when things get tough, and they're going to get tough in this business, you focus on your job. You focus on that day, hour by hour. Then you go to bed, wake up all over again, you focus on your job and don't let anything else get to you. I've seen it happen to others. This job can chew you up."

Okay, Coach. I walked out of there unsure of what to think. Little did I know it was probably the most profound coaching advice anyone ever gave me. Countless times that advice helped me remain focused on my job, attend to what's most important, and get through the day better than the day before.

• • •

When I became a head coach, I knew exactly what I was going to do. I played for a meticulously organized and disciplined program at Kent State. I worked in the same program at Washington. What we did at those schools was going to work at Toledo.

Nick Saban and I only occasionally talked socially, but we'd always visit at the annual coaching convention and catch up other times throughout the year. I have such respect for Nick. He was so sharp and genuine and sincere with his players. On the outside you'd see this serious, tough, bad-ass-looking guy, but he could relate to players on a personal level. He cared about them—and still does.

But my new staff at Toledo was used to doing things under Nick. I wanted to run things differently. There were some good coaches on the staff I inherited. Greg Meyer was the offensive coordinator and he'd later serve the same role under Gary Barnett in their historic turnaround at Northwestern. Phil Parker coached our defensive backs and he'd go on to have great success as Iowa's defensive coordinator. Dean Pees coached the defensive line and would have a long career in the NFL. Tom Amstutz, a Toledo lifer who grew up in the town and played for the Rockets, stayed on and later became our defensive coordinator.

About a month after I settled into the job, Nick had all of his old staff over to his house in Toledo and he invited Vicki and me, too. At one point, everyone cleared out of the kitchen and it was just Nick and me. He had to get something off his chest. "Gary," he said, "why have you changed so much stuff at Toledo? I had everything so organized." I told him, "Nick, I'm going to do it my way. You did it your way. I'm doing it my way." We got into a slight argument—until finally, Miss Terry, Nick's wife, came into the kitchen to break things up. "What are you guys doing in here?" Then we both smiled and moved on to another conversation.

I held firm. This wasn't going to be a democracy. I didn't survey each coach and ask them how they wanted to manage the program. There was none of that. This is how our organization is going to run. It's going to be done my way on a daily basis. It's all about the process and the program. There was a method to the success we were having at Washington. We never beat USC or UCLA for recruits. It just didn't happen. But we were getting players drafted that weren't even being considered by the L.A. schools. Our approach worked. We looked for size, strength, and speed potential guys. We wanted athletes. Through our player development program we could turn them into good players. We'd do the same thing at Toledo.

Nick was influenced by Coach James, but he worked for other coaches, too, including Earle Bruce at Ohio State and George Perles at Michigan State. I always go back to that conversation Nick and I had back in graduate school. He told me, "You have to find a good horse and ride it." Well, I did.

I got the Toledo job right before spring break. They had just tied for a championship, so things were going pretty well. But I was still the third head coach in three years, and for any organization, that's

Left to right from top:

My first grade class photo.

My eighth grade class photo.

Christmas 1963 with my sister, Kathy, our maternal grandmother, Nana, and my brother, Greg.

Here I am in 1965 with my grandmother, Nana, and younger brother, Greg.

Me as a teenager. I attended Kenmore High School.

I was fortunate to play for a couple great coaches, including Dick Fortner, who coached Kenmore High School to the Akron city championship in 1969, my senior year.

Kenmore High School didn't have a great football tradition, but under coach Dick Fortner we captured the 1969 city championship in Akron with a victory over rival Garfield. I played receiver before moving to tight end in college.

I served as a co-captain as a senior at Kent State in 1973.

I earned All-MAC honors as a senior at Kent State and was named honorable mention All-American.

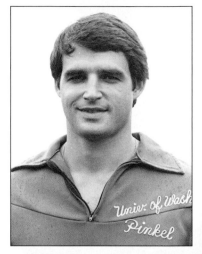

Top left: *I joined Don James' coaching staff at the University of Washington in 1976 as a part-time assistant coaching tight ends, and after a detour through Ohio I was back in Seattle two years later. I returned as a full-time assistant and would become the Huskies' offensive coordinator and quarterbacks coach through the 1990 season.*

Top right: *I like to say I got my doctorate in coaching from Don James, shown here after one of his many wins at Husky Stadium. This one happened to come at my expense: in 1991, my first season as the head coach at Toledo, we lost to Coach James and his Washington team that would go on to win the national championship.*

Bottom: *In the early 1980s, the Washington football coaching staff was coined the James Gang, and sometimes we looked the part. Here's our staff, led by head coach Don James (on horse), including myself (far right) and offensive coordinator, and former Mizzou head coach, Bob Stull (right in red)*

Left: *I landed my first head-coaching job at the University of Toledo in 1991, back in the state of Ohio, back in the Mid-American Conference. (Photo courtesy of the University of Toledo)*

Top right: *Frank Lauterbur, here visiting one of our practices, was a valuable source for me during my time at Toledo. Coach Lauterbur won three conference championships as the head coach at Toledo and stayed engaged with the program and our staff after he retired from coaching. (Photo courtesy of the University of Toledo)*

Bottom right: *We opened the 2000 season with a game I initially opposed to putting on our schedule, but the 24–6 victory at Penn State in front of a national TV audience was the start of 10-win season and delivered some national attention to our program. (Photo courtesy of the University of Toledo).*

There was nothing easy about the challenge we faced at Missouri when we arrived from Toledo for the 2001 season. It took three seasons to reach a bowl game and seven to win our first division championship. (Photo courtesy of the University of Missouri)

Brad Smith, our quarterback from 2002 to '05, was the catalyst of our program at Mizzou. When Brad played his final home game, here against Baylor on November 12, 2005, I knew we were losing a great player and leader who played a pivotal role in our program's success. (Photo courtesy of the University of Missouri)

We needed the biggest rally in team history to secure our first bowl win, a 38–31 comeback win over Steve Spurrier and South Carolina in the 2005 Independence Bowl. It was Brad Smith's final game in a Mizzou uniform. (Photo courtesy of the University of Missouri)

Led by two senior captains, Lorenzo Williams (99) and Martin Rucker (82), we finished the 2007 season with a huge victory over Arkansas in the Cotton Bowl, the final touches on a 12-win season that included a Big 12 North Division championship. We finished ranked No. 4 in the AP poll. (Photo courtesy of the University of Missouri)

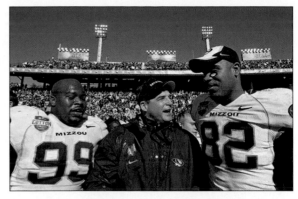

We had so many great players come through our program, including these three offensive stars from left: receivers Danario Alexander and Jeremy Maclin and quarterback Chase Daniel, a Heisman Trophy finalist in 2007. (Photo courtesy of the University of Missouri)

Here's a rare smile in my postgame press conference. It must have been a victory. From 2005 to '11 there were many, as we went to bowl games seven straight seasons. (Photo courtesy of the University of Missouri)

Winning our home games became a priority at Mizzou, and from 2006 to '11, we won 31 of 37 games at Memorial Stadium. (Photo courtesy of the University of Missouri)

We played in 11 bowls at Missouri and nine in a span of 10 seasons, including this one, a Cotton Bowl victory over Oklahoma State after the 2013 regular season. (Photo courtesy of the University of Missouri)

Me and my Harley Davidson Road Glide motorcycle, which often served as my recreation when there was time. (Photo courtesy of the University of Missouri)

a sign that there will be dysfunction. I wanted to hit the ground running. I wanted my coaches working 10-hour days every day until we had everything installed. But that just wasn't going to work. These assistant coaches needed some time off. They had just finished the 1990 season and recruiting. We met individually and I told each one that I'd keep them for one season for sure. I was very demanding. They probably thought I was a pain in the ass, but I wanted things done my way—so it would become our way. And I refused to deviate from that way. But I tried to be fair and consistent, just like Coach James. I wanted these coaches to always know where they stood. A few guys left on their own. They could probably sense I wanted to make changes.

My first week on the job, I worked 18 hours a day while everyone was on vacation. I'd be there at eight in the morning and work until 2 AM. I was working on pure adrenaline. I was just so excited about this opportunity. It wasn't like I had all these decisions to make about how I'd run the program. I had a plan.

My first weekend in Toledo, a few buddies from Akron came up to welcome me back to Ohio and pull me away from the office. I was exhausted and slept until two in the afternoon that weekend. I needed some rest. I wouldn't get much more.

• • •

Frank Lauterbur, Toledo's head coach during the team's glory years, lived in town and wanted to stay engaged in the program. He led Toledo to consecutive unbeaten seasons in 1969 and 1970 then went to coach at Iowa and later in the NFL as an assistant. He moved back to Toledo after he retired from coaching, and I embraced him and encouraged him to be around our coaches and players. Right before our first spring practice of 1991, I was freakin' wired. It was my first practice as a head coach and I was ready to run through a wall. Coach Lauterbur walked into my office that morning and said, "You know, Gary, I love spring ball because there's no pressure."

What? No pressure? Are you kidding me, Coach? Years later, I told him he was crazy for saying that.

I was about ready to explode with all my plans and all the things I knew we needed to get done. That's how I handled that entire first season. You never know what it feels like to be a head coach until you're bunkered down in the job. I believed in what I was doing, but I wasn't surrounded by people I knew well or had coached alongside in the past. I made it clear after that first practice how we were going to do things differently. Those coaches looked at me like I was crazy. But I made it very clear to them, "I'm not criticizing you guys out of anger or disrespect, but we're going to coach a certain way here." You have to do it within your personality, and we were going to develop certain practice habits that would make Toledo a better program.

We talked for almost an hour in the kind of staff meeting that would normally take about five minutes. I was bound and determined that we would do everything exactly how I wanted it done. We weren't taking any votes.

We opened my first season with two wins, a loss, and a tie, followed by a trip to Washington and Husky Stadium. The Huskies were ranked No. 3. Coach James' team was loaded. A national championship was not out of the question. Mark Brunell had blown out his knee during spring practices and Billy Joe Hobert had taken over as the starter. As the bus pulled into a place filled with great memories from my time there, my focus was on my Toledo team. The first half was grueling. The Huskies controlled the game. In the second half, Coach James signaled the quarterbacks to let the clock run down to one second on the play clock every single snap. He wanted to get that game over as quickly as possible. A couple times I remember Brunell looking over to our sideline and not smiling but just nodding to me, like he was saying, "We're taking care of you here, Coach." Washington would go on to win the national championship. We barely got in their way. The final score was 48–0. Our offense never even entered the red zone.

At the time, my players at Toledo didn't know me that well because I was so rigid and still trying to find my identity as a head coach. I was probably trying too hard to act like Don James. I wanted to run his program, but I wasn't doing it in my own skin. After the game, my focus was getting to Coach James to shake his hand and congratulate him on the win, but it took about five minutes because all the Washington players swarmed around me on the field. I never really got a chance to tell those players good-bye because I left so abruptly. But they were so kind after the game. Steve Emtman, Lincoln Kennedy, Billy Joe, Mark Brunell— so many guys came up and shook my hand and gave me a hug on the field.

Not until years later had I watched that moment on video. It was an awkward scene. My Toledo players witnessed the Husky players embrace me and must have thought, "Okay, this guy must know what he's doing. Maybe he's not all that bad." They saw that player-coach reception and maybe that gave me some credibility in their eyes. Coach James was brief after the game. That's just how he was. We talked for a few seconds and we went our separate ways.

We finished the season 5–5–1. Washington went undefeated, won the Rose Bowl, and finished first in the coaches poll, giving the Huskies a share of the national championship with AP poll champ Miami. I was thrilled for Coach James and all those players I had recruited and coached. Back in Toledo, I had problems to solve, starting with my staff.

Five of the nine assistants I inherited from Nick's staff coached only that first season under me. I was demanding with my staff but always in a respectful way. I was never a screamer or name-caller.

I never wanted to create uncomfortable situations. But a couple coaches retired or left the staff.

For the 1992 season, I brought in Mike Dunbar as offensive coordinator and quarterbacks coach. He had been a successful head coach at Central Washington and understood the culture I was trying to build. He'd occasionally brought his Central Washington staff to Seattle and traded notes with the Washington coaches, so he had an understanding of the program I was trying to build at Toledo. Maybe most important, he knew how I coached quarterbacks. Dave Christensen joined the staff that year as offensive line coach. He played for Coach James at Washington and worked under him as a grad assistant. When Dave walked in the door he knew what I was doing because of his experience with Coach James' program. I didn't have to train him. I added Dave Steckel from Lehigh to help with the defense. Matt Eberflus, a Toledo player my first year as coach, joined the staff as a defensive assistant. He was a bright, young guy who grew up in Toledo. He was really sharp. He reminded me of myself when I was a young coach. He believed in what we were doing with the program. If you played for me or worked as a grad assistant, you had an idea of what we were trying to build. Craig Kuligowski, another former Toledo player under Saban, came on to coach on offense and later took over the defensive line. Cornell Ford and Brian Jones joined us from smaller schools. Later, I'd add Bruce Walker and David Yost, both offensive assistants.

Yost came to us as a grad assistant on the defensive side. In 1997, Dunbar left for the head-coaching job at Northern Iowa, so I promoted Christensen to coordinator—but I needed a quarterbacks coach. I interviewed a bunch of candidates but didn't like any of them. I needed to have a gut feeling on a coach before I'd hire him. Mike told me, "Gary, you need to interview Yost because if you don't promote him I'm hiring him at Northern

Iowa." That really grabbed my attention. So I brought in Yost and asked him some questions about the job. After about 30 minutes, it was obvious. He had what I was looking for. I could train him for the job, and I had that gut feeling that he could handle it. You're only as good as your staff, and handing Yost the quarterbacks was our best move. He didn't play college football—he went to Kent State, my alma mater, and joined the team briefly as a walk-on long snapper—but playing experience didn't matter to me when it came to hiring coaches.

By then the bulk of my staff would be the core that followed me from Toledo to Missouri, and some of them coached with me for 20 years or more. That kind of staff continuity is incredibly rare in college football today.

They were very loyal to me. In almost every case when an assistant left my staff he was advancing his career and went to a better job. The staff is so critically important. We've all got to be singing the same lyrics to the same song. It has to be how Toledo runs its program, not how Gary Pinkel runs the program. There is nothing worse than having staff dissension. That happened a few times over the years, and one thing I learned from Coach James is you have to address those problems immediately. They don't take care of themselves.

In our second season at Toledo we had a landmark win over Purdue, Toledo's first ever win against a Big Ten team. We went 8–3 and finished strong with five straight wins. The MAC still only had one bowl partnership back then, so unless you won the conference, which we didn't in 1992, you stayed home for bowl season.

• • •

In August 1993 we were preparing for our third season at Toledo when I got a phone call from Seattle. Coach James had announced his resignation. I was shocked, crushed, and, more than anything, angry.

The Pac-10 Conference had just punished Washington for NCAA violations by Husky players, including a two-year postseason ban. Billy Joe Hobert, the team's quarterback, had accepted a loan from a booster that the university never knew about, especially the coaches. The league also barred Washington from earning TV revenue, restricted scholarships, and put the program on probation for two years. Washington had cooperated with the investigation, but the school believed the sanctions were too excessive. Coach James was so disgusted with the penalties that he resigned. He stepped down with more wins than any coach in conference history.

I was sitting in my office when I got the call that he had resigned. I started crying. I couldn't believe it. This was a man of high integrity. I didn't think it was right the way the program was getting criticized. It was a very sad situation. I called him and could barely talk. He just said, "This is the right thing to do. I feel very good about it." He also got to save all his assistants' jobs. The school promoted defensive coordinator Jim Lambright to head coach.

I was very angry. The players were angry. Everyone was angry at how it was handled. But it's a classic example that life doesn't always go your way.

I got my doctorate in coaching from Don James. I watched everything he did. How he talked to the team and to his coaches, how he responded to everything that happened, good and bad. Fortunately, Coach James' reputation wasn't smeared by the sanctions. That was always my biggest concern. I didn't want this to impact his legacy.

When I was still a young coach at Washington, Coach James took us to the annual coaches convention one winter and invited me to sit with a group of his coaching friends. Lavell Edwards from BYU, Bobby Bowden from Florida State, Joe Paterno from Penn State, Michigan's Bo Schembechler. Are you kidding me? How am

I sitting at this table? That day Coach James introduced me to the game's greatest coaches. That moment symbolized what he did for me and my career over time. I owed him so much.

• • •

Back in Toledo, we slipped to 4–7 in 1993. The last thing you want to happen after you taste some success is to take a step backward. Internally, things weren't going well within the team. Our players hadn't fully invested in the program. We had a good young running back in Wasean Tait, but we turned over the ball too much.

Around this time I was out to lunch with a close friend, Pat Gucciardo, who played at Kent State a few years before me and was the longtime successful coach at Whitmer High School in Toledo. We were clearly struggling at Toledo. I was not handling those struggles well.

I joked during lunch that I was going to eat as much grease as I could so that I would die of a heart attack. That's how stressful this job had become. Pat heard me say this and he leaned over, real seriously. "I know you don't want to make any changes, Gary, but I think it's time."

No way. Not me. "Gooch," I told him, "I am never going to change. Never. I've seen this program work. I am not going to change."

To this day Pat calls it "the defining moment." And it really was. A lot of coaches in that situation would have blown up what they were doing and started changing things. I wasn't going to change. The structure, the schedule, the discipline—it all worked. It worked when I was a player at Kent State. It worked when I was an assistant at Washington. I was going to make it work at Toledo.

Pat knew I was stubborn. He kept pressing. "Maybe you need to look at things here and ask yourself if you're doing it the right way."

I hit my hand on the table and yelled at him, "I'm not going to change!"

Pat cared about me. This was serious. He knew I was distraught over the struggles we were having to win games. He knew how intense I was every second of my life. But if I was going down, I was going down my way.

We recovered with a six-win season in 1994, but we were giving up too many points and losing games we should have won. We struggled to win close games. Coach James rarely called me to give advice, but that next summer he made an exception. He thought I was coaching too conservatively. "Sometimes you need to make some calls on game day in order to win," he told me. "You're coaching not to lose."

In 1995, I was a little more aggressive with game-day decisions and we won a lot. Our only blemish during the regular season was a 28–28 tie at Miami. That year we didn't have to worry about many close games, at least during the regular season. With a loaded offense, eight of our first 10 wins came by double digits.

Coach James' advice came in handy when we played Eastern Michigan later that year. They spotted us a 21–0 lead, but Charlie Batch drove them back and got them within a touchdown in the fourth quarter. We faced a fourth down deep in Eastern Michigan's territory. I got the punt team ready. There were about two minutes left. Then I vividly remembered Coach James saying I had to start coaching to win. The safe play was punt and play defense, but I didn't think our defense was sound enough to rely on that strategy. I called off the punt team, put the offense back on the field, and we converted the first down. Charlie Batch never touched the field again.

When plays like that work you have to make decisions with confidence, but the circumstances have to be right. You must have intelligent reasoning behind a call like that.

The offseason leading into the 1995 season I could start to see our program coming together. We had Wasean Tait at tailback, the

MAC MVP, and Ryan Huzjak at quarterback, who'd go on to rank among the school's greatest passers. In the regular season finale we beat Ohio in the Glass Bowl to clinch the MAC championship outright. As our fans took down the goalposts, I officially accepted our invitation to the Las Vegas Bowl. It would be Toledo's first bowl game in 11 years—and one of the most historic bowl games ever.

Before the 1995 season, the NCAA had sent a letter to every head coach explaining rule changes for the upcoming year. I don't think I ever saw it, but the big change was the introduction of overtime for bowl season. For years, the lower divisions in the NCAA had used overtime to decide tie games, but the major college divisions had held out and settled for ties at the end of regulation. That changed in 1995 when overtime was introduced for the postseason.

We would face Nevada in the Las Vegas Bowl, set for December 14, the earliest bowl game on the calendar that year by almost two weeks. Sure enough, we were tied when Nevada kicked a field goal to even the score.

Mike Dunbar, our offensive coordinator, had coached in overtime games in Division I-AA. Before the game, knowing overtime could be in play, our staff discussed our strategy when we went through our game-planning checklist. Normally we'd go over the checklist two days before the game. In this case, we moved it up a day so we had more time to prepare. The overtime rules weren't like the NFL's sudden death overtime. Instead, each team got the ball at the opponent's 25-yard line and got four downs to score or get a first down. Then the other team got the ball at the opponent's 25-yard line with a chance to answer. If the game was still tied after the first overtime, the teams did it all over again.

We went into the game planning that if it went into overtime and we won the coin toss, we would go on defense first. That way you know what you need, either a touchdown or just a field goal, based on what the other team did during its overtime series. Dunbar's strategy was to go for the big pass early. I was more conservative: get a first down. If you get a new set of downs you increase your chance of winning. If you hit the big play to win the game, that's great. But I was a little more practical. Our plan offensively was to get a first down before anything else. That doesn't mean you can't throw for a first down, but if you get a first down, you get four more shots. I see a lot of people throwing for the end zone on first and second down. In 1995, we had Wasean Tait, a gifted running back from Detroit who finished as the nation's No. 2 rusher. He was talented enough to play for Michigan or Michigan State but undersized just enough to land at Toledo. But when you're faster and quicker than everyone else on the field, it doesn't matter how big or small you are.

We won the toss and chose to go on defense first. Nevada kicked a field goal to take a three-point lead, but we answered with a touchdown, thanks to Wasean's game-winning run. It was a 40–37 victory, the first Division I overtime win in history.

We finished 11–0–1 and ranked No. 24 in the final AP poll. Undefeated national champion Nebraska was the only other Division I-A team to end the year without a loss. That was such an important season for our program. We won a championship, we won a bowl game, and the system we worked so hard to install and build produced success on a conference and national level.

We lost Wasean to a serious knee injury in the 1996 opener at Indiana, and our offense wasn't nearly as explosive that season. We won seven games but finished a game behind Ball State for the MAC championship.

After the breakthrough 1995 season, job offers started coming around. Minnesota called after the 1996 season and we set up an interview at the Detroit airport. At the time, though, our sons

the eulogy, I remember saying that my mom never said a bad thing about another person. We weren't allowed to do that.

She was such a good person. She lived her life by the golden rule. I'd give my kids the same lessons and always say they came from my mom.

The next Saturday we beat Western Michigan at home and my players gave me the game ball in the locker room. It was such an emotional week. The funeral was on Thursday and that's when I normally give the team my weekly Thursday talk. That week it was a Friday talk.

• • •

We finished with seven wins in 1998 and made it back to the MAC championship game where, again, we lost to a very good Marshall team. After the season the University of Washington contacted me about interviewing for its head-coaching job. Jim Lambright had winning records every season after replacing Don James but the school wanted to go in another direction. I had promised myself I wouldn't take another coaching job until all my kids graduated from the same high school—with one exception. All three kids still had friends in Seattle from our time living there. Blake, our youngest, was still a sophomore in high school, but the adjustment would be easier if we moved back to Washington.

I thought I would have a good chance to get the job. I was a Don James guy and had built a winning program on my own. I went to Seattle and interviewed for the job. I felt like the process was going well. My good friend Chris Tormey, the head coach at Idaho and another former assistant under Coach James, was another candidate.

Barbara Hedges, the Washington athletic director, called me on Thursday to say I was still a candidate. I took that as a positive sign. I was feeling good about my chances.

Then she called back Saturday morning. Washington was going in a different direction. They were moving away from the Don James coaching tree and going with Rick Neuheisel, the coach at Colorado. It was disappointing. As I reflect back on that, there's no one they could have hired who would have run the Don James program how I would have done it. I played for him. I coached for him. I applied the same principles and structures at another program and won a lot of games. I knew it worked. Unlike some of the other coaches who left Don's staff to run their own programs, I stayed true to his system. I was a disciple. And I would have installed the same elements back into the program at Washington where Coach James had so much success.

In some respects I can understand where they were coming from. They wanted to break away from the past. I just didn't like getting the call on Thursday and then getting hit in the face with the bad news two days later. I was okay with the decision. I wasn't really angry. I had a good job and figured another great situation would come around when the time was right. At least I hoped.

In 1999, we had a great running back, Chester Taylor, who'd go on to a long career in the NFL. At quarterback we turned the offense over to a sophomore, Tavares Bolden, a good young player from Cleveland. I thought he had great potential, but he wasn't living up to our expectations. He was missing classes, and if you're going to play quarterback in our program, you have to set the standard. Quarterbacks don't miss class.

I had a meeting with Tavares, just the two of us, and I got after him about his lack of commitment. I told him, "You'll never play here, much less become a great quarterback, if I can't count on you. That means you go to class. You stay out of trouble. You become the hardest worker on our team. That's what our quarterbacks do. If that doesn't happen, you'll never, ever play here."

My goal when he walked out of that meeting was that he left shaking. That was the reaction I needed to see. And I got it. In those settings, your voice goes where it needs to go. I had to create the necessary environment to get his attention.

During the 1999 season, we had another defining moment, but this one didn't involve greasy burgers and fries. The Mid-American Conference had six teams when I was a senior at Kent State. By 1999, the MAC had 13 teams with two divisions. It was harder to sustain success year after year because there were so many quality programs in the league. We had just lost to Louisiana Tech at home to put our record at 3-5. We had three games left, which means we had to sweep all three games to finish with a winning record.

After the Louisiana Tech loss, I told the team, "Guys, I want to make something very clear. What we do wins. And it wins championships. We're not changing anything here. If we all get on board, we're going to win."

Later that night, I buried my head in my hands and must have cried for five minutes. I was emotionally distraught. We had been to back-to-back conference championship games, but here we were 3–5 with three home losses. One more loss and we'd have a losing record. That would have been devastating. All the work we put into building a consistent winner, the last thing you want is to take a step back. It hurts recruiting. It hurts your support. We couldn't afford the stigma of having a losing season. Even in the tough years here, we still win. That had to be our identity.

At that moment, if someone had walked into my office and told me we'd win 13 of our next 14 games, I would have lost my mind, kicked them out of my office, and told them to never come back. But that's exactly what happened. You truly never know when greatness is around the corner. It's no different than Mark Brunell taking a snap from under the guard. He had no idea his career was about to take off. "You persevere and you battle."

We had three games left to salvage our season, starting with Central Michigan in Mount Pleasant. If we lost we couldn't have a winning season. This game was emotional because so much was at stake, but like always, I had to keep my calm demeanor on the sideline. I always told my players that bombs could be going off, but you can always look at me and see that things are under control. "When you're wondering what the hell's going on, look at me and chill out." That was my message.

One last time before kickoff, the team came back in the locker room after warming up. I went around and shook hands with every player like always, but then I had to go back outside. If those players had caught a glimpse of me, it wouldn't have been a good scene. I wanted to win that game so badly that I was ready to explode.

We won the game then finished with wins over Northern Illinois and Western Michigan. Those games weren't close either. We won by a combined 73 points. In today's bowl arrangement we would have qualified for a bowl game, but the MAC only had one bowl tie-in back then.

More importantly, those wins created the momentum we'd need heading into the offseason. Starting with the Central Michigan game, Toledo won 23-of-26 games, all with Tavares at quarterback. He became the leader and playmaker the program needed.

• • •

Around 1998, our athletic director, Pete Liske, told me we were going to schedule a game at Penn State. Why Penn State? Easy answer: Pete played quarterback there in the 1960s. He was an outstanding AD, but I didn't like this idea. I told him, "I don't want to play at Penn State. Why Penn State? If we're scheduling a Big Ten team, let's give ourselves a chance to win and play somebody else." A down year for Penn State at that time was 9–3. We had just gotten crushed at Ohio State. I didn't want to relive a game like that.

I met for coffee with Pete and our president to discuss the schedule. I lost the argument and wasn't happy about it. I thought

I had earned enough credibility to make those decisions or at least have some influence.

So we were stuck with playing Penn State for the first game of the 2000 season—in Happy Valley.

I called in the captains that Monday before the game and asked them, "Okay, guys, how do you want me to approach this week?" We could have played up the Big Ten vs. MAC angle. It's another chance for the little guy to knock off a Big Ten powerhouse. Those guys looked at me and said, "Don't do anything differently at all. Nothing." That surprised me. Our approach to the game was really important, but they insisted this game was about us, nothing else. We weren't going to play the disrespect card. This wouldn't be about David vs. Goliath. We were just going to play the game—the game I didn't want to schedule. But it turned out to be a turning point for Toledo football and my career.

It was an incredible game, and on national TV, no less. We had such a good team. Coming off that three-game winning streak to finish the 1999 season, this bunch had confidence. Did they know we'd win the game? I don't know, but they believed we could. With five minutes left in the game, for the first time in my coaching career, I took my pen and wrote five slashes. One, two, three, four, five. One for every minute left in the game. When a minute would pass, I'd mark it down. We're up 18. At this point, I'm in some disbelief. Toledo doesn't come into Penn State and win—not with Joe Paterno on the other sideline. The clock hits the five-minute mark, slash it off. Four minutes, slash. Three minutes, slash. My players probably thought I was taking notes or preparing my interview for the media. They had no idea. Two minutes, slash. One minute, slash. Then the seconds tick down...and we win the game 24–6. It was the first time a MAC team had beaten Penn State in 12 tries.

A few players hugged me as the celebration began and I ran on the field to look for the rest of our team. And where were they? In line to shake Joe Paterno's hand. The entire team! So what do I do after the biggest win in my career? I get in line with everyone else. I guess I have to shake JoePa's hand, too. The TV crew came over to interview me, but by then I was already in line. At that point, I can't lose my place. Finally, I got to Coach Paterno. He was very gracious and shook my hand. That put a national spotlight on our program. Maybe we knew what we were doing after all.

Several years later I was in Hawaii at a resort walking around the pool and there's Coach Paterno. He was still coaching at Penn State. It was the first time I'd seen him since we played. I had to say hello and pay my respects. I made my way over to him and said, "Coach, I'm..." and he stopped me. "Coach, I know who you are," he said. "You know what, I kept telling people that you were better than us. Your team could have competed in the Big Ten that year." I was blown away. Joe Paterno remembered me?

We had another great season and by year's end had tied for the division championship, finished 10–1, and were nationally ranked. But we'd be remembered as the Toledo team that took down Penn State.

• • •

By then, Blake, our youngest son, was a senior in high school, so it was time to start considering other options if they came my way. For 10 years we had built the program at Toledo with a goal to win championships—not to get out of town for a bigger and better job. A lot of coaches take those jobs for that very reason, but that was never my approach. Shortly after the Penn State win we started hearing from schools that might be interested. Later in the season, I started talking to Arizona State, Maryland, and Missouri. I interviewed at Arizona State. They had fired Bruce Snyder, and I figured my Pac-10 experience would be a plus for the job. I had a good feeling about the situation. Maryland left me with some concerns. My gut told me it wasn't the right time or place, and I wasn't sure how they felt about me.

Missouri's athletic director, Mike Alden, had only been on the job a couple years, but he knew me from his time working at Arizona State when I was at Washington. He had followed my career over the years. He called me the week we were preparing for our final game against Bowling Green, which came on a Wednesday. The next day, we met at a hotel in Toledo.

A man named Brad Epple had flown the jet that brought Mike and his contingent to Ohio and he sat in on Mike's interviews. Years later Mike told me that Brad came out of our meeting and told the others, "Well, I'm done. We don't need to talk to anybody else. That's my guy. It's not even close."

Missouri had fired Larry Smith, who had guided the Tigers to consecutive bowl games in 1997-98, but the program had problems sustaining the success.

But I wasn't the only coach Missouri was considering. Mark Richt was a candidate. He had been Florida State's offensive coordinator and would leave for the top job at Georgia. Jon Hoke, Mizzou's secondary coach, was in the running. Gary Darnell, the head coach at Western Michigan was another, along with Jim Chaney, the offensive coordinator at Purdue.

Mizzou flew me into Columbia to meet with Chancellor Richard Wallace for a second interview, and Mike made sure to have the pilot fly us over Memorial Stadium to get a view of the field. We had to avoid the team facility while Mike tried to keep the visits a secret. We talked about staffing and I said I'd prefer to bring all my coaches from Toledo. The search team flew me back to Toledo then huddled in Chicago at Gino's East to feast on deep-dish pizza and decide on their next head coach.

Missouri had only two winning seasons in 17 years, but in the coaching industry, people always talked about the program's potential. It's the only Division I program in the state. There were recruits all over in a state with two major cities, St. Louis and Kansas City. Why can't you win here? In the 1960s, Dan Devine proved for a decade that you can win at Missouri. But ever since then, other coaches couldn't consistently win. A lot of people cautioned me against taking this job, but it was appealing to me.

This became the job I wanted. Around the same time, Arizona State hired Dirk Koetter, a former Mizzou assistant who had been the head coach at Boise State.

Meanwhile, Alden and his crew were making decisions over pizza. Mike told me he was going to call me at a certain time. I was having lunch in Toledo and couldn't keep my mind off the phone call. I'm waiting…and waiting…and waiting. The phone never rang. I called my agent, John, and told him to call Missouri.

"You tell them if I don't hear back from them in 15 minutes," I said, "I'm withdrawing my name for the job. I'm out." I had just gone through this with Washington and I wasn't going to let it happen again. If I'm Missouri's second or third choice, that's fine. I'll get another good job some other time. Toledo's going to be good for the next few years. I told John, "I'm not pulling a power play here. I'm just being honest. I cannot go through this again."

John called Mike, who said they were still talking to another candidate or two. At that point, I think Mike understood my urgency. He called right back and apologized. I explained that I couldn't go through this process any longer. He understood…and offered me the job.

I had a trust with Mike right away. If the AD had been just an average guy who I couldn't connect with, I wouldn't have taken the Missouri job. I felt like Mike respected my track record. It wasn't about Xs and Os and being a brilliant play-caller on offense. It was our structure, our organization, our commitment to certain standards. I told Mike, if I took his job, at some point me and my coaches were going to be criticized for having a Mid-American Conference staff. That never bothered me, but I knew it would happen.

When Mike hired me, he mentioned Mizzou's men's basketball program. "I've got a good young basketball coach here," he said. "But with your experience and background, I don't have to work as much to help you like I do this other guy. He's really good, but I need to help him more." That, of course, was Quin Snyder, who won big early at Mizzou.

I believed in our program, but Missouri needed to show commitment. We couldn't be the lowest-paid staff in the conference. We needed the right facilities and resources. But I liked Mike Alden. I told him, "This job is going to be difficult. And I'm going to need your support. There's going to be a point some time down the road when people here are going to say, like they have for decades, 'Get this guy out of here and bring in somebody else to coach the team.' When that happens, I'm going to need you." I was right on that one.

Mizzou vs. Kansas

November 24, 2007

Kansas City, Missouri

The No. 2–ranked Jayhawks vs. the No. 3–ranked Tigers. Bitter enemies playing for the Big 12 North and the No. 1 ranking in the national polls. The Border War had never been bigger.

Team Meeting
Thursday, November 22, 3:30 PM

"Let's look at Kansas. They're the only undefeated team in the nation. They are playing very good football. They lead the nation in turnover margin. They have not turned the ball over in their last four games. We are going to hit their ass even harder than they've been hit this season! Our goal is to play the most physical game of the year. For our offense and defense, we know KU. We know what we have to do on both sides of the ball. We will prepare to play our best game of the year.

"This rivalry is one of the longest in the nation. They've played this game for 114 years. They don't like us and we don't like them. You play this game for every player who has played in this rivalry for the last

114 years and every fan and alum. KU is in our way. We have to maintain our composure so we can stay in total control.

"You should be very confident because you know how to prepare and as you guys say, overprepare... because you believe in each other...because you trust your teammate and trust your coach. You know we are a really good football team. And when we play our 'A' game, nobody can beat us. And we are going to play our best game of the year Saturday night. We started a six-game mission five and a half weeks ago. We have five pressure-packed victories. Game six is up. It's Kansas. They are in our way and we HAVE TO TAKE THEM OUT!"

FINAL: Mizzou 36, Kansas 28

The game lived up to the hype as Chase Daniel stepped into the Heisman Trophy race and we captured the Big 12 North Division.

5

Mizzou: Building a Winning Culture

BEFORE I MET MY TEAM AT MISSOURI I had to do something I absolutely dreaded. I had to say good-bye to my players at Toledo.

It was awful. The night I made the decision, word had gotten out that I was leaving. I told the staff I had taken the job. I had just hired an assistant coach, but I wasn't taking him to Missouri. He just wasn't ready for that kind of job. I called the rest of my coaches and asked each one, "Are you in?" They all probably wanted me to take the Arizona State job instead, but they were all on board. That was a relief. But the next morning was difficult.

I called a meeting for 8:00 AM. I had to pull into the stadium through the back entrance because there were some reporters and TV vans hanging around. Nancy, my secretary, helped me sneak into the building and avoid all the cameras. She was an emotional wreck. You get really attached to the people you work with every day, and Nancy had been my secretary since I first came to Toledo a decade earlier. She put up with me through some dark days, and sometimes in this business you don't have a whole lot of friends. But I could always count on my secretaries, Nancy Frazier at Toledo and Ann Hatcher at Mizzou. They were so important to me.

The team gathered for a meeting and I could barely hold back my emotions. I told them, "I've been here for 10 years. This is a great opportunity for me and my family." Nothing I could say would make them feel better, but I had to face them and tell them the news in person. It was the right thing to do. Some coaches skip town without having that difficult conversation. But we are a team, coaches and players, and consideration, respect, and trust is part of that relationship. We had just won 10 games and would have another great team coming back. There was a lot of anger that we were leaving. A few players stole some items out of the locker room. That was really hurtful to me—until I spoke with my son Geoff, who was a student at Toledo and knew a lot of the players. He told me, "Dad, they're angry because they love you and they want you to stay. That's what this is about. That's the way you want it to be." That conversation really helped me. Not too many coaches stay in that league for 10 years, but I was fortunate. We flew out later that day for Missouri.

I knew Larry Smith before I took the Missouri job. We coached against him when he was in the Pac-10 at Arizona and USC. He had done a great job taking Missouri to back-to-back bowl games. I called him right after I got the Mizzou job. He wished me well and told me it was a tough job. My old coaching colleague Bob Stull had advice, too. He had been Mizzou's coach before Larry. After he left our staff at Washington he eventually landed in Columbia and didn't have much success there. The climate was much different at the time. Academic standards were different for athletes. Facilities were in poor shape. But he always believed it was possible at Mizzou. Bob told me, "That place has potential."

Everyone always said that. Missouri has good high school football. It's the only Division I school in the state. I heard it all the time. Why can't Missouri win at a national level?

One thing I did with my players and staff was I made it really clear in our first meetings that we would never say anything negative about Coach Smith. We'd never complain about anything. When you make that transition, that's the right thing to do. However, we inherited some problems. At my introductory press conference a theme started to develop. Over and over again people asked me, "Why are you doing this?" Someone seemed to imply, "Why do *you* think you can win here?" It was almost like the next Missouri coach was expected to fail. The message was clear that is the climate here. That's what happens when you have two winning seasons over 17 years. The press conference ended and Mike Alden took me over to the team facility. I didn't get to see the building during my interview because they wanted to keep the process a secret. But when we got to the building the first thing I noticed was the parking sign: HEAD COACH. Most college football programs have the head coach's name on his parking spot. I figured out really quick that this place had flipped coaches so fast they don't even change the sign.

I've told this story a million times, but while I was meeting the media and donors at various functions the first few days, David Yost, my quarterbacks coach, was in the office working. He had flown in with me from Toledo to get a handle on our recruiting situation. I was at a hotel in Columbia waiting to meet more fans when Yost called. "Coach, do you want the good news or the bad news?"

"David, just give me the news," I said, using a serious tone.

"Okay, the good news is we have one cornerback on scholarship. The bad news is he's having surgery tomorrow morning."

At that moment, I sat down in a chair and went numb. Welcome to Missouri. Here we go.

We had to start working immediately. The great thing is when you have a structured staff that knows the process, you can get going right away on installing your program. I didn't have to train the staff. They believed in the program. Their passion helped that process. I brought most of my Toledo staff to Missouri: Dave Christensen, Brian Jones, Bruce Walker, David Yost, Tom Amstutz, Cornell Ford, Craig Kuligowski, Matt Eberflus, plus Dave Steckel, who had been at Rutgers for a few years. I figured that both coordinators, Christensen on offense and Amstutz on defense, would be considered for the head coaching job back at Toledo. The job eventually went to Tom, a former Toledo player and longtime assistant coach there. He did a great job there with the teams we left behind. I had more than a few friends in Toledo ask me, "What are you doing leaving all that talent?" We had 17 starters returning from a 10-win team. There was certainly no rebuilding job in Toledo after we left. Tom guided Toledo to two MAC championships after we left.

I didn't have that luxury when I took over at Toledo and inherited Nick Saban's staff. But at Missouri, I was surrounded by loyal soldiers. My guys thought the same way, they talked the same way.

I kept Andy Hill from the previous staff and that was a great decision. He was a Mizzou guy, a former player for the Tigers, and he was popular with the players, high school coaches, and our supporters. I really liked my interview with him and I thought it was important to have someone in our meetings who knew Mizzou and could help us with the transition. He was on the staff before I arrived and he'd stay after I left.

Our first recruit was Justin Smith, a junior defensive end who was coming off an All-American season. Right after I got the job I met with Justin and we had a good talk. He was thinking about entering the NFL draft—for good reason. He was an outstanding player for Coach Smith. Obviously it would be great for our team if he came back for the 2001 season. He might be the best defensive player in the country. I called some people I knew in the NFL and I kept hearing back, "He's a top 10 pick in the first round if he comes out this year."

When we sat down to talk about his decision, I had to be honest. I had to look at his situation like he was my son, not a player in our program. I said, "Justin, do you feel you're ready for the NFL?" He said he was. "Okay," I told him. "I've done some checking and everyone says you're a top 10 pick. If you feel like you're ready, and I was your dad, I'd tell you, 'You have to go.'" And he went.

People flipped out when Justin later said, "Coach Pinkel said I should leave." Of course, we would have loved to have him on the team, but I had to do what was best for the player. That's my obligation as a coach when you recruit players—and in this case, when you inherit a player. You tell the parents of these players that you're going to take care of them like you're their father. And that's how I had to approach Justin's situation. I remember hearing the media say at the time, "We'll see how good a recruiter this guy is if he can keep Justin Smith on campus for another year. We'll see." Yeah, well, that's not how I do things. This kid's decision wasn't about Gary Pinkel. Years later we'd face similar situations with some of the great players we recruited and developed, and I always took the same approach. It's about the player and his future.

Oh, by the way, Justin was the No. 4 pick in the 2001 draft and spent 14 years in the NFL, made five Pro Bowls, and put up Hall of Fame numbers for the Bengals and 49ers. We never coached him at Missouri, but we sure were proud of everything he accomplished.

• • •

I had to make a strong impression with my new players. Almost every time I raised my voice at players, it was calculated. Not to say I didn't lose my temper at times, but for the most part those blow-ups were planned in advance. For my first team meeting I had one hope: I wanted a player to show up late. Wish granted. Thank you, Jamonte Robinson. He was a linebacker in the program, great kid. But he popped in late to our first team meeting. I flipped out on him. "Don't you ever, ever, ever be a second late for my meetings or I'll throw your ass out!" And I did. I had to instill the message. We were going to be disciplined. We were going to be accountable. We were going to be responsible. One second late is late. I didn't realize what kind of impact that first meeting would have, but for years players from that first team would tell me they walked out of the room knowing things had changed.

After I got settled in, my old friend Coach Lauterbur told me, "They don't know that they don't know."

I walked away from that conversation thinking, "What the hell is he talking about?" Then I realized his point. When you take over a new program after a coach gets fired, all the returning players must be thinking they're not the problem; it was the coaching that wasn't any good. Give us a new coach and we'll be fine. The reality is it's probably a combination of both factors. Mistakes are made in recruiting and you have players who aren't good enough for the team to win. Maybe the coaching wasn't very good either. But the past doesn't matter. We had to establish our standards. Not rules, not regulations. Standards. This isn't the United States Army. We had standards and they were consistent. Our players would know exactly where they stood. We loved them but didn't back off discipline. You can't run a disciplined program without sticking to the standards and the details. By our third year, the players started talking like me. My family pointed that out to me. They'd hear our players talk in interviews and they noticed. It goes back to your staff, too. You can't have three coaches handle discipline issues one way and another three coaches handle problems another way. If a running back is two minutes late and gets disciplined differently than a linebacker who's also two minutes late, that causes friction within your program—not when you're winning but when you're going through struggles. We needed consistency. And consistency would lead to trust. When you start to develop trust, your players climb on board to your process.

At Toledo, I was the players' third head coach in three years. The program there was winning, so this change was difficult for the players. I changed a lot of things they were doing and they wanted some stability.

I walked into an entirely different environment at Missouri. It was a losing culture. That mentality impacts how you think and act, and when adversity comes, everything gets magnified.

We understood the culture had to change. We had to demand excellence and attention to detail. We had to get these kids to understand that all the tiny details of our program had to be important to them. This losing culture was similar to the situation Coach James walked into at Kent State when I was a player. But unlike Coach James, I came into the Missouri job with a track record of success as a head coach. I knew we could clean this up. But it was going to be very difficult.

Our first winter conditioning workout illustrated the situation we inherited. We had strict standards for these 6:00 AM drills. For one, don't even think about putting your hands on your knees when you get tired. Players rotated through three different stations and had to follow commands at each one. They had to start and finish each drill the right way every time—just like a football play. These players had no concept of the discipline we demanded. One of our first workouts, we had probably about 20 players leave the field and climb the stairs toward the exit of the Devine Pavilion because they wanted to quit. I told them, "Go ahead. Because we're not going to change." They all came back down and finished the drills.

All the while, I kept my eyes on my staff. They looked so frustrated. They couldn't believe how undisciplined these players were compared to what we left behind at Toledo.

Weeks earlier when I told my Toledo coaches I was taking the Missouri job, I told them there would be nothing easy about this challenge. Yeah, we were moving into a bigger conference with more bowl bids, more money, more exposure. But this job was going to be hard. That's why a lot of people thought I was crazy. Five straight Missouri coaches had been fired from 1977 to 2000. They had just two winning seasons in 17 years.

After that first workout, we talked to the players, then the staff went into the coaches' locker room. Almost every one of the assistants had his elbows on his knees and his head in his hands. It was like a state of depression had swept over the staff. I had to say something. "Guys," I told them, "there's a reason why we're here. Now you know."

After that day's workout, I began to believe my friends might have been right. I was crazy.

• • •

Once the staff was in place we had to start recruiting. For the most part, coaches received us pretty well as we toured the state. But there was one high school in St. Louis that wouldn't let us in the door. We arrived and they told us, "Our coach doesn't want to see you." I realized then that we had some problems in terms of public relations. It was enlightening...or maybe I was just naïve. We believed in our program, and I had great faith in the system I had learned under Coach James and all the schools where his system had success. But that didn't really resonate on the recruiting trail in Missouri. You quickly learn that no matter how strong that sales pitch sounds, you inherit all the problems from the previous regime. When you have just two winning seasons in 17 years, that means you're rifling through coaches. All this baggage piles up, and the only way you lighten the load is to run your program with honesty and integrity. You have to treat people the right way, starting with your players. If you start there, you build trust. I realized walking out of that high school that we had to build trust. I told the rest of the staff, "Don't expect people to jump on board with blind faith."

In our first recruiting class, we had some success around the state, especially in the St. Louis area. We were fortunate to sign Damien Nash, an elite running back and a national recruit out of East St. Louis. We knew there was a chance he'd need some time at junior college, but it was crucial to sign him. It made a bit of a statement for our program, that we could come in without having coached a game at Missouri and sign the area's best player. Missouri wasn't on Damien's radar before we came along, and that goes back to the trust factor we were trying to establish. We got some positive feedback early. We got our share of national recruits from around the state in those early years before we'd have any success on the field. The next year we landed Dedrick Harrington, a national recruit from Mexico, Missouri, who chose us over Notre Dame.

We didn't come to Missouri with a program that we hoped would work. We knew it would work. And that's exactly what we told players and their parents. "I don't care what happened in the past at Missouri. We're going to win here—and we'll win for the same reasons we won at Kent State, at Washington, and at Toledo. It works."

We believed we could teach players the proper fundamentals to play the game at the highest level. We recruited speed, strength, and quickness potential. With our proven development program, we would build great players out of great athletes. That was a different sales pitch for a lot of recruits.

We realized shortly after I took the job that there was some friction between the African American community and the Mizzou program, particularly in St. Louis. That was something we had to address. In March 2001, not long after national signing day, Demetrious Johnson, a former Mizzou player who had influence in the St. Louis area, reached out to me to talk about the problems that had lingered for years. Demetrious and some other former Mizzou players, Don Johnson and Kevin Potter, helped organize a meeting at the Marriott in St. Louis by the airport. Norris Stevenson, who in 1958 became the first black scholarship football player at Mizzou, also helped organize the event. Norris would become a close friend and a great asset in the St. Louis community. It was important that our program recognized Norris' legacy and his significant place in Mizzou history. We established a scholarship fund on his behalf and made his name a more prominent fixture around the program, including the Norris Stevenson Plaza of Champions, which we unveiled in 2001 on the west side of Memorial Stadium.

Mike Alden and I invited each and every former player from the area to talk about these problems. At the meeting, we needed dialogue. Most important, I had to listen. The turnout was awesome. I spoke to the group and told them we all had to be honest. This was our shot to make a strong first impression and start the healing. There was some tension in the room. A few harsh comments were made. The discussion was raw and emotional. Many of the black players felt a disconnect with the program.

I finally had to stand up and say something. I told the room, "Listen, I've coached a long time and coached all different kinds of kids. But I can't say how a black player feels. I'd like to think I can, but deep down, I don't know what that's like." We had to respect the different backgrounds and perspectives. It turned into a real honest, productive meeting. It was good for our program. That's when some healing started. After that you started seeing more former players coming back to the program. We started seeing bigger crowds at our player alumni reunions at the spring scrimmage. That was important for me to make those connections. We had to reconnect with the past to see a better future. We realized that day we couldn't just pop into the community every couple years and pay lip service to these ideas. We had to consistently build relationships. We assigned Cornell Ford to be our primary recruiter in St. Louis, and he developed trust with the high school coaching community and over time cultivated strong relationships.

• • •

In our last year at Toledo we had a quarterback on our radar, an elite athlete from Youngstown, Ohio. Decent quarterback, tremendous athlete. Little did we know Brad Smith would change our lives forever. If I had been the head coach at Ohio State, this guy would have been on the top of my list, but he wasn't picking up much attention from the so-called power conferences. Mid-American Conference schools were interested, but not the Big Ten or Big 12 schools. He was such an outstanding athlete, we thought he was talented enough that we could train him into a good quarterback. Why didn't Ohio State see the same thing? If he would have signed with the Buckeyes and become their quarterback, they would have won at least one national championship. I firmly believe that. If Ohio State or Michigan would have shown much interest, I figured he'd be gone in a heartbeat. But those offers never came. Fortunately, we were the coaches who saw Brad's potential.

By December we had settled into our new jobs at Missouri, but we hadn't forgotten about Brad. We soon discovered that the church played a critical role in Brad's life, and we figured out that the church would play a critical role in his college choice. A man named Bishop Norman Wagner presided over Brad's church in Youngstown. He was obviously an important figure in Brad's life. Matt Eberflus and

I went back to Ohio to visit Brad, and Bishop Wagner arranged a meeting for us and members of the church to discuss Brad's future. We talked for more than two hours. I was really impressed with this man. The congregation had done its homework on Mizzou and its new head coach. The bishop looked at me and said, "I know everything about you. Everything. I know more about you than you know about yourself." He was probably right. He knew where I went to high school and college. He knew the details of my coaching career and my background working with quarterbacks. He knew all about my family, too. Finally, the bishop delivered his good news. "I'm going to allow Brad to go to Missouri," he told us.

Hallelujah!

Of course, I didn't want to jump up and celebrate in the church, but we were happy for obvious reasons. Maybe Brad would prove all those Big Ten schools wrong and turn into a starter for us.

Bishop Norman looked at me and said, "Coach, you have no idea what you've got in this kid."

I beg your pardon? I think my track record spoke for itself when it came to quarterbacks. I said, respectfully, "Well, yes..."

He interrupted me.

"Coach, you have no idea."

After the meeting, Matt and I left the church and headed back to the airport. It was one of the most unique recruiting visits either of us would ever make. "You know," I told Matt in the car, "if he turns out to be a great player, that scene's going to make for a good story someday."

The Bishop was right. We had no idea!

We signed Brad and took a close look at him that first summer to see what kind of athlete he was. We looked at his passing ability. I knew we'd really struggle that first year. To throw him into the mix as a true freshman, that didn't make much sense to me. Halfway through the season some coaches on the staff wanted me to change my mind and make him the quarterback. "We're not going to play him. Period," I told them. I knew they were upset with me, but that's okay. He wasn't ready, and if we played him it would be a waste of his year of eligibility.

Right after the 2001 season, I met with Brad and told him, "Listen, you've got to become a great thrower. You've got to throw every day. That's the only way you're going to become a great quarterback."

In the middle of January, I was driving past the facility coming home from a movie and the lights were on in the indoor facility. I pulled into the lot to flip off the lights—and there's Brad. He's got trash barrels lined up all around the field. He's taking drops and throwing passes into the barrels. "Hey, what are you doing, man?" I asked him. "I thought someone broke into the facility."

"Nope, I'm just working, Coach."

That was a good drive home. I just remember thinking, "Wow, if this guy's got that kind of work ethic, who knows how far he can go." There weren't too many days he didn't work like that. It was a great visual aid to our team.

I thought he could play the position. Did I think he'd last eight years in the NFL? I had no idea.

• • •

We went through our first cycle of recruiting, offseason conditioning, spring practices, and preseason camp, and it all led up to our first game. An old familiar opponent came to Memorial Stadium for my first game as head coach: Bowling Green. They weren't just a Mid-American Conference team but our main rival at Toledo.

We spent 10 months working toward that first game...and got hit by a truck.

The year before, my final game coaching Toledo, we smothered Bowling Green 51–17. After the season, I left for Missouri and

Bowling Green hired a new coach. I didn't know Urban Meyer at all. He was a fellow Ohio native and had been Notre Dame's receivers coach before landing his first head-coaching job. His debut game would send him on the road to a Big 12 school. Little did we all know what would unfold.

MAC schools lived for games like this, as our players soon discovered. I knew the possibility. Our staff knew. Most of us had just spent a decade or more in the MAC. We'd gone to Purdue and Penn State and taken down heavy favorites. But our first Missouri team wasn't good enough to overlook anybody. Bowling Green proved it with a 20–13 upset.

I was devastated. Why did I come here again? Everyone told me not to make this move. Maybe they were right. In moments like that, those thoughts resurfaced. What had I gotten myself into? But times like that always brought me back to my dad and the message he gave me at Toledo. His advice was so simple but so profound. When doubt crept in I could hear his voice. "Gary, go fix it!" That got me back to focusing on my job. I went in the next day and went back to work. We had to demand excellence. We had to fix it.

We won the next week against Southwest Texas State then got flattened at home against Nebraska. But we won two of our next three, both on the road, at Oklahoma State and Kansas, and stood at 3–3. A week later, No. 7 Texas rolled into Columbia with a cast of star players, especially on offense. The score was closer than most people expected at 35–16. It wasn't Texas' best effort of the season but they played well enough to win.

I jogged off the field and as I stepped into the tunnel toward the locker room, our fans were cheering. They probably thought we'd lose by 40, but instead we looked respectable. I guess those fans were clapping for respectable. Are you kidding me? We're not going to feel good about ourselves for playing a really good team close. We're trying to establish standards around here, and we just lost by 19 points. I had to make a statement. I went off on the team, the staff, and myself and made the same point in my postgame press conference. "That's how losers think," I told the media. Also, that was a message directed to our fans. We had to train them, too. Get mad if we play poorly and lose, but don't celebrate losing close.

We lost four of our final five games, including a 24–3 loss at Kansas State, a place where Missouri teams had struggled for years. A week earlier, during a bye, our punter and backup punter were spotted at a bar. That was against our team rules. The next morning I decided we had to suspend them for the Kansas State game. Some of our assistants said, "Coach, we can't do that. We don't have anyone else to punt." Too bad. We must follow through with our standards, and if we didn't, it would have consequences down the road. The right thing to do was suspend the players. It wasn't the right time, but we had no choice.

Kirk Farmer, our quarterback, handled the punting duties in swirling winds that day in Manhattan. God bless Kirk. He did his best. But we didn't play well in any area.

The next week we played our season finale at Michigan State, a game that was rescheduled from earlier in the year after the 9/11 attacks.

The attacks happened on a Tuesday morning as we were preparing for our trip to East Lansing. Once the news broke, the first thing we did was contact any relatives of players or staff who were in the areas affected by the attacks. Once we got that settled, it was time to figure out what came next. Routine is so essential for coaches, but 9/11 put college football on pause. Initially, some conferences decided to postpone their games for the following weekend. The Big 12 and Big Ten decided to carry on with their schedules. I spoke out publicly against those decisions. For me, it made zero sense to play games that weekend. With the magnitude of what happened to our country, I thought it would be disrespectful to play a football game. By Thursday, the leagues came to their senses and postponed all games.

It made for an especially unique season for us because we were scheduled to have a bye after the Michigan State game, which meant we'd go three weeks between games after the attacks. At the same time, when we started playing the following week, it was great to see the role sports played in the country's healing process. For a few hours, football gave us a chance to forget about the devastation.

By December 1, 2001, we were 4–6. A bowl game was out of the picture. We headed north to play a physical Michigan State team. It wasn't even close.

At halftime we had players who didn't even want to go back out for the second half. It was cold and nasty, and Michigan State had a much more physical team. They hammered us 55–7. I remember going home and sitting on the edge of my bed by myself and the tears came bursting out. I was an emotional wreck. We finished 4–7 and got outscored 79–10 in our final two games. I might have gotten a couple hours of sleep, then I woke up around 3:00 AM. I walked around my house and thought about everything that had just happened. I had some players quit on me. Okay. Now what? I decided right there that would never happen again.

I called the staff in the next morning before they headed out recruiting. They were devastated, too. I told them, "I guarantee you what happened in East Lansing will never happen again. We might have some players quit in January. That's okay in spring ball or during the summer, but Missouri players will never quit on the field during the season." I made the same point to the players. We were going to crank up the intensity. We were not going to tolerate quitting. It was a defining moment for the program. It was an awful time for me personally, but we turned it into a positive.

• • •

Going into our second season we had a huge decision to make. Kirk Farmer was back for his senior year. He stayed healthy as a junior and did some good things for us. Kirk was a great kid. I loved the guy. But any time you make personnel changes, you do what's right for the team. You have to put the personal feelings aside. I told our staff the same. You can't run a business that way, and we couldn't run our team that way. I was conflicted. Do we go with the senior who had given Mizzou everything he had the last few years, or do we turn the offense over to the redshirt freshman, Brad Smith?

So I called Frank Lauterbur. The former Toledo coach always gave me great advice. I told him about our quarterback situation. The senior or the rookie? He said, "Gary, what's your gut feeling?" There's got to be a time when you rely on your gut. Don James used to say that all the time. Steve Jobs talked about that in his book. People in the business world have to make gut decisions. My gut told me to go with Brad Smith.

I'd probably get criticized for turning away from the senior, but that didn't matter. I didn't really get a good feel from the team one way or another. I think our players had a feeling Brad was a different kind of athlete. His abilities weren't on full display in scrimmages. You tagged him and he was down. But those six-yard gains in a scrimmage might turn into 30-yard gains if you have to tackle the guy to the ground. Both kids were such good guys and they handled the decision as I expected.

We announced Brad as the starter a week before our first game. Here we go. We were set to open the season against Illinois in St. Louis. Illinois was coming off a Big Ten championship season and had just played in the Sugar Bowl.

I thought you'd see a pretty good athlete make a few plays for us. But Brad was a redshirt freshman. Of all the guys on our staff, our defensive coaches probably knew best what to expect. They'd spent the last year watching him run the scout team offense. They were the ones lobbying me to play him the year before. "This guy's a freak!," they'd tell me.

The night before the game we had a walk-through at the Edward Jones Dome in St. Louis. From the dome, I rode to the team hotel with Chad Moller, our media relations director and my friend. It was a quiet drive. "I hope I made the right decision," I said.

"Me, too, Coach," Chad told me. "Me, too."

I wasn't concerned about Brad's ability, but could he handle the big stage in a rivalry game like this?

The next day St. Louis threw a coming-out party. Illinois was stunned. Our fans were stunned. I was a little bit stunned. Brad ran for 138 yards and threw for another 152. And we took down the Big Ten champs 33–20. What I remember most about that night was sitting in the front seat of the bus as we're pulling away from the Dome and thinking, *Wow. We've got something special here.*

My mind drifted back to the summer. I was playing golf with Coach James. He could tell I was frustrated. We were running the program, his program, but that first year was so difficult. We seemed so far away from our goals. He said, "Gary, you can think you're doing everything right, but if you don't evaluate your players and develop them, I don't care how organized your program is, it's not going to work. You need players. Get more guys drafted and you'll start winning more games." He was absolutely right. It would be years before we started shipping players to the NFL, but obviously we had a great young player in Brad Smith.

Our players were feeling really good about themselves. But I didn't handle them very well. We were 2–0 after a lopsided win over Ball State and headed to Bowling Green for a rematch. Not only were we playing Urban Meyer's team again—the team that beat us in my first Mizzou game—but we were going to their place, Doyt Perry Stadium, a place that seats about 30,000. And you can bet they wanted to see another upset of a Big 12 team, coached by the guy from Toledo, their archrival. Brad Smith was outstanding, but we couldn't stop Urban's offense. Bowling Green got us again 51–28.

As if things weren't bad enough, our plane didn't show up to take us home after the game. Like a sick joke, we were stuck in the Toledo airport. We waited for hours in the terminal, our entire team of coaches and players and staff. I was so mad about our performance. I wore the anguish on my face. And I wanted the players to notice. I wanted them to look like I was ready to beat someone up. I walked up and down the concourse. Down and back, down and back. I was just waiting for a player to joke around, to say something to set me off. I was in attack mode. I wanted them to see how upset this game made me. I wanted them to see how much I wanted to win. I should have done something different to have my team prepared for what was waiting for us in Bowling Green.

Two weeks later we hosted No. 3 Oklahoma. It was another breakout performance for Brad, who ran for more than 200 yards on Bob Stoops' defense. Oklahoma went ahead late in the fourth quarter and won by a touchdown, but it was the best we'd played against a nationally strong team in my two years on the job.

But we still didn't know how to beat good teams. We lost the next week at Nebraska and again the following week at Texas Tech.

I was so upset with how we played in Lubbock. I'm not sure I ever flipped out on my players more than I did that night after the game. I had already talked to the team, so everyone was at their lockers changing clothes. I was at my locker doing the same, except I was throwing stuff everywhere. I looked like I was going crazy. But I was under complete control. It was a calculated explosion. I had to make a statement. This was about what was acceptable and what wasn't acceptable. It was one thing to lose to Oklahoma and Nebraska. But this was Texas Tech, and we should have been more competitive. *If you can blow off this result, this effort, then you don't get it.*

We ended the losing streak with a home win over Kansas but lost three of our final four games. Overtime games became our specialty, which I suppose is appropriate considering I had coached the first Division I-A overtime game seven years earlier. We had at least one overtime game in each of our first five seasons at Mizzou, including the only back-to-back overtime games in team history in 2002, a home loss to Colorado followed by a road win at Texas A&M.

That victory in College Station felt like the start of something. That wasn't an easy place to play, but we persevered and hung on 33–27. We were getting better, we were getting closer, but we still didn't go to a bowl. So we were still frustrated. We weren't handling success very well, because we weren't used to winning. Our team still didn't know how to prepare. We needed to beat No. 10 Kansas State in the final game of the regular season to secure bowl eligibility, but it wasn't even close. They took us out 38–0. Our Missouri teams would get shut out only one other time in 15 years.

I knew if we struggled early our staff would face criticism—and we did after another losing season. I could avoid the outside noise because I always went back to the advice Coach James gave me the day I left Washington for Toledo: "Just focus on your job every day." That talk was probably the best thing that ever happened to me professionally, especially in this volatile, public job where you get evaluated and criticized all the time. Now that I'm out of coaching I've realized there's more criticism and scrutiny and analysis from the media and the fans than I ever imagined. Everyone has an opinion on everything coaches do. People who know nothing about football act like they do. But that's okay. That's one of the things that makes the sport so entertaining. Everyone has an opinion on everything.

But I focused on my team, doing my job and sticking to the process of the program.

For our players, I had to keep reminding them that what we do works. We were training players, training leadership, and teaching players how to think the right way, how to act the right way. Those lessons started to take root.

• • •

We started the 2003 season 4–0, Missouri's best start to the season since 1981. In our fourth game we needed overtime to hold off Middle Tennessee State 41–40. Our tight end, J.D. McCoy, made a diving, juggling catch along the sideline to convert a fourth down on a late possession, the kind of play that saves seasons and saves jobs. He's now a fireman in Oklahoma saving real lives. On that day, he might have rescued our season from something we couldn't escape. We came into that game 3–0 and ranked No. 23, the first time we had been nationally ranked since I came to Columbia. I guess I assumed we had everything covered. Sometimes you have to go through games like that to remind yourself how vulnerable your team can be any week against any opponent.

The good times didn't last; we lost at Kansas by three touchdowns the next week. We had a bye the following week, and I remember staying at home the next Monday morning, just wanting to stay in bed. I was just wiped out emotionally. We didn't play well. We didn't handle our success well. Now we faced a bye and had to get ready to play 10th-ranked Nebraska. That was one of those weeks where I thought about the advice my dad would sometimes give me. "Get up and do something about your problems. You're a leader. You're not allowed to have bad days." Most of all, "Go fix it!"

Once the staff returned from recruiting trips during the bye, we took the approach with our players that we were going to be positive. Just like Coach Fortner back at Kenmore High the week of the city championship. That game wasn't about Garfield. And this game wasn't about Nebraska. It wasn't about our past failures. It was about our chance to pull off the upset by playing our best. That Saturday we returned for the start of Nebraska Week practices, and the staff was shocked. What had gotten into our players? We were 4–1 and coming off a bad loss, but the players were focused on the next challenge. There was a collective feeling that we were still a good team. We just couldn't let something like that happen again. And for the first time since those players had arrived on campus, they had a feeling we could be a pretty good team, even after that loss to Kansas.

We needed a signature win for our program. We needed something to validate our strong start. We were better than the team that lost 35–14 at Kansas. Mizzou hadn't beaten Nebraska since 1978 and hadn't won in Columbia since 1973. This was our opportunity.

With an extra week to prepare, we finally earned that first signature win 41–24 over the Cornhuskers. We captured all the momentum late and outscored Nebraska 27–0 in the fourth quarter. The go-ahead touchdown was a fake field goal, a toss from backup quarterback Sonny Riccio to tight end Victor Sesay. That's a bold call, but we had to coach to win the game. We went into every game with a planned fake. But this was a game that we had to give our kids a chance to win. I told the team the same thing. "We're going for this win. We're not going to sit back and hope things work out for the best. We've got to create some plays." Those kinds of plays are emotional back-breakers to your opponents.

The fans stormed the field after the win and took down the goalposts. It was a historical win for the University of Missouri. We looked like we belonged on the field, and for me, that was important. The Mizzou crowd was crazy that night. We needed to start creating an environment at home games if we wanted to win more games like that.

With that win, the confidence level for our players started to change. We were slowly moving away from the losing culture. But I wasn't naïve enough to think a couple wins would have us turned around. When you have two winning seasons in 19 years, it doesn't happen that quickly. You might be able to flip things quicker at a program like Texas but not at Missouri. There's no way we'd sit back and announce that we'd arrived just because we beat Nebraska—especially with our schedule. Our reward for finally beating the Huskers? A trip to No. 1 Oklahoma. That was our dose of reality. They were a better team and won by three touchdowns.

For us to build a winning program, we had to start winning home games. Eventually, established programs win games at any location, but you've got to start with success at home. We started to create some traditions to build our home environment. I talked to Mike Alden about putting more emphasis on a consistent and unique logo. We were sending a mixed message with our brand by using the traditional block M logo in addition to our Tiger image. The Tiger head became our identity. We started the Tiger Walk. Fans greeted the team a couple hours before each home game as we walked from the team facility, across the Providence Road bridge, and down into the bowels of the stadium. We gave the stadium a nickname: the ZOU. We had to give the place some character to turn it into a place opponents didn't want to visit. We had to draw a line in the sand and say, "This is the ZOU. The past doesn't matter." We're all part of the past to some degree, we told players, but it's about everything that happens from this point on. "The past is not your burden," I told the team. "It's not my burden." The kids bought into it for all the right reasons.

Texas Tech came to town after the Oklahoma loss, and a victory would make us eligible for a bowl. To secure a spot in the bowl selection process in your eighth scheduled game is unique, but I was still concerned with the letdown factor. There was no letdown that day. Brad nearly ran for 300 yards in a 62–31 win. We clinched a bowl spot but the season wasn't over. We split our final four games to finish the regular season 8–4. We still weren't a consistent team, but we happily accepted our first bowl invitation, a date with Arkansas in the Independence Bowl in Shreveport, Louisiana, a place we'd visit frequently for bowl season. The Razorbacks controlled the game and won 27–14. Our kids just didn't play well. We hadn't learned how to flip that mental switch from enjoying our time at a bowl to playing the actual game. Over time, we'd learn how to handle those situations.

In the coming years, when I spoke publicly about my first few years at Missouri, I made a habit of talking about the situation we inherited. Our roster wasn't good enough to compete in the Big 12, and that losing culture had infected the program. In 2007, I made that same comment during a public speaking engagement. Afterward, a former player from those earlier teams came up to me. "Coach, I was really disappointed when you said we had personnel problems." I told him I was just being honest. "But you know," he said, "there were a bunch of us back then who really bought into you and your program." He was right. We might not have been loaded with great talent, but those guys were invested and made a difference in the future of Mizzou football.

Looking back, I'm so thankful for those guys who stuck around and battled for us. They started building the foundation. We needed kids like that. I appreciate those guys so much, because without them, more would have quit. Most kids like structure. They learn the discipline and apply it to the rest of their life. They feel more responsible and accountable, and that boosts your self-esteem. When it came to the weight room, it wasn't about just lifting weights all day long. It was about setting personal records. Under the watch of Pat Ivey, our strength and conditioning coach and one of the indispensable members of our staff, we saw guys change in the offseason because their bench press went from 310 to 365 and their 40-yard dash went from 4.9 to 4.7. They were like light bulbs walking around. You raise your self-worth through the structure and through the discipline. That process helped build our program. Our players got bigger and faster and stronger, but they also developed their psyches. Their confidence soared. This was the beginning of Mizzou Made.

We made it to a bowl game in 2003 on the backs of players we inherited, and they proved Missouri could win again.

The 2004 recruiting class was loaded with in-state prospects. It was a crucial recruiting time for us. We had to capitalize on all these local players. The stories we told three years earlier to recruits and coaches and parents were starting to produce results. The trust factor was paying off. For years people said you couldn't win at Missouri, but we had started to prove them wrong. People were noticing. Good things were happening. We signed all of the state's best players that year, including some who became crucial additions, such as Tony Temple from Kansas City, Will Franklin from St. Louis, William Moore from Hayti, and others.

When the 2004 season arrived, we faced something new— outside expectations. We were ranked No. 18 in the preseason poll. With Brad Smith back plus some proven playmakers around him, we expected our offense to be explosive. We wanted Brad to become a more polished passer. He didn't attend the summer passing camps or work with a personal quarterback trainer like you see with so many players today. We hoped to have more balance in the offense, and we expected he'd improve as a passer.

There was no way to sense we were heading into a setback season. Never did we announce the year before that our program had arrived, but we had clearly made progress. In 2004, things unraveled quickly. We opened with a 32-point win over Arkansas

State then faced a Thursday night game at Troy. We weren't ready for what hit us that night, a 10-point loss in Troy, Alabama, on national TV. That was devastating. We weren't mature enough to go into a game like that and play anything less than our best game. I should have done more. I don't know what, but I should have done more.

But we recovered and won our next three games. We were 4–1 and 2–0 against Big 12 teams before heading to No. 9 Texas. We did some good things against a team that finished with 11 wins, but we came up short 28–20. It was the start of a five-game losing streak. Our defense was one of our best statistically, but we couldn't do enough offensively.

We had some internal problems on that team. After a home loss to Oklahoma State, we had to suspend Damien Nash, our running back from St. Louis, after he questioned our play-calling in an interview with a columnist, and because of other issues. We had to find ways to win and resolve the problems we had internally. With Damien's situation, you don't want to hurt the team by holding a talented player out of games, but you also have to fulfill your team standards and do the right thing—or down the road it's going to hurt you. We had other problems, not just Damien. When you lose close games, guys bunker up and they're not in it for the team. Some players just don't understand or believe that when things get tough you're supposed to work together. You can't hide in the corner.

We headed to Nebraska the next week without Damien, our leading rusher. We decided to pull the redshirt off our freshman running back, Tony Temple. The trip began ominously when our plane skidded off the runway in Columbia the day before the game. We had to delay our flight until Saturday morning and made it to Lincoln just a few hours before kickoff. Things only got worse during the game. We couldn't run the ball and after just a few carries Temple hurt his Achilles tendon. We lost 24–3.

When things are going badly like that, you try to stay positive. You can't just start screaming at people. The players had to see me under control.

But away from the team, I lost my cool with the media a few times that year. We had a couple new beat writers that I let get on my nerves. We were struggling, and I felt they were overanalyzing me. I got edgy a few times and fired back at them. After the Nebraska game, I cut off my postgame radio interview with Chris Gervino, our sideline reporter and a local sports anchor. People were angry I snapped at him—my boss, Mike Alden, included. They were right to be upset. I later apologized to Chris.

During the season, Don James called me from Washington, which was rare for him. He had a friend in St. Louis who had read about some of the tension I had with the media. He read Don some stories over the phone.

He said to me, "Gary, you getting a little frustrated with the media?"

I told him, "Yeah. I've got these two young writers covering the team who..."

I barely got to finish my sentence.

"Gary," he said, "remember when things are going well you give all the credit to everyone else. When things are going bad, you take all the blame. You don't need to get into it with the media. Right or wrong, you don't need these problems. You can be completely right in your mind, but they'll always have the last say. When things go bad, take the heat and get back to work and make things better."

That was brilliant advice that I needed to hear.

Things didn't get better on the field. We lost the next two weeks, both at home, against Kansas State and Kansas. That took us out of bowl contention. Our program was steadily making progress our first three years and then we had this setback. Suddenly I had three losing seasons in four years. We won at Iowa State in overtime to close the season, but the year was still nothing short of a disappointment. From nationally ranked to staying home for bowl season. But I still believed in what we were doing.

After the final game, I met with Mike Alden at Lakota Coffee Company, my regular morning stop for coffee where I meet with some close friends. We had to evaluate the season. Mike wanted to analyze the situation but without micromanaging. He asked open-ended questions about the program's direction and our leadership. That was his way of asking if I needed to make staff changes. I could sense Mike was feeling some pressure. His hand-picked football coach had three losing seasons in his first four years. But in my mind, I was thinking, *Are you kidding me, Mike? Is Missouri going to do what it's always done?* When things get tough, Missouri fires the head coach and brings in the next guy. It had been the cycle for decades. I told Mike, "I will not make a change unless it's a necessity, unless it's the right thing to do for our team. I'm not firing a guy to take the heat off the head coach and the athletic director. I'm not making staff changes just to make changes. I see it happen all over the country, and I'm not going to do it."

These were good coaches. They were good coaches at Toledo, and they were good coaches the year before when we went to a bowl.

Mike was fine with my decision. I think he wanted me to make some changes, and I didn't have a problem with him asking me about making changes. That's his job. I also think he wanted to see how I reacted to the topic. Was I truly confident in this staff? If he sensed I was indecisive about making changes, maybe he would have pressed me harder. He didn't say I should hire this guy or that guy.

When I sensed people wanted change, I heard the same concerns we faced when we first came from Toledo. "You've got these Mid-American Conference coaches, and they'll never win in the Big 12."

Sometimes the right thing to do is fire an assistant. I made changes at Toledo. Some of Nick Saban's coaches weren't right for the plans I had. But this was different.

I told Mike when he first hired me that there would come a time when the pressure would rise and I would need his support. This was never going to be an easy job. We made it harder with a rough 2004. But like he promised, Mike supported me. The staff stayed intact.

Back at Lakota, Mike Alden said he especially didn't like the way I snapped at Chris Gervino after the Nebraska game. "Chris is a good guy, Gary," he told me. "People like him. My grandparents like him. You can't snap at Chris like that." He was right.

At that point, I told myself I'd never let a writer or someone in the media get me to lose my poise. I think I was pretty good with that the rest of my career.

Mike was always concerned about public image with every coach in our program and would always give suggestions on how I could improve in that area. I had great respect for Mike and appreciated that support.

Mizzou vs. Oklahoma

October 23, 2010

Columbia, Missouri

For our 2010 homecoming game, we hosted Oklahoma, the No. 1 team in the BCS standings. We were winless in six tries against the Sooners. That had to change.

Team Meeting
Thursday, October 21, 3:30 PM

"The strength of the team is its power when it plays as a fist. We have talked about what makes up the fist: trust, enthusiasm, work ethic, pride, and collective responsibility. The new component today is will, the will to win. This team has a tremendous amount of will. It showed up at our toughest moments this year. Oklahoma is coming to the ZOU for the first time since 2006, and they have no respect for us. The media has no respect for Gary Pinkel. The media has no respect for this coaching staff. The media has no respect for you. Bob Stoops has no respect for Gary Pinkel. Bob Stoops has no respect for this coaching staff. Bob Stoops has no respect for you. Oklahoma players have no respect for Gary Pinkel. Oklahoma players have no respect for this coaching staff.

Oklahoma players have no respect for you. Men, it's time that changes.

"To the Missouri football family: There comes a time when you have to make a statement about who you are and what you are about. The time is now. It's time to draw a line on the field and say in order to get across you're going to have to destroy me. You're not coming across this line because this is my team, because this is my city, this is my university, and this is my stadium. This is THE ZOU and WE ARE MIZZOU!

"Have fun Saturday at 7:10 kicking Oklahoma's ass."

Final: Mizzou 36, Oklahoma 27

Gahn McGaffie's game-opening kickoff return touchdown would set the tone for one of the biggest home wins in Mizzou history. We trailed in the fourth quarter, but Blaine Gabbert's touchdown pass to Jerrell Jackson rallied our team. Blaine had one of the best games of his career and passed for 308 yards.

6

Mizzou: Competing for Championships

WE DO WHAT WE DO. I've said that a few times over the years. It drove Mike Alden crazy. Sometimes he'd cringe when he heard me say it. It probably bothered the fans, too.

We do what we do because it works. This program I installed at Missouri was the same program Don James ran at Kent State and Washington. It was the same program I installed at Toledo. We have infrastructure. We have a daily process that is about attention to detail. That process applies to every part of the program and everyone who works in our organization. We had meticulous schedules and standards for everything: recruiting, practicing, academics, lifting, running, traveling, coaching. Everything operated according to a precise schedule that was mapped out to the minute every day, every week, every month. How meticulous? We had a daily schedule for the content that we tacked on the team bulletin board in the locker room. It was the graduate assistants' job to post the right information at the right time of day every day. The staple on the bulletin board had to be at a precise angle so the sheet of paper wouldn't tear. We left no stone unturned. Our stones were completely turned. And we didn't deviate from the plan.

But "we do what we do" doesn't mean we don't evaluate and don't change. We constantly analyzed and evaluated everything we did, and if we decided something needed to adjust, we made adjustments.

After the 2004 season, I explained to our players that we had to brush ourselves off. If you go to a bowl one season you're expected to go to a bowl the next season. If you don't, it feels awful. And it should feel awful.

As coaches, we see other coaches fired all the time. Sustained success in this sport is so difficult. When things go bad, it's tempting to scrap what you're doing and change your identity, change your process. But just like I told my friend Pat Gucciardo back at Toledo, I wasn't going to change our program. After our 2004 season at Missouri, Pat and I talked again.

"Gary, I'm not going to ask you again," he said, "but do you feel good about what you're doing?"

I did.

"Yeah, I do," I said. "And as you know, we evaluate everything."

I told the team we weren't changing. The coaches were going to work harder, and they were going to work harder.

I knew we were under pressure going into 2005, but I didn't dwell on it. Nobody put more pressure on me than I did. The pressure was self-induced. I had to learn how to keep the pressure from affecting my job. Were my coaches worried about pressure? We didn't talk about those things, but my staff knew me well enough that we weren't going to start throwing around magic dust to fix our problems. I just had to remind our players that our way works. We had to stay positive. I think back years later and we worked so hard to get to a bowl game in 2003, but then we struggled to repeat that success. We had to coach better.

We didn't change a thing when it came to the foundation and structure of our program, but when we did our 2004 postseason evaluation and looked closely at our offense, defense, and kicking game, we came to the conclusion we had to adjust our offense.

• • •

Our offense struggled in 2004. Brad Smith didn't run the ball as much, and he wasn't making the progress we needed as a passer. There was one team in the Big 12 that I spent a lot of time watching: Texas Tech. Mike Leach brought his no-huddle spread offense to the Big 12 and changed the game in our conference. I was in Big 12 meetings with Mike all the time, and it was pretty obvious we were very different guys. He was quirky but so intelligent. I had so much respect for him and what his team was accomplishing with that offense. They were going to bowl games every year. Our players were just as good as their players, so what was the difference? Their offense was better. After the season, I called in Dave Christensen and we started talking. I told him, "We've got to do something different." He felt the same way. He wanted to play faster. He wanted to spread out our formations. Those concepts are so common in today's game, but in 2005 only a handful of teams had truly embraced the no-huddle spread offense.

One of those teams was Bowling Green.

After the 2002 season, Urban Meyer left Bowling Green for Utah, but Bowling Green kept his offense in place and continued to win a lot of games under Gregg Brandon, who had been Urban's offensive coordinator. We flew Gregg and his staff to Columbia and they taught us their version of the no-huddle spread. We didn't want to dip our toe into a new offense. We wanted to dive in head first and fully submerge into a new system. We changed every aspect of our offense. Formations. Plays. Terminology. Signals. Everything. I thought it was one of the great installations of an offense I'd ever seen. I was so thankful for Gregg and those guys at Bowling Green.

We always said we'd never change the foundation of the program, but we always evaluated everything within the program. We'd go back and grade everything, from recruiting to spring practices to winter conditioning. We always tried to make ourselves better. The foundation doesn't change. The structure doesn't change. But the other side of being a successful team or corporation is that you've got to stay on the cutting edge of change. You can be the last one to change and get passed by, or you can be the innovator. You can't just live in a box. You have to adjust. At Nike, Phil Knight would preach the practice of relentless evaluation. How are you going to make yourself better? This was our answer.

Once we installed the new offense, we intentionally downplayed how drastically we changed the system with the media. You only get one chance to surprise your opponents, so we weren't interested in sharing all the nuances of our changes. These weren't subtle tweaks to the offense. We tore up the old playbook and changed everything. Four- and five-receiver sets. Shotgun formations exclusively. No huddles, ever. It was bombs away downfield. That's what we needed.

Our coaches believed the new offense would give us an edge on Saturdays, but there was more to it. It was good for morale, too. After that difficult 2004 season, our program needed a spark, an emotional boost.

• • •

We installed the offense before spring practices. After spring practices comes spring recruiting, and after recruiting comes camp season. After camps, coaches would get a chance for some down time.

A few weeks before preseason camp, my wife and I went to Las Vegas with some other couples for a getaway. While I was gone from Columbia, I was in touch with everything back home every day. I never delegated to the point where I was in the dark on what was happening around the program. I wasn't a micromanager; I just didn't like surprises.

On July 12, a Tuesday, we went for a long walk in the late morning. I didn't take my phone with me, which was incredibly rare. I'm on call all the time, and that thing never left my side. When we got back from our walk, I grabbed my phone and I must have had 10 calls from Pat Ivey, our strength and conditioning coach, and another eight or 10 calls from Rex Sharp, our team trainer. I had another four or five calls from Mike Alden, our athletic director, who was on vacation in the San Juan Islands. I said to my wife, "Something really bad has happened." I just knew it. There's nothing normal about that many phone calls.

I called Mike and Rex and Pat and they all told me what happened. Aaron O'Neal, one of our young players, a freshman linebacker, had died after a workout in Columbia. You can't be prepared for a phone call like that. We got on a flight home as soon as possible.

Aaron had just finished his freshman year. He redshirted in 2004 and was going to be a great player for us. He came from Parkway North High School in St. Louis. He was an exceptional young man with a big bright smile that lit up his face. I loved recruiting the kid and just loved everything about him. He was only 19 years old. How could this happen?

Once we got back to Missouri, one of the first things I did was travel to St. Louis with Cornell Ford, our assistant coach who had recruited Aaron. We had to go see Mr. O'Neal, Aaron's father. It was something we had to do. There were a lot of tears that day. It's a moment you never want to experience in this line of work. Parents entrust us to watch over their kids. There aren't many head football coaches who have had to make that visit.

There were so many questions to answer, so many things we needed to address. Weeks later I wondered in the back of my mind if our staff could overcome a tragedy like this, but our primary focus, after visiting with Aaron's father, turned to our team. How will our players recover? How will the players respond to losing one of their teammates, their brothers?

We got the team together and talked to all of the players. We had doctors talk to the players. At that point we weren't sure what had caused Aaron to die. When something like this happens, it's really easy to point fingers and blame people, but I believed in the people we had working for our program and the people working on that field that day. I was confident in our staff. They knew to recognize the warning signs when kids are struggling during a workout. I wasn't at the workout because NCAA rules prohibit coaches from attending those offseason drills. But I also knew what kind of people we had on our staff running those workouts. I trusted them to do their jobs the right way. Those guys, our trainers and strength coaches, were absolutely devastated.

We had to heal. Aaron's family held a funeral the next week in St. Louis. Later that week, we had a memorial service at Mizzou Arena. It was so difficult for our players, our staff. I spoke during the service, as did Mike Alden; Bob Bunton, Aaron's high school coach; and two of our players, Derrick Ming and Dedrick Harrington.

Initially that summer, all of our thoughts were focused on, number one, Aaron's family and, number two, our team. Hearts were broken and we had to comfort people through their loss. Over time, the legal process set in and also the potential effects something like this might have on our program. We worked hard to establish trust with recruits and parents, especially in the St. Louis region. In the back of my mind I thought about those potential issues right away. But at that time, I had bigger, more immediate, more personal concerns. How would our players cope with this tragedy? Our assistant coaches told our players to have their parents call us with any concerns or questions. If we got any of those calls, we had to be honest and handle things the right way. But I never had a parent call and accuse our staff of pushing kids too hard. That never came up.

So I felt pretty comfortable with how we handled that part of our program. Our golden rule was to treat our players like we would treat our own kids.

We couldn't discuss details publicly with the media. We were instructed immediately that we couldn't talk about what happened that day from a legal standpoint. That had nothing to do with anyone's guilt or innocence. The athletic department wanted to be more transparent, but it was one of those situations where the school's legal counsel and our public relations office came from different perspectives. We wanted to protect the school's image and talk about what happened that day; legal was more concerned with liability, which also made sense from the university's position.

Initially, the medical examiner said Aaron died from lymphocytic meningitis. Aaron's family later filed a wrongful death suit and identified the sickle cell trait as the cause for the vascular crisis that led to his death. Four years later the university reached a settlement with Aaron's family. Mizzou also used $250,000 to establish an annual endowed scholarship in Aaron's name.

On our practice plans that coaches carried around during practice, we always listed names of players who had asthma. If those guys had breathing troubles during the workout, our coaches knew to back off. You always push your kids, but you had to know better if their names were on that list. After Aaron died we began listing the names of players who carried the sickle cell trait. Our training staff also began mandatory sickle cell testing for all athletes, a year before the NCAA required the testing.

I never faulted Aaron's family for how they felt and the legal action they took against the university. I could only imagine if that was my son who died the way Aaron left us. Aaron's father is an incredible person, and it was no surprise Aaron was such an impressive young man.

• • •

It had already been a difficult year for me. On January 30, my brother Greg died suddenly after suffering a heart attack. He would have turned 47 the next day. He had the same disease as my sister and in some ways didn't handle the symptoms and struggles as well as she did. He was able to play wheelchair basketball, and I was so proud of him when I'd get to Akron to watch him play.

His team was good enough they won a championship. I still have his trophy in my case at home in Columbia.

• • •

In July 2004, we secured a verbal commitment from a quarterback out of Southlake, Texas, who would go on to change our program forever. Chase Daniel ran a similar no-huddle shotgun offense at Carroll High School, one of the elite programs in Texas. As poorly as the 2004 season went, we knew we'd have Chase on campus for 2005, Brad Smith's senior year. Did we adopt Chase's offense knowing he'd be our next quarterback? No, not at all. But the two systems paralleled each other—and the timing worked out perfectly. If Chase hadn't come to Missouri, we still would have switched to the no-huddle spread.

Chase was incredibly talented. He was a two-time Texas state player of the year, passed and ran for nearly 12,000 yards his final two years, and guided Carroll to the 2004 state championship. He learned how to win at high school's highest level of competition and was gifted in so many ways. He understood defenses.

When I met quarterbacks we recruited, I had to have a good gut feeling about the guy if we were going to seriously pursue him. I can't really define what I was looking for, but I had to sense…something. Some people call it the "*it* factor." For the most part, my gut feeling was usually right with the quarterbacks we recruited. In some years you might need to sign a quarterback for depth, and you don't have the strongest feeling about those intangible factors. But with Chase there were zero doubts. He impressed me in so many ways. His confidence, his character, his leadership. And, oh yeah, his right arm.

In December, after that lousy 2004 season, we made a visit to Chase's home in Texas. He had been committed to us for five months, but there are no guarantees in recruiting. In four years at Missouri we were 22–25 with one winning season. Chase had lost one game his last three years in high school. One loss. We lost *five* games in a row just a few months earlier. Was he still on board? How could we possibly keep this guy?

We walked in the Daniels' home and I acknowledged to Chase and his parents the struggles we had faced. We had some problems, and I didn't hide behind them. We had to own our problems. I told Chase and his mom and dad, "I'm confident we're going to win at Missouri. Our program has worked everywhere else. We inherited a tough situation, but we're right on the edge of doing some great things."

I'll never forget, Chase's mom, Vickie, let out a big sigh. "Okay, Coach," she said. "I'm glad you brought that up and talked to us about it." They were on board. We had our quarterback.

Shortly before national signing day in February, the University of Texas lost a committed quarterback, Ryan Perrilloux, to LSU. Texas had been Chase's dream school. His high school coach, Todd Dodge, played quarterback for the Longhorns in the 1980s. As we feared, Texas coach Mack Brown made an 11th-hour pitch to our future quarterback. Uh-oh.

I had to call Chase.

"Chase, is everything okay?"

"Coach, everything's fine," he assured me. "You want me more than they do. You were the first school to offer me a scholarship. I'm coming to Missouri."

That was obviously a great phone call for Missouri football, but it also made a statement about Chase. He didn't get caught up in the sudden interest and all the hype. He could have easily said, "Coach, Texas has always been my dream school. They finally came to their senses. I'm going to be a Longhorn." But he didn't, thankfully.

Chase's time would come, but in 2005 it was still Brad Smith's team.

• • •

The new offense changed our team, but we still struggled in some ways. We debuted the offense against Arkansas State at Arrowhead Stadium in Kansas City. Brad Smith threw for 300 yards and four touchdowns and nearly ran for 100 yards in a big win. The offense was explosive again the next week against New Mexico, but our defense couldn't get off the field. It turned into a 45–35 loss, another difficult defeat that proved our team still had a long way to go. Texas went on to win the national championship that year and we were one of the teams in their way. After losing to the Longhorns, we bounced back with a win at Oklahoma State, then came home to host Iowa State for homecoming.

We took a quick 14–0 lead with two defensive touchdowns, but Iowa State scored the next 24 points and had the lead late into the fourth quarter. Midway through the fourth quarter Brad had to come out of the game after taking a shot to his head. It was time to find out what Chase Daniel was all about. He led us on two long scoring drives in the final five minutes and tied the game with a touchdown pass with 20 seconds left. In overtime, we kicked a field goal to win 27–24.

The medical staff cleared Brad to come back into the game, but the coaches and I discussed it on the headsets and kept Chase on the field. We had all the momentum with him in the game.

After the game, a pivotal win for our program, I learned a lot about Chase Daniel. That was the most extensive playing time he'd gotten since high school, and it was easy to see we had a special player on our hands. There was nothing normal about the way he played as a true freshman. He won the game for us and might have saved our season. He might have saved our jobs, too.

After the game, I found him in the locker room. I had to warn him what was coming next. "The media's going to come after you now. Are you ready for that?" He knew exactly what I was talking about. I didn't have to explain what I meant.

"Yeah, Coach, I'll take care of that," he said. "We all know who the starter is."

He went out in front of the reporters and, of course, he was asked if he thought he should start the next game. Chase never blinked. "I'm the backup," he said. "Brad Smith is the starting quarterback." You can't have a kid handle that situation any better than he did. He wanted to make it clear he had no expectation to be the starter. It was the ultimate sign of respect for Brad, our senior leader.

Chase said the same thing Monday at our weekly press conference.

"Brad's the leader of this team and has been for four years," he told the reporters. "Nothing will change at all, and I don't want it to."

In Chase, we knew we had a guy who was at a different level in the way he thought about the game, the way he prepared for the game, the way he competed, the way he believed in himself. I thought he had those qualities, but you never know until you see the player on the field when the score counts. It took me back to 2002, when Brad was a freshman. We knew we had a guy in line who could play at a high level at the most important position on the field.

There was never any lingering controversy, mostly because of the way Chase handled those questions after the game. Brad went back into the starting lineup the next week and led us to another win—and not just any win. We beat Nebraska 41–24, oddly enough the same score of our milestone win over the Huskers in 2003. Brad was at his very best, with 234 passing yards, 246 rushing yards, and four touchdowns. We were 5–2, one win away from bowl eligibility. And we had our quarterback of the future on deck.

After the Nebraska win, our players were feeling pretty good. They probably enjoyed walking around campus and hearing the praise. But then we went on the road and lost to Kansas 13–3. It was only the second time we failed to score a touchdown with Brad at the controls of the offense. Kansas' defense had good game plans for us during Brad's four years. One loss turned into two when we lost the next week at Colorado. As a program, we still hadn't learned how to handle success.

We came home to play Baylor in Brad's last home game.

With six minutes in the game, we faced a crucial fourth-and-1. We were winning, but Baylor had trimmed our lead from 24 to eight and held all the momentum. At the time you never think this way, but looking back, our whole football program was on the line. If we don't convert this fourth down, Baylor would get the ball around midfield and, the way things were going, probably rally to win the game, or at least take us to overtime. The next week we had the season finale at Kansas State, where Missouri hadn't won since 1989. If we don't beat Baylor, we're longshots at Kansas State. Lose both and no bowl game—and maybe my job is in jeopardy.

In other words, we *had* to make this first down. We called a quarterback sneak into the A-gap. Brad picked up the yard, bounced it outside, and kept running...and running...and running. All I wanted was a yard and he gave us 56—and a touchdown. We won 31–16, and we were bowl eligible.

I just remember going home after the game and walking into my house where my family was euphoric, clapping, hugging, crying. We get so emotionally wrapped up in these games because they mean so much for our players and, ultimately, our careers. But they mean so much to our families, too. We lose that game and maybe we never get to see the Big 12 North championship seasons in the coming years.

But first, a bowl game. We finished the regular season 6–5 after another loss at Kansas State. Our reward is another trip to Shreveport for the Independence Bowl against another SEC team, this time South Carolina, in its first year under Steve Spurrier. It was the first time we ever met, but shortly after that game, we bumped into each other at the national coaches convention and talked for more than an hour. We had plenty to discuss.

Bowl games are tricky, especially for teams that weren't used to playing in them. We were in the second quarter, down 21–0, and I was miserable, taking everything that went wrong personally. I screwed this whole thing up. I still hadn't trained my team to have fun but be ready to play our best by game time. They still didn't get it! Then Markus King, a senior cornerback, picked off a pass on the goal line and returned it 99 yards. We added another touchdown right before the half and our locker room was crazy. We were down 28–14, but it was like we were winning the national championship game. In the second half we outscored them 24–3—three Brad Smith touchdown runs and a field goal—and won the game by a touchdown. It was the biggest comeback win in Mizzou history. Brad was vintage Brad in the second half, racking up more than 400 yards of offense and accounting for all of our offensive touchdowns. He went out on a moment that he deserved.

Chase played a series in the game, but even though Brad struggled in the first half, we stuck with our senior. A lot of friends asked me after the game why we didn't bench Brad. (I suspect they were bold enough to ask only because we won the game.) I just went back to the factors I always used to measure a quarterback. Was he still poised? Was he focused? Brad was in charge. We just had to encourage him. But I also realized that we would not have been playing in this game if not for Brad Smith. I felt with all he had done for us, I should give him an opportunity in the second half.

Brad finished his Mizzou career with a record of just 25–23. Nothing spectacular. If you were around Missouri prior to Brad's arrival, you'd understand the extraordinary circumstances.

It was a huge win for our program and a huge season. Mike Alden never said a word about my job security. At the time I never worried about job security. I never talked to my staff about it or my family. But looking back now, the 2005 season could have given us four losing records in five years. How do you convince your fans and your recruits that I'm a pretty good coach if we're home for bowl season four out of five years? Thanks to Brad, we never had to worry about that.

As our personnel was developing and maturing, Brad was still the catalyst. As much as anything he was just a remarkable young man. He was so special. He was a tremendous leader by the way he carried himself and treated others. He was a very strong Christian, but he never alienated anyone who wasn't. His form of leadership was to put his life on display to see how he lived on and off the field. You hear coaches say all the time that a good player leads by example. Brad's examples were simply the best. You can be the greatest coach in the world, but if you don't have great players you don't win games. Without Brad, without all the special things he did for our program, we might not have lasted long at Missouri.

• • •

When the clock hit zeroes at the Independence Bowl, some of our players celebrated at the 25-yard line. That was Aaron O'Neal's number. Aaron was on our minds throughout that year and beyond. For years to come, we came up with ways to honor his memory. We kept his locker intact and turned it into a memorial. In 2008, which would have been Aaron's senior year, a different senior wore his No. 25 for each game. From then on, a linebacker was assigned No. 25 and wore it for the length of his career. We had his picture up throughout the facility. We hung an "A.O." sign in the locker room and made sure to touch it every time we walked in or out through the door. It was important to hit the sign and touch Aaron every day.

When new players came into our program each year, we told them about Aaron and what he meant to our coaches and players. He was such a special kid. In a way we never could have envisioned, we had leaders in our program emerge from Aaron's death and its aftermath, guys like Lorenzo Williams and Martin Rucker. Our players loved Aaron, and you could sense they became united in trying to honor him. It was important, too, that they trusted our staff. They were hurt and confused, but they didn't come out and criticize our coaches for what happened on the field that day. Our coaches and players got closer in some ways because we all went through the grieving process together.

I realized then, too, I had to open myself up more to my players. I needed to talk to them, to hug them, to tell them I loved them. That came more naturally after we lost Aaron.

• • •

The 2006 season felt like the start of a new era. Chase Daniel was our quarterback. It was our second year in the new offense. We were starting to recruit and develop other playmakers to surround the quarterback. We started the season 6–0, the program's best start in 33 years. That made us bowl eligible before Halloween. That didn't happen very often at Missouri. We were learning how to win games but still didn't always know how to handle success. I was still apprehensive because we didn't quite know how good we were. But the players were starting to absorb the process of how to prepare and play well consistently.

We didn't lose to Texas A&M very often, but we lost down there when a fake field goal backfired. We cleared some hurdles that season, finally beating Kansas State. Missouri hadn't beaten the Wildcats since 1992. But we did that season, by 20 points at home. That was significant, even though Bill Snyder had stepped away from coaching that year. He had the Kansas State program right up there with Oklahoma and Texas and Nebraska as the class of the Big 12. We'd get more chances against Bill down the road.

We came home and lost a competitive game to Oklahoma—a game some might remember for Chase Coffman dropping a wide-open pass along the sideline. He never dropped a ball in his life, and by the time he left Mizzou a few years later he caught more passes than anyone in program history. But it's funny how you sometimes remember the plays that didn't go your way. He put on a show the next year at Colorado, one of the many great games he played for us.

We went to Nebraska the next week. You could tell from the opening kickoff they wanted us bad. We had beaten them two of the last three years and before we knew it, we were down 27–3. They'd win by a couple touchdowns.

After a bye week we headed to Iowa State. Shortly before the game, Mizzou announced my contract extension through the 2011 season. What followed was one of the craziest games of my career. We led at halftime but fell behind in the third quarter. We cut the lead to five early in the fourth quarter and began to march down the field. We got to the 2-yard line with 26 seconds left. On fourth down, Chase found a lane and plunged into the end zone for the game-winning touchdown. What a comeback victory!

But then came the flag—holding on Monte Wyrick, our right guard. Nobody calls holding down there on the goal line. It never happens. Never. I erupted.

We had one more play, but Iowa State sacked Chase and won the game 21–16.

I never, ever in all my years before or after that night complained about officiating after a game. But my players fought back after a bad start and put themselves in position to win the game. And the officials took it away from them. I was so proud of the way my team responded. We'd been in those situations before and came up short. I admitted to the media after the game that we didn't play well, but good teams still find a way to win and that's exactly what we did. It was devastating.

The next day I talked to Walt Anderson, the Big 12's coordinator of officials, and he apologized for the penalty. He said it was wrong. Holding never should have been called. We should have been given credit for the touchdown and the win.

I felt really good hearing that, especially for my players. We had lost three games in a row, but we stayed positive around our players. How could we be disappointed with them? We didn't play well, but we battled and did everything we could to win the game.

I didn't pay any attention to the media coverage that week, but I had to be aware of what my players were hearing and seeing. I knew I was getting some criticism for talking so much about the penalty. But it was important that my players hear me talk positively about the way they rallied at Iowa State. This was the one time I thought it was appropriate to talk about the officiating. They botched the call and took away what should have been a victory.

We had one regular-season game left, at home against Kansas. We carried a three-game losing streak to our biggest rival into that game. We were bowl eligible, but we needed a win in the worst way.

Heading into the game we thought everyone was timing our punts, so we installed a fake we thought we could use against Kansas.

Up three late in the third quarter, we called the fake on fourth down and got Kansas to jump offside. We took the first down and marched to another touchdown. We won 42–17 and after the game I was careful how I chose my words. I thanked all those fans and our administration and alumni that believed in my players all week long. I appreciated the contract extension, especially because they didn't wait until after the season to decide. It was a statement. It was a lesson for our fans. This wasn't a time to jump off board. We needed their faith.

We played Oregon State in the Sun Bowl, and it makes me sick to think about that game. We gave up the lead in the fourth quarter and lost by a point on a last-second touchdown and two-point conversion. Those losses tear your guts out. Aside from the outcome of that game, our team made progress that season. Plus, it was the first time we went to consecutive bowl games. But we still weren't winning consistently. That would change.

By 2007, we were clearly getting better. We were starting to have multiple all-conference players. Our depth chart was starting to look like it's supposed to look. Lord, it had taken a long time, but I wasn't a quick-fix guy. We were never going to load up on junior college transfers and take short cuts.

We resumed the Illinois rivalry in St. Louis that year. It seems like every one of those games is a breakout game for someone. In 2007, it was Jeremy Maclin's turn. He was a special playmaker out of St. Louis, but he hurt his knee the summer before his freshman year and missed the entire 2006 season. Had he played we might have won two more games—and maybe won the North Division. Against Illinois, in his first college game and in his hometown, J-Mac caught a touchdown and returned a punt for a touchdown. Boom, just like that, we had a great young player out of St. Louis and suddenly Chase had a new weapon in the offense.

J-Mac was a national recruit, just a great kid who was so grounded emotionally and mentally. We were able to get him to flip his commitment from Oklahoma, one of the best moves we made in recruiting. We needed a guy like that in the offense to join the great tight ends we had signed and developed, Martin Rucker and Chase Coffman. We had the running back in Tony Temple, an explosive playmaker from Kansas City. We suddenly had some skill players who perfectly fit this spread offense. The potential was there, but to translate all that talent into double-digit wins, something Missouri had done only once and not since 1960, we needed to think right. Around that time, we introduced the concept of "whistle to snap" to our players. Once the whistle blew to stop the play, what is your mind doing to prepare you for the next snap? We taught them how to think instead of just saying, "Hey guys, get focused." That had a great effect on those teams. Andrew Gachkar was a prime example. He came in as a freshman safety in 2007. He played some special teams his first year, moved to linebacker, and went from a decent player to an All–Big 12 player. He was never overly confident, but he embraced our "whistle to snap" teaching and became one of the best linebackers in the Big 12 and developed into an NFL player.

We needed to become a team that played its best every week. In 2006, we were still streaky, but the atmosphere was starting to feel right.

After beating Illinois, we went to Ole Miss and beat an SEC team with NFL talent. We dominated Nebraska 41–6 to open Big 12 play. Then we went down to Oklahoma and lost a close game. We had a costly fumbled exchange because of a signal breakdown on our sideline. One player got one signal; another player got another signal. We never quite recovered because of that simple coaching mistake. That's my fault!

But we recovered that next week and ran off a five-game winning streak, all against conference teams. We had confidence. We were finishing games the right way.

All along, as we're going through our best season in decades, we were very well aware that Kansas was winning all its games, too—though we played by far the tougher schedule with power conference teams Illinois and Ole Miss to start the year, plus a road game at Oklahoma. We didn't talk about it, but we knew what was coming at the end of the regular season.

We just methodically went through the season, and the more we won, the higher the stakes got each week. Those stakes were incredibly clear by the time we kicked off November 24 in Kansas City against the Jayhawks. Both teams were unranked in the preseason polls, but here we were in the final week of the regular season. Kansas was No. 2, and we were No. 3. A day earlier, No. 1 LSU lost to Arkansas. That meant the biggest matchup in college football on the final week of the regular season would be Missouri-Kansas. Who could have ever imagined? The winner would capture the Big 12 North Division and play Oklahoma for the conference championship. Beat the Sooners and we'd clinch a spot in the BCS national championship game. What an opportunity—for either team.

I knew it would be the biggest game in the rivalry's history and, let's be real honest, it would never be bigger than No. 2 vs. No. 3 with a chance to be the No. 1 team in the country and be in position to play for a national championship. All I wanted to do was win it because that game would be remembered forever. ESPN *College GameDay* was on site. Kansas City was electric. The environment outside Arrowhead was like the past Rose Bowls I experienced—just a little colder. When our Washington teams played in the Rose Bowl, our fans would come up alongside our caravan and beat the sides of our busses. The same thing happened that day in Kansas City. Our fans were going crazy while we're shuffling along at 2 miles per hour through the Arrowhead parking lot. Just a surreal environment. That's what big games feel like.

Kansas had such a good team. Their quarterback, Todd Reesing, had put up outstanding numbers all year. The defense had some NFL talent, especially at cornerback.

I've never gone back and watched that game on film. I'll probably get around to it someday. I've never gone back and watched any games—and I can't really explain why.

But people still talk about that game. The players, the coaches, the fans especially. On top of it all, it was such a great game, back and forth, so much drama. It felt like a national championship game, where both teams had everything on the line—and against their historic, hated rival. I've coached in conference championship games and big January bowl games, but the environment that day in Kansas City was unlike anything I've ever experienced.

I got to know Kansas coach Mark Mangino during our conference meetings. Good guy, good coach. I never quite understood why he got fired the next year, but I always respected what he did with that program.

I didn't know much about the Missouri-Kansas rivalry when I first got to Mizzou. At Washington, we had a great in-state rivalry with Washington State. Bowling Green was our big rival at Toledo. But nothing compared to the animosity, the bitterness, and the history that Missouri and Kansas shared for so many years. It didn't take me long to appreciate what it meant to our fans. That's why we've got to revive the Border War. There's no reason—none—these two schools can't work something out and play against each other in football and basketball. There needs to be a meeting on neutral ground in Kansas City where the leaders of both programs agree on dates and location. Let's rotate between Kansas City and then back on our campuses in Columbia and Lawrence. Let's play it the first or second game of every season, so it's always going to be a big game for both teams. In our early years at Mizzou, even when we were scuffling along to build our program, the Kansas game meant everything.

The two schools had been working to move the game to Arrowhead for a long time. The 2007 game was originally scheduled to be in Lawrence. I thought it was a great idea for a lot of reasons to move that game to the neutral-site field, much like we did for the Illinois game in St. Louis. We lost a home game out of the deal every other year, but the pay from the Chiefs was good and it gave us an NFL stage for our biggest game. People stood the entire game in the rain and cold. You can't create a better game-day setting.

We dominated early and led 21–0 in the third quarter, but Kansas stormed back and made it a game in the fourth quarter.

It wasn't the cleanest game. We had 14 penalties. Our kids were at an emotional level they had never experienced before. Our defense gave up a lot of yards through the air. Our kids were just so wired that it affected our focus at times. But Chase was extraordinary and our defense sacked Todd Reesing at the end of game to preserve a 36–28 win. He had this big patch of mud stuck in his facemask. That's the image everyone remembers.

With the win, we climbed to No. 1 in the national polls, the first time that had happened since 1960. How did it feel? I couldn't really say. When you're living in the moment, your focus quickly shifts to what's on the line in six days. You get the news you're now No. 1, you process it for about five minutes, then you move on to whatever's next on your daily checklist. I was very good at that. I never let my mind focus on the past. I didn't drive around town and let my mind wonder, "Wow, we're No. 1!"

Chase was on the cover of *Sports Illustrated* the next week, and that win all but clinched his invitation to New York for the Heisman Trophy presentation. So many exciting things were going on around our program because of that win and all the wins that put us in position to be No. 1. Do I wish I could have enjoyed the moment more? I don't know. Maybe some coaches can do that. I just never did. I turned the page. That's how Coach James handled those situations. He didn't spend any time celebrating or dwelling on what just happened, not when there were more games to play.

I'm not the first coach to feel this way, but for me, losing always hurt more than winning felt good. Did I deal with losses better the more I coached? I think so. I didn't handle defeat well early in my career, or even our first few years at Missouri. I really lost it when we didn't play our best. But did I learn to enjoy the wins more? Maybe just a little. But another thing I always admired about Coach James was how he handled Sundays after a game, win or lose. You didn't change the routine. After losses early on, I'd really get upset with players on Sunday nights. I'd be just as upset with me as I was the players. I just wanted them to have this freakin' desire to be successful, the same drive I had. Teams had to mature to approach big games like that. We had to realize the grit it takes, the mental toughness required to get there.

That 2007 team figured it out.

We made it to our first conference championship game to face a familiar opponent. Just seven weeks earlier we had lost at Oklahoma.

This time we'd meet in San Antonio. The stakes were clear. We win and we're playing for the BCS national championship. Our players came in with great confidence and played really well in the first half. We just couldn't finish. Back at Washington, when Bob Stull was the offensive coordinator and I coached receivers, he used to say every Saturday before the offense got on the bus, "Remember, the team that makes the fewest mistakes is probably going to win." It was simple but so true, especially when it came to critical mistakes in big games like this one. We threw a late interception and could never regain momentum and Oklahoma pulled away by three touchdowns.

We were obviously crushed by the result, but we knew we'd still land in a good bowl game. The Orange Bowl had a chance to take a team from the Big 12, and we were clearly deserving of a BCS bowl. Instead, the Orange Bowl settled on Kansas. Our fans and players were obviously upset. I was disappointed, too. We had just beaten Kansas a week earlier in an epic victory. There was no sense in pouting over the Orange Bowl. We had absolutely no control over their decision. They took a team we had just beaten at a neutral site. We were the division champions. We should have been in the Orange Bowl, but I knew politics were involved. This wasn't purely a football decision. Whether it was the bowl committee or Kansas or the league office, something didn't add up. We were newcomers to the bowl process, especially at the BCS level. So was Kansas. Maybe their administration had some relationships that worked to their benefit. I never understood the details. All we knew was the Orange Bowl took Kansas instead. Fine. Let's move on. Who's next?

Arkansas.

We went to the Cotton Bowl to play a team from the SEC. I had to make sure our players were still excited about that outcome. When I talked to them after the bowl selection process played out, I chose to be positive. We had to tell our team about the generations of Cotton Bowl history. We had to embrace the opportunity.

Before that, I joined Chase Daniel in New York for the Heisman Trophy presentation along with a couple of our coaches and Chase's family. I felt so fortunate to be in the room that night. Some great coaches never get to take part in that historic environment. You see it on TV your whole life, never realizing the room is so small and they've got assigned seating for everyone. I was so proud to be there with Chase. He finished fourth and had a great attitude about the whole process. He was honored to be in the mix. That moment gave Missouri more national respect, having one of our players on that platform.

As for the Cotton Bowl, some people might have wondered if our team would be motivated for that game after missing out on a BCS bowl. But we were motivated—and dominant. It was a great finish to the season. Tony Temple and our offensive line controlled the game in a 38–7 victory. After starting the year unranked, we finished fourth in the national polls, a great statement for how far our program had come.

• • •

I didn't coach very well in 2008. We began the year ranked No. 6 in the preseason, another great sign of respect for all the success we had in 2007 and all the returning talent on our team. Can you back it up and do it again? It wasn't the kids' fault at all. What would I have done differently? I'm not really sure. We lost four games in 2008, but we were better than a 10–4 team. We had so much talent. We had Chase Daniel back. We had J-Mac back. We had Chase Coffman back. We had Sean Weatherspoon and William Moore on defense and a lot of talented kids. We could have won 12 games again, maybe more.

We had a huge win at Nebraska to start 5–0 and climbed all the way to No. 3. Our guys were in a zone they had never been close to approaching at this level. We had won 17 of our last 19 games. The only losses during that stretch were two competitive games against an elite Oklahoma program. Looking back, when we got back from Nebraska, I should have said more to the team that Sunday night or that Monday. When you start winning like that, you'll have guys who all of a sudden back off just enough, just one notch. But one notch is significant. It was my responsibility to keep that from happening.

We came home to host Oklahoma State and threw three interceptions. Overall, we'd done well against that program, going 3–1 since we came to Mizzou. Our players might disagree with this, but there's a big difference between the hunter and the hunted. The roles had reversed at Mizzou. Teams in the Big 12 started to realize that to beat us they had to take their play to another level. Some teams were able to do that, and that's what Oklahoma State did that night. We still thought we were the better team, but we didn't do enough to win the game. We went to Austin the following week and lost to No. 1 Texas, a really good Longhorns team with a Heisman finalist in Colt McCoy.

All of a sudden after winning 17-of-19 games, we were on a losing streak, the first time we lost consecutive games since November 2006. I had to take a different approach. We had to focus on nothing but our next game, a 5:30 visit from Colorado. We couldn't be consumed with the rankings or the standings. Colorado had just come off a win over Kansas State. I came into our press conference that Monday and had one thing on my mind: "5:30 on Saturday." I repeated it over and over again. You can't use that tactic every week, but our kids grabbed hold of that sucker. They started repeating me all week to the media and on the practice field: "5:30 on Saturday, 5:30 on Saturday." It's all that mattered in our world. Our guys responded and took control of that game from the start, which ended as a 58–0 win. Now we're sitting there 6–2 and in control of the North Division. We got on a run. Baylor, win. Kansas State, win. Iowa State, win. We clinched the North in Ames, Iowa, which meant we'd have back-to-back games at Arrowhead Stadium, the regular-season finale against Kansas and the Big 12 championship game.

We had a couple losses but still felt confident against Kansas—maybe too confident. I was really disappointed in how we played.

We trailed by 16 and came back to take a late lead, but our defense couldn't get a stop. Kansas won 40–37. We had already clinched the Big 12 North, so we'd be coming back to Arrowhead a week later to face No. 1 Oklahoma. That did not go well. It was a rough day for the Tigers and another loss.

We still weren't used to winning at this level in big games like that. It showed up at times that season. I thought I could have done more to have our team ready.

It was back to Texas for our bowl game, this time to the Alamo Bowl in San Antonio to play Northwestern. It would be Chase Daniel's final game, and we had a few more players who were thinking about entering the NFL draft. We were fortunate to make just enough plays to rally and win in overtime. We must have had a thing for overtime. That made us 6–1 in overtime games at Missouri.

It was still a great year. We won 10 games, which had only been done once before in team history—in 2007. But we had so many players back from that 12-win team. I just wish we could have done more. We were too talented to lose four games.

Along with a talented senior class that changed Mizzou football forever, it was Jeremy Maclin's final game with us. He entered the NFL draft that offseason, but not without a lot of thought and discussion. Just like Justin Smith eight years earlier, I told J-Mac that if he were my son, I'd advise him to make the move—as long as he wanted to make the move. He went to the Eagles with the 19th pick overall. We had six players drafted that year, the most for Mizzou in 28 years. That was another sign that our program was developing talent and earning respect.

That offseason was unique because both our coordinators left for other jobs. To that point, I hadn't lost an assistant coach in our first eight years at Missouri, a string of staff cohesion that was unmatched around the country. It was so critical for the success and continuity we had in our program. My staff was a group of great teachers and great recruiters who loved training and helping our kids grow and mature. Dave Christensen, our offensive coordinator and offensive line coach, had been named the head coach at Wyoming before our bowl game. It didn't come up very often for me, but when you're the head coach, you're always looking at your staff and trying to map out plans if one of your assistants leaves, especially if it's a coordinator. My philosophy was heavily influenced by Don James. If you have an internal candidate on your staff ready to promote, that's the ideal situation. But you have to be honest with yourself. Is he ready for the promotion? If not, you've got to look outside. I felt really good about David Yost taking over as coordinator. He had been our quarterbacks coach at Toledo and for our first eight years at Missouri. He had helped develop Brad Smith and Chase Daniel into all-time greats at Mizzou. Christensen thought Yost was ready. I did, too. It was similar to years earlier when Bob Stull left Washington's staff and Coach James promoted me to run the offense.

A lot of head coaches like to look for high-profile names to fill coordinator jobs. They want to capture some buzz. That was never important to me. I was never concerned with perception because that first impression with a hire doesn't last, good or bad. It's all about results.

When you bring in older, established assistants who have worked with other head coaches, they tend to struggle with this system and this process. They can be set in their ways. We have specific ways of teaching and coaching and communicating. There's no compromise. That's why I valued experience and familiarity with me and our system. If you can hire young guys that are dying to be great coaches and they understand your program, they become soldiers of the program. That was my vision. That's why I always looked internally first.

Then after signing day in February, Matt Eberflus, our defensive coordinator, left for a job with the Cleveland Browns. He came to me and said he was contacted by the Browns. Eric Mangini was the head coach, and Rob Ryan was running the defense. They wanted Matt to coach linebackers. Matt told me he'd really like to coach in the NFL. I was surprised by that. I never had that urge to coach in the NFL. So I talked to one of the coaches in Cleveland about Matt. I thought he was absolutely qualified, but I was honest with Matt.

"If you take this job and decide you want to get back into college coaching, you'll be able to do that," I told him. "But I don't think it's a good move if you want to become a college head coach. Because more head coaches come from the college game than they do the NFL. You have to be aware of that." He'd be giving up a coordinator position to be a position coach. But he put a lot of thought into it and it turned out to be a good move for him. He later went to the Dallas Cowboys and has been a valuable part of their staff. He's a really sharp coach and has a great future.

I had to do some soul searching before deciding on what to do with the staff. We had three position coaches on the defensive side that had been with me for a long time and were outstanding coaches. I went with Dave Steckel, our linebackers coach, and that was a very good move for our program. He did such a great job for us.

Back at Toledo, Dean Pees was our defensive coordinator in the early years. He had worked with Stec earlier in their careers, so on Dean's advice we brought in Stec to coach our defensive line and later our linebackers. He had great energy. He'd served in the Marines and he came from great bloodlines. His older brother, Les, had coached in college and the NFL for a long time.

Like Yost, even though I decided to promote Stec from the staff, it wasn't an automatic decision. I really had to think about these moves. Were they our best options? I believed they were.

We had to make a few staff additions. I promoted Barry Odom from director of operations to safeties coach. Barry had played at Missouri and spent a couple years as the head coach at Rock Bridge High School in Columbia. We needed an offensive line coach to replace Christensen, and Barry had a connection to a coach at LSU, Josh Henson, an offensive assistant under Les Miles. We brought him in to coach our O-line.

A few years later, Barry left the staff to become the defensive coordinator at Memphis. Immediately, I had three coaches in my office urging me to hire Alex Grinch, a former grad assistant from our staff who was out with Christensen in Wyoming coaching defense.

He was a good young coach, but there was one issue—he was my nephew, the son of my sister Kathy. I had one rule when it came to hiring staff: never hire your friends. It's a tough business and you never want to have conflicts with a close friend. There's a line there you don't want to cross—even more when it comes to family. I'd never been in position to hire a family member as a full-time assistant, so I had serious reservations when the opportunity came up.

One of my coaches told me, "I know you don't hire family or friends, but Alex is the right guy for this job." Five minutes later another coach came to my office, "Coach, I'm just telling you, your nephew is a damn good coach. Go get him."

Alex was similar to Eberflus and Odom. Young, intense, really sharp. I was tempted to make the move, and my staff finally convinced me it was the right decision. I'm sure there was a perception out there that I was only doing my nephew a favor, but I was the guy in our building who needed to be persuaded this was the right move—not the other coaches. It turned out to be a great move, and Alex's work with us was rewarded in 2015 when he landed the coordinator job at Washington State, where he's done great work.

I intentionally created some separation between me and my coaches. I didn't hang out with them socially. I always wanted to have caring relationships with my staff, but there was a professional line I didn't want to cross. I wanted family to be important to my coaches. At Washington, we'd coach from 7:00 AM to 11:00 PM most nights, which left you very little time to see your family. That's why

I changed our schedule when I became a head coach. I wanted our coaches home with their family by seven in the evening. I thought that would help us have success. You could have a healthy family life and still coach to win football games. It helped that technology advanced so much we didn't have to spend as much time crunching numbers by hand. But I'd say all the time, if you could guarantee me that we'd win games by staying at the office until 2 in the morning, I'd stay until four in the morning. But I thought it was just as healthy for our coaches to get out of the office and come home to their wives and kids. I believe that factored into why we had such continuity on our staff. Our coaches would go to the annual coaching convention and talk to guys from other staffs who complained about never being home, never seeing their kids grow up. Our coaches didn't experience that in our environment.

With our reshuffled staff in place, we stepped into 2009 with new pieces on the field, most notably at quarterback.

Mizzou vs. Kansas

November 26, 2011

Kansas City, Missouri

It was our final Big 12 regular-season game and our last game against Kansas for the foreseeable future. It had already been a difficult year for me personally, but another win would bolster our bowl credentials.

Team Meeting
Thursday, November 24, 3:30 PM

"When I arrived on campus I learned about the Kansas game. You inherited this rivalry. The responsibility was given to you and me. They don't like us and we don't like them. If you see a KU T-shirt or license plate, it should piss you off, even for just a moment. If that doesn't happen to you, you have not figured it out.

"You will remember every KU game that you were a part of for the rest of your life. This is my 11th as head coach and I vividly remember each one. Often we talk about how we play for each other. We do. In a Kansas game we play for a lot more. You play it for every Missouri Tiger that has ever worn the uniform. The rivalry game is bigger than you and me. The first meeting you had as freshmen I said to every one of you: 'This will leave your mark at Mizzou. You will leave with a win-loss record, a bowl record, a championship game record, and your KU record.' And this game has huge ramifications on them all. This is a big game and you've been trained for a big game. This game is different. You and I must take it personal. The bottom line, it's your responsibility and mine to do everything in our power to play our best, bring our 'A' game, and win. Kick their ass!"

Final: Missouri 24, Kansas 10

In our final Big 12 regular-season game, the Jayhawks were no match. James Franklin recovered after three first-half interceptions, and we clinched our third straight win to end the regular season. The Arrowhead Stadium crowd chanted "SEC! SEC!" as we closed out our final win in what soon became our former conference.

7

Mizzou: Reload & Redeem

YOU ALWAYS WANT TO HAVE A QUARTERBACK ON DECK. You won't always have that, but we were fortunate with quarterbacks. After Chase Daniel, we had Blaine Gabbert next in line. Blaine was everything you looked for in a quarterback, and that's why so many programs recruited him out of Parkway West High School in St. Louis. He was first committed to Nebraska, but we convinced him to change his mind. He joined the program in 2008, and we played him some as a freshman behind Chase. Our whole philosophy was to have at least one quarterback ready to take over. We did the same thing at Washington year after year. Blaine was very athletic for his size. He could run for a big guy. He was the prototype quarterback with the big, strong arm. But he was hurt a lot in high school, so he was relatively inexperienced when he came to us.

Blaine had played some as a freshman, but just like Brad Smith and Jeremy Maclin, his breakout game came in St. Louis against Illinois. Blaine was impressive in his first start: 319 passing yards and three touchdowns in a 28-point win. It was cool to see him play that well in his hometown. (We were fortunate in those NFL stadiums on both sides of the state, St. Louis and Kansas City. I always thought those games were good for the state and the whole region.)

Coming off 2007 and 2008, we continued to have high expectations. We had lost a lot of players to the NFL—six players were drafted in 2009, and Chase made the NFL as an undrafted free agent—but at this point we weren't calling it a rebuilding year. I'd go into every year thinking we'd win all of our games. I'd never start the season, count up the games I thought we'd win and lose, and put a note in my desk that read, "We're going 7–5 this year." I just couldn't bring myself to set expectations that we'd lose a game—even when we were not very good. I'd never do that. Maybe I would have emotionally handled the losses better if I had set myself up for some disappointment, but I wasn't wired that way.

I was concerned about Blaine feeling like he had to be the next Chase Daniel but also concerned because we lost a lot of great players from the 2008 team, including three of our best receivers in J-Mac, Tommy Saunders, and Chase Coffman, our All-American tight end. We still had some good young receivers on the team and had no idea Danario Alexander would become an All-American as a senior. Every quarterback is different. You just try to call plays that you believe work best for him.

Blaine had a strong first few weeks—then Nebraska came to town for a Thursday night game. It was a nasty, rainy night. There had been flash flooding around the state that week. A power outage took out our new scoreboard in the north end zone. On the field, Nebraska defensive tackle Ndamukong Suh controlled the line of scrimmage. Blaine badly sprained his ankle on one of Suh's sacks, an injury that affected him for most of the season. He was a tough kid, though. Blaine was so determined to play through that injury. He was such a team player.

I was conflicted. Ultimately, the team's medical staff always made the final decision if a player can play, but we had to make sure Blaine was functional. He gutted through the middle part of that season on one leg. It was hard to be playing with a hobbled quarterback during a brutal stretch of games. Nebraska, Oklahoma State, and Texas. He was stubborn when it came to that ankle—but a good stubborn. He would barely acknowledge the injury to the reporters who covered the team. He refused to make any excuses. I really admired that. Blaine was a lot tougher than I thought he was before I got to know him. At one point I brought him in my office to talk. "Blaine, I'm not sure you can play," I told him. He was on the verge of tears. "Coach, I can play." Maybe if we kept him out one game he would have been better for the next three, but you never know.

He was adamant on staying on the field. We won a lot of games those two previous seasons and lost a lot of players from those teams, so we faced both high expectations but also the reality that our players weren't as experienced as the guys who led us to all those wins in 2007 and 2008.

After three straight losses, we were sitting at 4–3 and then we bounced back nicely with a win at Colorado. Then Baylor came to Columbia and ran all over us—with a backup quarterback, not even their future Heisman winner Robert Griffin III, who was hurt. Now we were 5–4 headed to Kansas State. We had never beaten Kansas State with Bill Snyder as coach. Danario was having a great year for us, but he took it to another extreme in that game with 10 catches for 200 yards and three touchdowns.

I remember talking to Bill after the game. "Where did 81 come from?" he asked me.

That was my first win over Coach Snyder, and that was significant for me. I really admired him and the way he built his program. He and Coach James had a great relationship. I probably never talked about it publicly, but when you're fortunate to beat a great coach who you really respect, you savor that experience. His teams were always so well-coached.

Danario was such a unique athlete. He had that tremendously long stride and could really accelerate for a bigger guy. If his knee had stayed healthy, he would have been a first-round draft pick. With better knees he would have played 10 years instead of three. You can put him right up there with J-Mac as the best receivers we had at Missouri.

So much of football is confidence, and losing streaks were so damaging. We had to address the adversity. We got some of that back with some late wins over Iowa State and a walk-off field goal win over Kansas back at Arrowhead.

Against Kansas, we were down a point in the final minutes but had the ball in the red zone. I told our running back, Derrick Washington, not to score when he touched the ball. We didn't want Todd Reesing back on the field. The Kansas quarterback had already thrown for almost 500 yards. We would play for the field goal. I told our staff on the headset, "We're playing for a field goal here. I don't want to score a touchdown."

They couldn't believe me. "What do you mean you don't want to score a touchdown?"

"I don't want Reesing back on the field. If we miss this field goal, it's on me. I'll take the heat."

You learn over the years there are certain guys who are so good you don't want the ball in their hands with the chance to beat you. Fortunately, Grant Ressel made the field goal as time expired.

We won the game to push our record to 8–4. That was better than some other Big 12 teams that were in the mix for the same tier of bowl games. Some people were disappointed we got picked for the Texas Bowl in Houston. Iowa State was 6–6 and went to Phoenix for the Insight Bowl, which was perceived as a better bowl. I tried to reinforce a positive angle. You shouldn't be disappointed about going to a bowl. At the same time you want to make sure your administration is being proactive with the process. You weren't allowed to lobby the bowl committee members, but just a few years earlier we suspected Kansas had done some negotiating to get into the Orange Bowl ahead of us.

Bottom line, we still had to show up for our game and we played terribly against Navy. When the matchup was announced I knew this was going to be a huge game for Navy, a chance to play a power conference team in an NFL stadium. For our team, this had the makings of a letdown game. But it was my responsibility to make sure that didn't happen. That game was on me. If you don't play your best, a team as good as Navy can beat you. And that's just what they did. It's a difficult game defensively because Navy's triple option was unlike anything we'd seen during the regular season. But that was no excuse. We were a much better offensive team all season than we were that day. We scored a touchdown on the game's first possession, a little bubble screen to Danario that went for 58 yards. But sometimes that's not good enough. Maybe we got overconfident. Navy whipped us the rest of the day 35–13. I never made too much out of bowl losses. It was a transition year for our program. We played with a banged-up first-year starting quarterback and still managed to win eight games.

◆ ◆ ◆

In that offseason the Big Ten Conference announced it was going to explore expansion. I got worried as more and more talk surfaced about conference realignment. I didn't know where Missouri would land in a game of musical chairs. There was a lot of conversation about some schools going to the Big Ten and some going to the Pac-10. If leagues started poaching the Big 12, where did that leave Missouri? I didn't come here from a smaller conference to suddenly start coaching in another smaller conference. So personally, I had a lot of concerns.

I could sense the tension and the inequality starting to surface during our Big 12 meetings. Texas controlled the conference. People can deny it all they want, but that was the truth. For a guy like Tom Osborne, Nebraska's athletic director and the school's legendary football coach, to come out and say the league wasn't acting in its best self interests, that was significant. And from there Nebraska left for the Big Ten. It was a bold move.

Could that have been Missouri's spot? At the time I thought the Big Ten would have been a great place for Missouri. It was very competitive, very respected. At the time, I never once thought about the possibility of Missouri moving to the SEC. I knew the SEC was a great conference with great teams. But we fit the Big Ten. Geographically we touch states with teams from both leagues, but we're a lot closer to more schools in the Big Ten. When all the talk started, I didn't suspect the SEC would have interest in Missouri. We were still a long way from that scenario unfolding.

Mike Alden and I talked about the Big Ten. He always let me know everything that was happening. He had a meeting in North Carolina with folks from the Big Ten. The Big Ten would have been okay for Missouri, but I still would have been disappointed if things couldn't work in the Big 12. The Big 12 was a great league. We had great rivals. We had great competition. It was just so disappointing how they let it fall apart, to the point that Colorado wanted out and joined the Pac-10 and Nebraska wanted out and joined the Big Ten. Then Texas A&M wanted out and joined the SEC.

Texas had launched the Longhorn Network instead of finding a way to create a Big 12 Network. The TV revenue had always been distributed unevenly in the Big 12, with a larger share going to the teams that were on TV more often. More than anything, I got a sense for how Texas felt about the rest of the conference when we sat down for Big 12 meetings. They operated on their own agenda. It doesn't matter what kind of company you're running—when you have that kind of inequality in terms of control, they'll all implode eventually. I made some candid comments to the media about the league's state of affairs that probably bothered some people, but I was just being honest about the revenue-sharing and decision-making that was affecting the league. People at other schools felt the same way; they just didn't want to say it out loud. Mike Alden probably wished sometimes I had taken a more measured tone, but that's just how I felt.

• • •

When we faced challenging times in our program, I often heard the voice of my dad giving me the simple message whenever times got tough. "Fix it, Gary." He was a master at fixing things himself—radios, computers, you name it.

I lost my dad on February 6, 2010. It seemed like he could survive anything. At 55 he underwent triple bypass surgery and later lived through an aneurism. When I was coaching at Toledo, he was diagnosed with cancer, which doctors traced back to radon exposure. I'd drive over to Akron for a day or two and take him to his cancer treatment. But he lived on until his health deteriorated beyond the point where doctors could fix him. He was 83 when he died.

• • •

By the time we opened preseason camp for 2010, the Big 12 was down to 10 schools. By August, we were focused on football. Unfortunately, adversity came before we broke camp. On the day of our final scrimmage of the preseason, we had to suspend Derrick Washington, our senior running back who had just been voted a team captain. Derrick was accused of sexually assaulting a female tutor, who then issued a restraining order against him. That led to a felony charge, a conviction, and a prison sentence. By then, he was long gone from the program.

This wasn't the first incident for Derrick. Two years earlier he was questioned by police about a sexual assault accusation. When I learned of that, I went through our normal protocol. I alerted Mike

Alden, who then told our chancellor and other school officials. Derrick was never arrested or charged with a crime for the 2008 incident, which came to light years later in an ESPN report about Title IX regulations.

Like always, with Derrick's incidents, I just wanted information so I could pass it along through the proper channels. If it's a case of he said–she said, I can't do anything with that as a head coach. In those cases, I can't make a ruling on accusations that don't lead to charges—unless I know for certain that something wrong took place. We had another case years later with a star player where I learned more information about an incident from people I trusted.

In 2010, when we suspended Derrick, I told him, "This is really bad. Two years ago and now this? This is serious. The police are investigating. We've got problems here." You don't want to falsely accuse a player, but you have to be aggressive verbally because you want to know the truth and you want the player to understand how serious these accusations are.

We never would have allowed Derrick to be voted a captain if we thought the situation would have gone that direction. He went down to Dallas for the Big 12 media days shortly before this unfolded, and obviously we wouldn't have taken him on the trip if we expected the restraining order. Parents give me their sons and expect me to treat them with fairness and handle situations the right way. We had structures set in place should a player be arrested for a felony and then charged. You want to do what's right and deal in honesty.

When it came to discipline issues, the voice of public opinion was never my guiding light. I never made decisions based on how the media or the public would perceive the situation. You have to plan how you'll deal with the questions and the scrutiny, but you still have to do the right thing. Sometimes the right thing is protecting your player. Sometimes you have to suspend him or remove him from the team.

We needed a win badly on November 10, 2012, and we got one at Tennessee, a four-overtime thriller and a 51–48 Mizzou victory, our first SEC road win. (Photo courtesy of the University of Missouri)

Our 2013 team had great leadership and character, including senior receiver L'Damian Washington (No. 2), here smiling for the team photo at the Cotton Bowl in Arlington, Texas, where we'd beat Oklahoma State for our 12th victory of the season. (Photo courtesy of the University of Missouri)

I was blessed to have a group of hardworking, loyal assistant coaches throughout my career. Here's our 2008 Missouri staff.

I had been diagnosed with lymphoma in the spring of 2015 but decided to coach that season, here in our season-opening win over Southeast Missouri State. (Photo courtesy of the University of Missouri)

In what turned out to be my final coaching win in 2015, we rallied to beat BYU in Kansas City the day after I had to tell my players and coaches about my plans to retire.

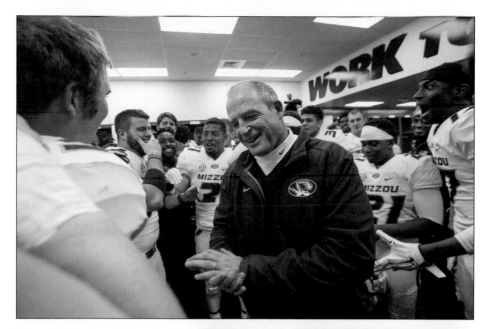

Top: *Our team celebrated what would be my final coaching win in 2015, a comeback victory over BYU at Arrowhead Stadium in Kansas City.*

Right and below: *On November 16, 2015, we held a press conference at Mizzou Arena to discuss my retirement plans. It was an emotional day for me as I was surrounded by family and colleagues.*

Top: *On June 27, 2015, Missy and I got married in Naples, Florida, joined by family and close friends. Here I am with all eight of my grandchildren on our wedding day.*

Left and opposite: *Missy and I on our wedding day, June 27, 2015, in Naples, Florida.*

My first home game and first time watching the team from a press box suite. My entire family by my side (missing from photo: Baby Chace Pinkel). 2016.

Taking time to vacation in New York City's Time Square with my new blended family Mira, Jace, and Missy. July 2016.

My children. From left, my son Geoff and his wife, Jen; my son-in-law, Josh, and my daughter, Erin; and my daughter-in-law, Jenny, and son Blake. Fall 2016.

Top left: *Retirement brought me opportunities to speak to multiple groups, one of the most special being the Toledo Rockets football team before practice.*

Middle left: *The MAC Hall of Fame award was very special. I'm pictured here with some of my dearest longtime friends and former teammates.*

Bottom left: *A pre-game good luck to my old friend Nick Saban at the 2015 Cotton Bowl, Alabama vs. Michigan State.*

Bottom right: *Mike Alden, former Mizzou Athletic Director, recaps my head coaching career at the launch party for the newest ZOUNation publication. Spring 2016.*

At the Legendary Coaches wall in Toledo.

On the set of the SEC broadcast of the SEC Championship Game as announcer.

By 2014, Mizzou had made major policy changes to clarify how employees report sexual assaults. The university also hired a new full-time Title IX coordinator to handle those allegations. I welcomed the changes because now a structured system would be in place that took the coaches and the athletic department out of the decision-making process. We were criticized in how that situation unfolded, but long-term, I was glad we were able to bring some awareness to the importance of the Title IX regulations. In 2017, the Association of American Universities recognized Mizzou for its efforts to combat sexual misconduct and commended the school's Office for Civil Rights & Title IX.

As for our team, our players weren't naïve when it came to Derrick's situation. But the fewer problems you have off the field, the better team you're going to have. All those distractions take their toll on the unity of a team. But you also have to recognize that we're dealing with kids and kids make mistakes. I'd always tell people that if their son or daughter makes a mistake, you don't automatically throw them out of your house. There's a price to pay for mistakes, but then, hopefully, it'll make you a better man. You learn and grow, hopefully. Whenever a player gets in trouble with the law, as a coach you are concerned about embarrassment that might be brought on the program. But I dealt with each situation head-on. A lot of coaches at other schools would overlook issues, but we never made decisions on discipline issues based on how it would impact wins and losses. We had to dismiss a handful of talented, valuable players over the years. Some people say you hurt the rest of the team when you suspend a player for a game. If it hurts the team that he's not playing, then the bigger message is even clearer—don't hurt the team. We were very consistent when it came to discipline. We also didn't ignore problems. I told our coaches all the time, "I want to know what's going on." A lot of coaches delegated the discipline to the assistant coaches, but that wasn't my style. I handled discipline issues so that we kept things consistent. It's better for team morale that way. It didn't matter if you were at the top of the depth chart or a walk-on.

On the same day we suspended Derrick, our scrimmage ended with a major injury. Munir Prince, a defensive back who transferred to us from Notre Dame, was knocked out during a punt return and experienced temporary loss of feeling in his upper and lower extremities. I quickly made it over to the hospital. I didn't know if he was going to make it. Was he going to be paralyzed? It was horrific, just frightening. It's not your son, but it is your son. That's your role as a coach, like it or not. When you recruit these players, you look their parents in the eye and make that promise: "I'll treat your son like I would my own." Thank God the doctors eventually came out and said he was going to be okay. Munir decided to end his playing career, but he earned his degree and is now a college coach. What a day that was.

Once the season began, we had to replace our 1,000-yard rusher, but we had Blaine Gabbert back at quarterback and a committee of running backs. After we opened with another win over Illinois in St. Louis, we hosted a talented San Diego State team and fell behind early in the fourth quarter. The lesson that night was simple—never give up. With a minute left, we trailed by four and T.J. Moe caught a short pass in the flat, found an alley down the sideline, and went for 68 yards and scored the game-winning touchdown.

I've had some good fourth-quarter teams, and the key to winning games like that wasn't just believing in yourself. It's not about the rah-rah-rah. It's about playmakers. Somebody has to make a play. Once we got into the SEC, we played so well in the fourth quarter in 2013 and 2014. I told those teams all the time, "We're mentally tough. We're at our highest level of focus in the toughest parts of the game in the fourth quarter. But you still have to make plays." In the San Diego State game it was T.J. The agony of defeat quickly became the thrill of victory. We did not play our best game, so you have to remind your players in the wake of the celebration. But it's so much more fun fixing those problems after you win a game, especially a game like that.

We started to get on a roll. We shut out Colorado. We won big at Texas A&M. Our reward was a huge home game against Oklahoma. They were ranked No. 1 in the BCS standings. For the first time ever, ESPN's *College GameDay* came to our campus and set a record for the biggest crowd at the on-site studio on Francis Quadrangle. That was a big deal for our program and our university.

We had never beaten Oklahoma. We had played well against the Sooners in some regular-season games, but they also got us twice for the Big 12 championship. In my Thursday speech that week I talked to our players about respect. In the Big 12, you earned respect by beating the great teams.

The atmosphere was electric that night and it only got better when Gahn McGaffie returned the opening kickoff for a touchdown. Blaine was outstanding. We took the lead in the fourth quarter and our defense made enough stops down the stretch in a 36–27 win.

I was very fortunate to have a lot of big wins in the ZOU. This was the first time we had ever beaten a No. 1–ranked team. I was so proud of our team. It was as big of an environment as you can get in a regular-season game. I remember coming out of the locker room and Blaine was sitting there on ESPN's set on the field. You want your program to experience days like that. You've got to have big wins if you want to elevate your program.

That night, I was just thrilled on the drive home. It was about 11:00 PM. I decided to call Coach James. I never called him after any other game that I coached. It was 9:00 PM on the West Coast and he'd still be up watching a game. All I wanted to do was thank him. We had a lot of tough wins at Mizzou and those huge wins were so rewarding. We talked for a few minutes, but then he ended our call with this: "Now you know what your toughest problem is going to be?"

"What's that, Coach?"

"Next week," he said.

Are you kidding me? That's it? I get one of the biggest wins of my career and he wants to warn me about next week?

Well, he knew what he was talking about.

We played at Nebraska the following week. We won our last game there in 2008 by five touchdowns. Needless to say, we had their attention. We didn't play our best and they played really well. It was a brutal back-to-back schedule for us. At one point during our time in the Big 12 I called the league office to ask about our schedule. Every year that we played Oklahoma we played Nebraska the week before or the week after: 2002, 2003, 2006, 2008, and 2010. Why was that? Oklahoma was always our toughest cross-division opponent and Nebraska was our toughest division opponent. Back-to-back, every time. Whining aside, we still had to come to those games with our highest level of play. We didn't at Nebraska in 2010 and they beat us by two touchdowns.

The next week we went to Texas Tech. We had beaten them three times in a row. We scored on the first possession and then our offense went into hiding for the rest of the game. It was a lot like the Texas Bowl against Navy the year before. I could feel it on the sideline. Our guys thought we were on cruise control. From that point on, we played poorly on offense. Sometimes scoring so fast becomes your own worst enemy.

We had gone from this epic win over Oklahoma, thinking we were about to have another 2007 season, and then it was whack, whack. We were 7–0…and then in an instant we were 7–2.

My senior players had a lot of meetings to attend in my program. Once the staff got through signing day, I met all the time with the current juniors who would be seniors in the fall. We'd have regular meetings February through April to discuss leadership and their roles in the summer and fall. Those guys were responsible for relaying our talks and our decisions down to the younger players in their position groups. Once we got into the season I met with the seniors every Monday. I valued their experience, their leadership, their voices, and their trust. They would have a record at the end of their Mizzou careers, and I reminded them of that all the time.

The Monday after the Texas Tech game, one of those senior leaders and team captain, Kevin Rutland, a cornerback from Texas, said he needed to talk to me. He came into my office, shut the door, and looked me dead in the eye. "Coach, this team is in a funk. It's been that way since the Oklahoma game. We've got to do something to get out of this."

So I listened. We freakin' cranked up the intensity that week. We always practiced hard, but this was different. We had to get the funk out. It's like when you take a nap in the afternoon. You wake up after an hour and you're still groggy. Your head is swimming in gunk. That was our football team. They wished the season had ended after Oklahoma so they could go home and celebrate. Instead, we had to shake things up.

We played Kansas State the next week, a team that had just beaten Texas. But we finally played close to the level of the Oklahoma game. We beat Kansas State by 10, then won at Iowa State the next week 14–0. We played Kansas again at Arrowhead and dominated 35–7. Coach James was right. It was all about the next week. How would we respond? We responded, but it took us a few weeks to respond the right way.

At the end of the regular season, we tied with Nebraska for the division lead, but the Huskers went to the championship game because of the head-to-head tiebreaker. We still earned a great bowl matchup against Iowa in the Insight Bowl. Blaine had a career night until a late interception into coverage, his only mistake in the game. I told the team after the loss that the interception didn't kill us. It was the return. We let the defensive back go 72 yards for a touchdown. It was a great learning experience for Blaine, but he was a wreck after that three-point loss. First thing I had to do at the postgame press conference was take the heat off Blaine. If we had made the tackle on that return, maybe we would have won that bowl. It turned out to be Blaine's final college game. He left for the NFL draft, which didn't surprise us at all. Same for Aldon Smith, our defensive end. Again, no surprise. They both had NFL talent and received high draft projections. Both became first-round NFL draft picks. For the Tigers, we had just won 10 games but we had to reload quickly.

◆ ◆ ◆

After the 2010 season, Michigan was making a head-coaching change. I didn't necessarily want to move, but Michigan's representative had reached out. They said to me several times, "Gary, you had this program at Kent State and then you saw it work at Washington. You took it to Toledo and it worked. Now you're doing it at Missouri, a place where you're not supposed to win like you're winning. If you drop your program into Ann Arbor..." And then their representative paused and said, "You get to recruit any...player...you...want." He paused between each word to add emphasis. That was the comment that grabbed my attention.

At the time, and this is still true, Michigan carried more of a national presence. It's a place where you can consistently win at a national level. Not that we couldn't at Missouri, but Michigan has a stronger brand and more resources. I felt the temptation. He told me to bring my agent down to a meeting at the national coaches convention in Dallas. At that point, the reality set in. This could get serious. Do I really want to make this move? I sat up in my hotel room all night until early in the morning. Then I called my agent. I told John, "I want to stay at Missouri." We canceled the meeting.

Do I regret it? Do I regret never going to an established national program like Michigan and installing our program? I don't know how to answer that.

Late in my time at Toledo, I had a player who was a transfer from Ohio State. He walked into my office and said, "Coach, I'm just telling you, if you ever take your program to Columbus, Ohio, you'll win a bunch of national championships." Wow. Was this kid serious?

I told him, "Listen, you're a starter. You don't need to say these things." He wouldn't let up.

"No, Coach, I'm being perfectly honest. You'd win national titles there."

If nothing else, when I look back it makes me think about where things led in my career. I have no regrets about staying at Missouri. We got the program to the point where we made a lot of progress and won a lot of games. We had national respect.

• • •

Even though he became a first-round pick, I couldn't help but wonder what Blaine Gabbert could have done with another year in college. He had all the measurables, but he was still fairly inexperienced. He was hurt a lot in high school then started just two years in college, half of which he played on a bad ankle in 2009.

But for us, we had to move on. James Franklin was next up. He played some as a freshman behind Blaine and gave us a true dual threat. He was a unique player in more ways than one. He told me once, "You know, I'm not sure I want to play in the NFL." That gave me some pause. It wasn't a bad thing, but he didn't necessarily approach the game like a lot of his peers. Great kid, great player. He won a lot of big games for us.

In 2011, three of our first five games were on the road, at Arizona State, Oklahoma, and Kansas State. We were competitive but lost all three. We finally won the next week against Iowa State, but we couldn't get on a roll. We lost to Oklahoma State, won at Texas A&M, lost at Baylor, and beat Texas.

The Texas win was bittersweet. Finally, we beat the Longhorns on my watch after five tries. But we lost our best player, running back Henry Josey, who was having a breakthrough year, already hitting 1,000 yards through the season's first nine games. And he was just a sophomore. But he suffered a crippling knee injury along our sideline, so bad we wondered if he'd ever play again. I spent most of that night visiting Henry in the hospital. He was crushed. It was crushing for our team. And the week was just getting started.

• • •

The next Wednesday, I had dinner out with some friends and then went to a friend's house for a couple glasses of wine. After that I drove around for a while on Highway 63. Sometimes I'd like to get in the car, listen to music, and just drive along the same roads where I'd ride my motorcycle. I was driving well below the speed limit when a police officer got behind me and turned on his lights. I sped up but didn't signal a lane change.

He pulled me over and I went numb.

I declined one of the roadside tests because my Achilles' tendon was bothering me. He had me say parts of the alphabet and count backward, but I didn't do so well with that. I had called Bogdan Susan, my attorney and friend, who lived nearby, and he came and talked to the officer. By then I was in handcuffs in the backseat of the patrol car. A million thoughts were racing through my mind. I'd never been in a police car in my life. I'd never been in handcuffs.

I told the officer, "My whole world's about to change."

It's not like I had a lot of experience in that situation. That was never something I ever imagined would happen to me. They had to take me to the hospital for a blood test. Thankfully, they took off the cuffs there. Later I was processed at the police station.

I didn't contest the charges. I pleaded guilty to first-offense DWI. The results of the blood test were never released. I was going to pay the price no matter what that number read.

When I got home I called my agent, John. He said, "Gary, you've built up enough goodwill, but you've got to take responsibility. You've got to stand up and take the bullet. What are you going to do tomorrow morning?"

"I'll probably stay home."

"No, you're not," he told me. "You're going to get up and go to the office. They have to see you."

He was right.

As the night became morning I called Mike Alden, our athletic director, my boss. Before we could talk, I had initially texted him about the DWI and that I was unbelievably sorry. At first he thought I meant a player had gotten arrested. Nope. It was me.

Obviously it was devastating for me personally. I never got in trouble in high school. Ever. And the reason why was my sister Kathy and my brother Greg. The last thing my parents needed was me getting in trouble. They were so consumed with taking care of my sister and brother and their disease that I never broke the rules. I waited until I was almost 60.

I was incredibly embarrassed. I let down our program. I let down the university. Most important, I let down my family, my kids, and grandkids. And I let down my other family, my team—my coaches, my players, and all the people in our program.

I couldn't get past the thought of how much I hurt people. I had never hurt anyone who trusted me. That thought crushed me. It was so difficult just to get through the day.

The next day, I met with my staff and they just stared at me, like, "What are you talking about, Coach?" They were shocked. They probably went through a brief scare thinking I might be fired, which would have totally disrupted their lives and careers. You make one bad choice and you impact everyone around you.

I just prayed that I had stored up enough goodwill and credibility through my whole career that I could survive this.

Later I met with Mike at his office. He didn't waste any time.

"We have to suspend you," he told me.

Of course. I understood. He was disappointed. But nobody was more disappointed than I was.

"I get it," I said.

I was suspended for a week, including that Saturday's home game against Texas Tech, a crucial game because we needed one more win to become bowl eligible. I was suspended for a week without pay and donated that week's salary to the MU Wellness Center. My salary was also frozen for a year, and I was not eligible for any bowl bonus for the season. The financial impact would be more than $300,000.

But this wasn't about losing money. I wasn't upset at all with the punishment. They could have cut my salary in half. I let down thousands of people with my decision to drive that night. They believed in me and I let them down. No punishment they wanted to give me was too big. I put Mike through hell with that decision—not just Mike but the administration and everyone associated with the program.

My players always respected me for how we ran our program and how we treated people, but now I had to face them. Before our practice that Thursday, I told the players. Obviously, they knew what had happened from the news reports. I went into our team meeting and broke down in tears. I apologized. It was just an awful moment in my career. When people trust you and respect you and you screw up like this in such an irresponsible way, it's just a devastating feeling.

As the day went on I realized I couldn't feel sorry for myself. I couldn't mope around. Deep down, I wanted to walk away for a month, just escape and not have to experience all this hurt and grief. But I knew my players were going to watch how I handled this situation. My leadership was crucial. We always say you lead by example, and that's exactly what I had to do. I had to lead after the incredibly difficult situation that I had gotten myself into.

The terms of my suspension said I couldn't be at the team facility for the week. My secretary, Ann, put together some stuff from my office, and I took it and left for the week. That afternoon I went to lunch at Panera Bread and got stopped by a few people, there and other places, like the gas station and the grocery store. A few didn't hold back. "Coach, we're really disappointed in you. We know you'll handle this right, but we're disappointed." I apologized to anyone who approached me. I wanted to run and hide and not face another person. But I couldn't. My kids and my players had to learn something from this. They had to see me respond.

I spent game day with two of my closest friends, Hal Cook and Al Speicher. We went down to my condo at the Lake of the Ozarks to watch the game on TV. It was such a weird feeling watching my team play. It was also excruciating, because it was senior night and I wouldn't be there to greet each senior when he was introduced before the game. If we would have lost the game it would have been my fault, but a young defensive lineman named Michael Sam clinched the win in the final seconds with an interception just shy of the goal line. If we had lost the game, that would have been my loss to endure forever. My staff kept the team together all week. Dave Steckel served as interim head coach, and Dave Yost ran the show on offense. They asked me if I wanted to drive to the stadium after the game and address the team in the locker room, but that didn't make sense to me. That was their moment.

The next Monday we had a press conference at my attorney's office. We were scheduled to play Kansas the next Saturday, and I wanted to address the media before the game so I didn't take anything away from our preparation. A reporter asked me if I had a drinking problem. No, that wasn't the case. I made a bad decision that night. If I could go back and erase one night of my life, that's the one, without any question.

After the arrest I talked to my sister. Kathy was so understanding. My kids were great, too. "You will overcome this," they told me. "You made a mistake. We've all made mistakes." It's pretty humbling when you're 59 years old and your kids are counseling you.

What I didn't expect was a knock at the door of my home that next Tuesday. It was Beau Brinkley, our long snapper.

"Beau, what are you doing here?"

"Coach, can I come in and talk?"

Of course. He came in and sat right next to me on my couch— not across from me, but next to me, just a few feet apart. He looked me right in the eye.

"I'm going to do what you did to me," he said. "It was the best thing that happened in my life."

I was completely stunned.

"Coach, I got a DWI a couple years ago," he said. "You brought me in your office and told me, 'You've got a choice how you're going to handle this. This is going to make you a better person or it's going to make you worse. One or the other.' When you said that, I looked at myself and changed things I needed to change so that would never happen again.'"

He gave me a hug. Not a quick hug but a long hug, for like a minute.

"Coach, I love you," Beau said. "Everything is going to work out. The team's got your back."

Then he walked out the door.

I sat there absolutely numb. Tears fell down from my eyes. Wow. It was one of the most touching moments of my life.

We all get judged when we face adversity in coaching. This was different than losing a game or anything you can experience on the field. But the goal was the same. I kept telling myself one thing over and over again—earn your respect back. My response was going to define who I was in the eyes of these players, my coaches, my bosses, our fans.

The suspension ended Thursday. We had two more days before we played Kansas at Arrowhead. I wanted my players to see me, see my face, before anyone else in the building. It was Thanksgiving, so they didn't have class that day. I stood in front of the locker room and hugged every single player when they got to the door. I thanked them. I told them I appreciated their forgiveness and I loved them. I had to bare my soul. I had to show my players I took 100 percent responsibility. And I had to earn their respect back. And their trust.

From that point on, it had to be business as usual. We had to move on. They had to move on.

I had never been in trouble before as a kid or as an adult, but I had to deal with players getting in trouble all the time. This made me more sensitive to players dealing with problems. I became more understanding. Before the DWI, I ruled with an iron fist. There was no tolerance for any misbehavior in my program. After that I changed. I still held players accountable. We still had consequences for poor decisions. You break the team standards, you paid the price. But how I interacted with them, how I dealt with them had to change. I had to be more compassionate, more empathetic. Sometimes I'd use my mistake as a reference point. "Remember when I got in trouble with the law? You now have a choice in how you're going to handle this. You can earn your respect back just like I did."

Finally we got to Arrowhead to play Kansas. It was our last game in the Big 12, our last Border War against the Jayhawks. Three weeks earlier we had officially joined the SEC and would start playing in that conference the next season. We said good-bye with a 24–10 win.

• • •

We went back to the Independence Bowl for a third time and beat North Carolina to finish off 8–5, a step back from the previous year, but we'd go into the new year confident we could compete in the SEC.

For me, personally, it had been a difficult year. In January, Vicki and I separated. We would get divorced later that year.

I wanted to make it through life without getting divorced, but it happened. When I told my agent, John, he gave me very good advice. He had other clients go through similar stages of life. "Brace yourself," he said. "This is very, very difficult. Make sure your kids always know what's going on. Keep in mind, too, no matter how great your family is—and you've got a great family—issues are going to come up. Those issues always come back around if you don't address them."

Our kids were understanding and supportive. This decision was not shocking to them. Vicki and I just hadn't been getting along for quite some time and had grown apart.

I had to tell my players, too. I wanted them to hear it from me. In the spring we put out a statement to the media saying we were separated. I thought we had to be transparent. For a couple months I moved in with my daughter and her family until I bought a new place. It was a challenging time for me and my family. Just like on the field, your personal life experiences wins and losses. But ultimately in each experience, no matter the score, you learn and you grow and become better.

Mizzou vs. Vanderbilt

October 5, 2013

Nashville, Tennessee

Coming off a disappointing debut season in the SEC, we began league play in 2013 with a trip to Nashville.

Team Meeting
Thursday, October 3, 3:30 PM

"I know you're excited about playing and competing in the SEC. We learned a few things about it last year.

"Number 1: It's great playing and competing in the best conference in college football.

"Number 2: We get to play and compete at the country's greatest stadiums.

"Number 3: It's no big deal. It's just like the Big 12. It's still college football. You play against really good teams with good players. That was the challenge and opportunity in the Big 12, and it is no different in the SEC.

"It's still about preparation. It's still about being a physical team. Let's have some fun, not just in this game but the remainder of the season. I want you to have fun competing. I don't want you worrying. I want you playing on your toes and attacking. If you make a mistake, screw it and get back to having fun competing for the next play.

"Men, you have been grinding since last January. You are finishing the preparation for this week's opponent. Now it's time to get in the blocks and run the race. The men in here will not be denied. Have fun playing. Have fun competing. This team needs you. Have fun kicking their ass!"

Final: Mizzou 51, Vanderbilt 28

James Franklin threw four touchdown passes as an explosive offense made it first statement in the SEC on our way to a division championship.

8

Mizzou: Welcome to the SEC

IN THE FALL OF 2011 TEXAS A&M HAD ANNOUNCED PLANS to leave the Big 12 for the SEC. That left the Big 12 with nine schools. The SEC had 13. It was logical to assume the SEC wanted another school to even out the membership. By then Missouri had gotten involved in discussions with the SEC. I had my concerns. The SEC was by far the country's best football conference. Our program could compete in the SEC as long as the university committed to competing in the SEC.

I told our chancellor, Brady Deaton, "Don't do this unless you're going to invest. Do everything you can to stay in the top half of the league in everything you do. Otherwise, we'll get run over." That was true then and remains true.

We couldn't even think about making this move unless we were serious about constantly investing in facilities. It's like hiring a coach or an athletic director. Those decisions aren't quick fixes. Neither was this. This decision was going to guide the university's athletics maybe forever. Brady and Mike Alden and the curators had to understand you can't join the league and then sit back and relax. "You have to keep investing," I insisted.

That was my input. I also knew from a coaching perspective that it was going to be much more difficult to win because there are more quality teams. That turned out to be very true.

Once we committed to joining the SEC, we had to plan as a coaching staff how we'd adjust. We always recruited to win championships, so it's not like we had to drastically change what we were doing. But you learn pretty quickly that the line of scrimmage is significant in the SEC. When we started analyzing the SEC, I'd say two-thirds of the league had elite players along the line of scrimmage. You always need a good quarterback and talented skill players, but you can't win without the right combination of size and speed and athleticism up front. We had to recruit and develop our players at a high level in the Big 12 to compete with Oklahoma and Texas and Nebraska. In the SEC you just had more quality opponents that were elite up front.

We left the Big 12, and right after we finished recruiting for our 2012 class, I attended an SEC meeting in Birmingham where I was sitting alongside Les Miles, Nick Saban, Steve Spurrier, and all these SEC coaches. I had met most of them. Obviously, I knew Nick from our time together at Kent State. The league was full of great coaches, all good guys. They were all concerned about being healthy for spring football. That was the conversation. Looking back, it was such a concern because this league is so physical. The Big 12 is physical, too, but there are just more big, physical teams in the SEC. That makes staying healthy a premium. You're going to get beat up. Alabama's depth was at a different level than Missouri's. That's when I started to realize the importance of staying healthy in this conference and how vital depth becomes.

In a way, my time at Missouri will be defined by the SEC move. I'll be remembered as being part of the decision, part of the transition.

I loved coaching and competing in the Big 12, but I was really concerned about its stability. I was worried that Texas was going to pull out and join the Pac-12, as well as Oklahoma and Oklahoma State. What was going to happen to us when the music stopped? All these comments from the leaders at Texas and Oklahoma kept triggering more speculation and more discussion. The welfare of our athletic department was at stake.

Once we joined the SEC, Mike Slive, the league's commissioner, told me our success in football was a big reason the league chose us to become that 14th member. The state of Missouri touches multiple SEC states, and we had the two big TV markets in St. Louis and Kansas City, but I don't believe the SEC would have chosen us had we not made so much progress as a program.

Right away we had to start preparing for all of our new opponents. Each assistant always had his own team that he'd study during the offseason. He was called the headhunter. He'd spend the spring and summer analyzing that opponent, staying on top of any roster news, injuries, coaching changes, scheme changes. He had to be an expert on their personnel and their systems. It was similar to when the staff first got to Mizzou. We had to investigate more and collect as much information as we could on our new opponents in the Big 12. Instead of just studying two or three games of film, we'd analyze four or five so we really got to know these teams we were about to face. You study coordinators when you're game-planning, but when you join a new league you've got all new coordinators to study. The scouting reports were more thorough and intense that first year.

Our first SEC game was home against Georgia. It was a huge game for so many reasons. We stayed at our normal hotel on Friday night, the local Marriott in Columbia. Surprisingly there were Georgia fans everywhere we looked. They were so kind and excited to be in Columbia. I had never seen anything like that. That was a new experience for our team.

We had James Franklin back at quarterback and some young playmakers around him. In front of a sellout crowd at the ZOU, we played really well the first half and held the lead until late in the third quarter. But then Georgia captured all the momentum with some big plays and we couldn't respond. It was a "Welcome to the SEC" moment for us.

That season my biggest message to our players was we needed to focus on us, our team—not these other guys from the SEC. We can't control what anyone else does. I emphasized that more in my later years at Missouri, especially once we settled into the SEC. Our players were about to play at some historic stadiums, places they would tell their kids and grandkids about in 30 years. Every game in this league is bigger. Games were big in the Big 12 but not like they are in the SEC. Life in the SEC sounds different, looks different, tastes different. Our players started to learn that once we played games at places like Georgia and Tennessee and Florida. But it was still about us and our team preparing the best we could. I didn't want to blow things out of proportion. The media did enough of that on their own; I didn't need to add any pressure. The question we'd have to answer was whether we had the depth to hold up physically in this league. It was almost like we were doomed before we started. There was a perception that the league was more physically demanding, and we learned that was absolutely true.

After losing to Georgia we hosted Arizona State, part of a two-game series with the Pac-12 school. James Franklin had taken a bad hit on his shoulder against Georgia, the same shoulder he injured earlier in the spring. He had an opportunity to take a high dose of ibuprofen before the game and play through the soreness, but that wasn't something he wanted to do. It wasn't for any religious reason or ethical reason. He just didn't like taking medicine. I was really torn with that, but it was his decision.

Unfortunately, right before kickoff the ESPN sideline reporter asked me about James' decision not to play on live TV. I'm usually protective of my players, but I let it slip that he didn't take the medicine and decided not to play. I regret saying anything publicly about it. I really do. It's not like I planned to tell the world that James didn't want to use anything to help the pain. The sideline reporter knew he had declined the medicine, and she asked me to confirm. But that's no excuse for what I said. I'm better than that.

I never asked a player to do something he didn't want to do. I never even talked to James about that decision before the game. But I certainly regret making that public. I was frustrated.

James was an incredibly tough player on the field. He had a unique personality, but he did some great things for us when he could stay healthy. After the way he played in 2011, we thought he'd follow the same course of our last couple quarterbacks who played in the NFL. We expected him to take off and become a great player in 2012. But he couldn't stay healthy. Corbin Berkstresser, another tremendous kid and a devoted team player, had to start four games as a redshirt freshman. He just wasn't ready to be thrown into an SEC schedule. We won the Arizona State game with Corbin at quarterback but then lost our next three SEC games to South Carolina, Vanderbilt, and Alabama. A lightning storm sent us into the locker room for more than an hour in the Alabama game—the first time I'd ever coached against my old teammate and friend Nick Saban—but we struggled to keep pace with his team in a 42–10 loss. We bounced back and beat Kentucky, had a close loss at Florida, then outlasted Tennessee in four overtimes in Knoxville.

James was in and out of the lineup that year but we had other injuries, too. Still, if we had won one of our last two games, against

Syracuse or Texas A&M, we would have played in an eighth straight bowl game. As much as we struggled, we were still in the hunt.

Only three games in my 15 years at Mizzou had we been eliminated from bowl eligibility at kickoff: the season finales in 2001, 2004, and 2015. Otherwise, we were always playing with a chance to secure eligibility or had already locked up enough wins to play in the postseason.

Under normal circumstances we would never schedule Syracuse for a game in November, but when we changed leagues some games got shifted around and we needed a nonconference home game at the last minute. We had already played two quality nonconference teams in Arizona State and Central Florida, and here we were needing one more win to get eligible for a bowl game after going through a gauntlet of Georgia, South Carolina, Florida, and Tennessee. Realistically, this was probably our last chance to get a sixth win. The following week we'd play our regular-season finale at Texas A&M. They were having a much better debut season in the league behind Heisman Trophy winner Johnny Manziel. That means we essentially had to beat Syracuse at home to secure bowl eligibility. Their program had struggled for a long time, but this was one of their best teams in almost a decade. They had an NFL draft pick at quarterback. We had a first-round draft pick on the defensive line—but not that night.

Sheldon Richardson, the best player on our defense, an All-SEC defensive tackle and a future first-round draft pick, had to fulfill what we called awareness training, which was punishment for being irresponsible academically. He skipped his awareness training, so I made him confront the whole staff. He had an attitude during that meeting. That's something we couldn't tolerate. So we had to suspend him less than 48 hours before a critical game.

There were a handful of times in my career that I suspended players for disciplinary reasons where other coaches at other programs probably would have found a way to keep the player on the field. To me, I had to do the right thing. Ten years later I didn't want to question my decision-making. I looked at those situations like this—if the third-team right guard breaks a rule, would I suspend him for a game? Absolutely. If the starting defensive tackle breaks the same rule, would I suspend him for a game? Yes. Case closed. Those decisions aren't that difficult. You do the right thing.

Sheldon later apologized to me, and I think in some ways he matured. But as a coach you've got to make the right decisions—and sometimes they don't help you win games. He played with an edge and carried that edge with him away from the field. Sometimes it got him in trouble. But he was a likeable kid. People from NFL teams called me before the draft and asked if he got in trouble a lot. He really didn't. There were just one or two minor incidents.

It's fascinating to think about why one athlete with great ability can handle success and another one can't. Derek Jeter wrote in his book that the one thing that guided him during his career is he never wanted to hurt his mom and dad. I've found that players who play for themselves struggle. Those who play for God, for someone in their family, anyone other than themselves, usually come back to earth and experience success. It's not all about me. Aldon Smith has had personal problems and legal issues in the NFL. I've tried to pass that message to Aldon along with others who have come through our program. Aldon didn't have any disciplinary problems in school, but he has struggled since he left. Success can be difficult to manage.

Sheldon didn't play in the Syracuse game. We lost after giving up a last-minute go-ahead touchdown. James Franklin left that game early with a concussion. That meant we had to win our final game of the year to keep our bowl streak alive—and without our starting quarterback. We headed to Texas A&M, where Manziel was about to put his Heisman campaign on ice. The Aggies were 9–2 with wins over Alabama, Arkansas, Auburn, and Ole Miss. We had played pretty well at Kyle Field over the years but not that night. We lost by 30. It was the end of a very difficult year for us.

After the game ended, everyone wondered how we would respond. We were in the SEC now, so what were we going to change to adjust? After the game I made it simple: "We're going to do what we do." That had to be another moment where Mike Alden cringed, but I was just being honest. We evaluated absolutely everything we did in our program. We never assumed everything was working without carefully evaluating it. Every year we wanted to improve 3 percent to 5 percent. But I also knew from past seasons that when things get tough, you don't just start changing your program for the sake of change. You bunker down and embrace the things that are most important. If at any time from 2005 to 2011 we would have had injuries at the quarterback position like we had in our first year in the SEC, then I might not have made it to 2012.

You never heard me say, "Oh, this league is too hard and too difficult. We need to change this and change that to keep up with everyone else." My players needed to see an enthusiasm from me about the league. We had to focus on ourselves and make the most of the opportunity. I wasn't going to panic over being in the SEC.

People wanted me to recognize how difficult it was for us in the SEC, maybe more than we could have expected. But the next two years we were division champions. It's not like we changed our program so we could compete five years down the road. If we stayed healthy in 2012 or I would have done a better job coaching, we would have played in a bowl game and the transition wouldn't have seemed so bumpy. All we needed to do was win one more game—and not necessarily an SEC game. The costly loss that season came at home against Syracuse.

I'm sure people expected some staff changes after the season, but that wasn't my plan. I trusted and had faith in our coaches. A few days after the season, David Yost called me and said he wanted to step down. He was burnt out. He had just dealt with all the quarterback problems all season. If your team has quarterback problems—high school, college, NFL—your team has problems. That 2012 season really affected him.

I tried to talk him out of leaving. I absolutely didn't want to make a change. Dave was a great coach and a great recruiter. The kids loved him. I wanted him on our staff. He was remarkably committed to the job. He had zero ambition to being a head coach. He had no use for the publicity and attention. After he got into the coordinator job, he didn't necessarily regret it, but he was essentially the head coach of the offense. He was good with the media, but it was part of the job he didn't want to do. At this level if you're a coordinator, you're training to be a head coach, but that was never his plan.

So we lost a good coach. When we had a staff opening, I always looked at my coaches first. The summer before every season I would think about the contingency plan. Who on my staff would I consider for a promotion if we lose a coordinator? I interviewed Andy Hill, Brian Jones, and Josh Henson on our staff and considered some outside candidates. We went with Josh for the coordinator job and moved Andy from receivers to quarterbacks. The worst thing you can do when you have adversity like we faced in 2012 is panic. The outside perception was we were overwhelmed in the SEC, and we had better change the program or we would get buried.

I didn't care about the outside opinion when it came to staff. I'd call Coach Lauterbur or Coach James for advice. Or maybe I'd look back at similar situations at Washington or Toledo and recall how we handled the staff.

We just emphasized who we were and what we were about. We had to communicate that with our players. I think it gave the players confidence that we didn't make drastic changes.

After the season, Mike Alden said to me, "I just want you to know I've been asked a few questions by our president about the direction of the program." He didn't go into a lot of detail. The president of the university system was Tim Wolfe. His message was subtle. He wasn't talking to Mike about firing me, but he might have been laying the groundwork.

I told Mike, "I get it. I appreciate you being honest with me."

That didn't change my approach one bit. Mike said he had given zero thought to a coaching change after 2012. Zero. I knew I had his support. I didn't tell anyone what the president said to Mike except my girlfriend, Missy. Nobody else needed to know. My coaches worked hard regardless of the circumstances. They didn't need that pressure on their back.

• • •

After our first year in the SEC, I reflected on a conversation I had with Jim Harbaugh when he was in his first year as the head coach of the 49ers. It was a profound statement that defined my approach with our players. I first met Jim at a coaching function in Phoenix when he coached at San Diego University. I knew Jim's dad, too. Years later he came to Mizzou's pro day to scout Blaine Gabbert and Aldon Smith in preparation for the 2011 NFL draft. We talked quite a bit that day. He had just left Stanford for the 49ers, going from a program that he had built into a national power to a league where it's supposed to be an even playing field across the board. I figured making that jump was going to be difficult for Jim. I mentioned to him, "You're going to have your challenges, right?"

He looked at me with that intense Jim Harbaugh glare and said, "Coach, we've got great players. They've got great players. We compete. They compete. It doesn't get better than this as a competitor." He was almost in a cold sweat. He couldn't wait for the competition. He embraced those challenges. It inspired him.

I was so impressed with his answer. Later that fall we made the decision to join the SEC and the more I thought about how we should approach this challenge, the more I kept coming back to

Harbaugh. We were now playing the best teams in the best stadiums. We had to embrace that. I had to embrace that. That's the message I had to get across to our players. "This is an opportunity to compete against the best. We're now part of this great league. It doesn't get better than that." That had to be our attitude.

Business as usual wasn't going to work for us. We couldn't just strut into this league and act like nothing had changed. Harbaugh has no idea what kind of impact that conversation had on me, and on our program, but his philosophy became our mindset.

You also have to stay healthy in this game. Missouri's not a program that can afford a run of injuries like Alabama might be able to afford. I believed in what we were doing. We just focused on the structure and the routine. I stayed positive.

I liked the senior leadership we had going into 2013. Our players never panicked after 2012. They weren't afraid of this conference. They thrived on competition. They understood we had talent. It's not like everyone walked all over us that year. We went toe-to-toe with Florida. We won at Tennessee. We beat Kentucky. Earlier in the year we beat Arizona State with a backup quarterback. We were competitive in other games. We just didn't handle injuries very well. We had 12 players undergo surgeries during the 2012 season and six more after the season.

That next offseason, the leadership in our program took over. I think of L'Damian Washington before anyone else. Here's a tremendous kid from Shreveport, Louisiana, who came from a challenging background. His single mom died of a heart attack while he was in high school, leaving L'Damian and his brothers to care for each other. He became one of our strongest voices, one of our most impassioned leaders. The kids took stock in the program. Leaders emerged, including Justin Britt, Mitch Morse, E.J. Gaines, Marvin Foster, and Michael Sam, among others.

• • •

In the spring we had one of our crossover dinners, where players were split up into groups and went to a coach's house for dinner. During the dinners we'd go around the room and talk one at a time about our backgrounds, about our families. You become much more understanding about your teammates and your coaches. We did it again in August during preseason camp. After the August meeting, I got a call from Craig Kuligowski, our defensive line coach. "Michael came out in our meeting," he said.

"Excuse me?"

He said, "Coach, Michael told the players he was gay."

"Whoa. Okay."

Some people probably suspected Michael was gay. His close friends on the team knew. That's not something I spent a lot of time thinking about. A couple years before, I was in a Big 12 coaches meeting and a few of us were talking about this very topic. We all said some day there's going to be a gay player who comes out to his team. Each one of us was probably thinking, "It'll happen to somebody somewhere—but not me."

Well, it turns out I was the coach.

The next morning I brought in our captains: L'Damian Washington, James Franklin, E.J. Gaines, and Andrew Wilson. By then everyone had heard what Michael said the night before.

"Okay, guys," I told them, "talk to me."

L'Damian did most of the talking.

"Coach," he said, "first of all, most of the guys knew this already. It's not a shock around here."

I asked him if we should have a team meeting to address the topic.

"Coach, I don't think that's necessary."

Over the years you learn to listen to your players. I could have done things my way—or run things by the team leaders first and get a feel for the pulse of the team. So we decided against a team meeting. I wanted to bring Michael into the office before we did anything else. I told them I needed communication from them twice a day. They could go through L'Damian if they wanted. I needed feedback. I needed to know what was going on within the team. There was a sense of calm while talking to the captains. It was like a true family. We weren't a bunch of individuals taking sides. With that team, it was becoming obvious we had great kids who truly cared about each other.

Next, I had Michael in the office. I hugged him, told him I loved him. Now, let's talk.

"Okay, what do you want me to do?" I asked him. "L'Damian didn't think it was necessary to have a team meeting to address this. If you want to have that meeting, we can do that."

He didn't think it was necessary, either.

Did he want to come out publicly and talk to the media? He wasn't sure it was the right time. He asked what I thought.

"This is about what you want to do," I told him.

There was no way I could tell him what to do. But I felt like we had to discuss what would happen if this went public. Chad Moller, our media relations director, talked to Michael, too. Mike had been in contact with a reporter from the *Missourian*, the newspaper that's published by the students in the journalism school. Michael was considering coming out in an interview with the paper. We were prepared to support Mike in whatever path he wanted to take. But Chad made him aware how big this story was going to become. We'd help him any way we could.

"This is going to be national news," I told him. "Every game we go to you're going to be asked about this. If you can handle that, that's fine. As a team, we'll find a way to handle it."

Michael seemed unsure about what he wanted to do. He said he'd get back to me. He came back later with a decision.

"Coach, I don't want this team to have that distraction," he said. "I'll do it sometime after the season is over."

I was okay with that.

"Once the season is over," I said, "just give me a timeframe and I'll stand right there next to you when you want to talk about this publicly."

I brought the captains back into my office to give them an update. We had a few minor issues in the locker room between players that we addressed right away. Otherwise, it was business as usual. I was so proud of my team in the way they handled the situation that season. I was proud of Michael.

Any day during that season a story could have come out about Michael's sexual orientation. A teammate could have tweeted about it or posted something on Facebook. That possibility was always there, but it wasn't something I worried about. I never woke up thinking, "Today might be the day." You just don't have time for those concerns during the season.

After the season, Michael told the world he was gay in interviews with ESPN and the *New York Times*. It became an international story. Michael didn't do many interviews during the season, but still, outside of our program, people were shocked that his story never went public during the season. After he came out, I did national TV and radio interviews, and the hosts couldn't believe that 126 players on a football team never said anything publicly to the media or posted something on social media. They asked me, "How did you keep that from happening?"

I didn't know the answer. We just tried to be honest with each other in our program. It just speaks to the kind of men we had on our team. It spoke to a team culture of tolerance, acceptance, love and, more than anything, respect. We were going through the grind of the season in the toughest conference in America. Michael's news could have been disruptive, but nobody in that locker room put any selfish thoughts or opinions ahead of the team. I never had to hold a meeting where I told the team, "Don't you dare say this to anybody."

For me, it was never about my personal beliefs. It was about respect, being respectful to people—and in this case, being respectful to a player on my team. I would like to think that message resonated with a lot of people. Maybe some people didn't like the idea that we had a gay player on our team. Maybe they were uncomfortable that we respected him and loved him. But I didn't care about those opinions. I'd like to think, in a small way, we helped change attitudes when it comes to protecting and respecting another person.

It was such a big moment for sport. Not just for Mizzou or the SEC or college football. Michael was on the cover of *Sports Illustrated* the next week. While the personal story was all about Michael, his courage and his challenges, it also reflected something very positive about our team and our culture. We taught respect in our program. That year, it proved our players were listening.

I had a lot of people, good friends, tell me our handling of that situation helped them understand this topic better. It probably wasn't easy for a lot of people to accept, the idea of a gay player in college football. I'd like to think we helped change minds.

On top of all of this, Michael had an outstanding season. He broke our team record for sacks. He was named the SEC defensive player of the year. He earned unanimous All-American honors.

Michael wasn't highly recruited. He became a productive college player who made huge plays for us during his career. He was a classic example of what we called "Mizzou Made," an unheralded prospect who developed in the program, getting bigger, stronger, and faster in our system. After college, he wasn't considered a great NFL prospect. Fortunately, the St. Louis Rams drafted him in the seventh round. I thought that was significant, that a franchise gave him a chance. He was eventually cut during training camp and resurfaced with the Cowboys, but he never played in a regular-season game. That couldn't take anything away from what Michael achieved at Mizzou and the impact he made in sports and throughout society.

• • •

We started the 2013 season 5–0. That's how many games we won the previous season. But then we headed to No. 7 Georgia for the first time. It was a day game in one of the loudest places we had ever played. It was such a great environment. On that day, that team embraced the Harbaugh mentality. Our players understood how strong of a program Georgia has been historically. I made sure they knew, too. It was my first time coaching in Athens. We loved the opportunity to play on that stage. We focused on us, not Georgia.

We found a way to win even when our starting quarterback left the game with an injury. Maty Mauk, a redshirt freshman, came in for James Franklin and did just enough to manage the game in the second half. We called a memorable trick play, a receiver pass from Bud Sasser to L'Damian Washington that went for a big touchdown. E.J. Gaines, our all-conference cornerback, also left that game with an injury.

But that team was fearless. We won 41–26, a huge game for our confidence.

I didn't make any grand statements after the game. I didn't tell the players, "Hey, you just won at Georgia. You can beat anyone." I kept the focus on our opportunities. "I told you guys this is a great league. Next week we play No. 22 Florida. Here we go. It doesn't get better than this."

First series of the game, Maty, in his first start since high school, hit a deep pass to L'Damian and a play later threw a touchdown to Bud. Two plays and we're on top. Before long we were in charge and we won the game 36–17 to go 7–0.

A week later, No. 20 South Carolina and Steve Spurrier came to town. Could we beat three nationally ranked teams in a row? We got out to a 17–0 lead, but they rallied and took the game to overtime. A missed field goal was the difference and South Carolina won 27–24.

• • •

Earlier that week came devastating news of the death of my former coach and mentor Don James. I flew out to Seattle for the memorial service. I was honored to give one of the eulogies. I knew he was struggling with his health. He'd been diagnosed with pancreatic cancer. I called him one day that fall, but he didn't answer, so I left a message. A couple days later, Ann came into my office to tell me he was on the phone. I figured he was too sick to use the phone, so I was blown away when he called me back. His voice was slow and soft. We didn't talk long, but I got a chance to tell him how much I loved him and how much of an impact he had on my life. He had influenced thousands of the kids he coached, and it was important for me to tell him just that. He told me he loved me, too. I had to take it all in after we spoke, because I knew we'd never talk again. He died two days later.

• • •

When you lose a game, you want nothing more than to avoid a losing streak. After the South Carolina game, we bounced back and beat Tennessee at home. We became very good at handling adversity. It started in the offseason when I talked to the team about how we'd manage through the tough times that were sure to hit us at some point during the year. We had a structured plan for how we were going to handle adversity. And when adversity struck, we went right to the plan. Those lessons and those messages filtered down through the players on the team. We headed to Kentucky the next week and won big behind Maty and Dorial Green-Beckham, our big, talented freshman receiver. From Springfield, Missouri, Dorial was rated the No. 1 recruit in the country when he chose Missouri on national signing day in 2012. He became a more productive player for us in 2013, but we'd only get to see glimpses of his potential.

The more we saw Maty play as a redshirt freshman, the more we got excited about the future. What's this guy going to be like once he's more experienced? At 9–1 we went to Ole Miss the next week with James Franklin back at quarterback. We were ranked No. 8 in the nation and our confidence was starting to peak. In Oxford we won behind our running game. We stayed patient and just kept pounding away.

Then we came home to host Texas A&M in the regular-season finale. The incentive was simple—win the game and we win our first SEC East championship and we would go to Atlanta to play for the SEC championship. We were ranked No. 5 in the country. We were playing Johnny Manziel. It was a sold-out crowd. It doesn't get any better than this. This was one of Missouri's biggest games in the history of Memorial Stadium—maybe the biggest ever. I didn't back away from the enormity of this game. Publicly, I built it up this way all week. I didn't deliver the same message to the team, but I knew they'd hear what I told the media. Sometimes that's how you indirectly send messages to your players. It was calculated. We had to embrace the moment—and we did.

This team was unique. They were on a mission all year long. Yeah, it's the SEC. It's a great league. But we were a great team.

The Texas A&M match was a tight game, back and forth through three quarters. In the third quarter, L'Damian caught a go-ahead touchdown that was initially ruled an incomplete pass, but he immediately got my attention and motioned to throw out the challenge flag. Well, that's an NFL thing. I didn't have to throw a flag to get a review. But he was right. Touchdown. Texas A&M answered with a score to tie the game early in the fourth quarter. Finally, with three minutes left, Henry Josey delivered the final blow, a 57-yard touchdown that put us ahead for good 28–21. Fans stormed the field

Who could have imagined such a season would unfold? We were picked sixth in the SEC East preseason poll—and finished No. 5 in the country.

After the season, Kony Ealy, another great defensive lineman to come out of our program, decided to enter the NFL draft a year early. Henry made the same decision. He had recovered from that horrific knee injury two years earlier and rushed for 1,100 yards and 16 touchdowns. He had one more year of eligibility, but he was scared to death he'd get hurt again and never have a chance to play in the NFL. I was bothered that he made the decision without talking to me. That never happened before with any other player. Those decisions are personal, and that's why I always made those conversations about the player and his future. I never told players how their decisions were going to impact the team. If I thought they were crazy to leave school, I would tell them. I think Henry probably didn't want to hear my opinion, because I thought he should have stayed another year. But once I talked to him after he made the announcement, I understood how he came to his decision. With everything he had gone through with that knee injury, and such a grueling recovery process, he was worried this was his chance to make it in the NFL. Unfortunately he didn't get drafted but bounced around a few rosters during the preseason.

• • •

We lost some important players from the 2013 team—Franklin, Josey, Sam, Ealy, E.J. Gaines, L'Damian Washington, Marcus Lucas, Justin Britt—but we had some experienced playmakers coming back, including Dorial Green-Beckham, our leading receiver from the 2013 team. Unfortunately, Dorial had some problems off the field. In January, he was arrested for drug possession in Springfield but was never charged. In the spring, there was an incident in Columbia where he was accused of assaulting a female. The alleged victim decided against pressing charges, so he was never charged or even arrested. But we had the police report and all the details. The media had the police report, too. The allegations were all right there. We suspended Dorial while we looked more closely at the situation. Ultimately, I had to remove him from our program.

Unlike other incidents we had with athletes in the past, in this case I had multiple people whom I trusted dearly tell me what happened that night of the incident. It was not acceptable behavior. Had no one told me what really happened, I wouldn't have had enough information to discipline Dorial. But I knew the details. I had to do what was right for him, our team, and the integrity of the program.

I told our staff we had to remove him from the team. Some coaches resisted. They said we didn't know if everything that allegedly happened really happened. But I knew. I trusted my information.

We had healthy discussions like that about a wide variety of topics. If it's a two-point conversion, we need to talk about it and get our thoughts on the table. Don James and Bobby Bowden always talked about the importance of the staff meeting. Around that table, I wanted information. You talk things out. In this case, I could sense frustration from some of our assistants. I couldn't change what I knew. Once we stepped out of the staff meeting, we were all on the same team. The discussion was over.

You always want to help kids. But I have to live with my decisions. I had no choice with Dorial.

I brought him into my office and shared the news with him. It was incredibly emotional. He was devastated. I thought he was a great kid. But I also thought he needed some help outside of football. I wish I had done more to help him earlier in his career if I had known more. Sometimes you make discipline decisions on a player based on precedents that you established years earlier with a different player. But in this case, I couldn't justify keeping him on the team.

Dorial wanted to transfer somewhere so he could immediately play that season. Oklahoma called about him, and I told Bob Stoops he was a great kid who could use some counseling. I love Dorial. It was hard for me to take that action, but at the same time, it wasn't a hard decision for our program. He crossed a line with his actions. I told Bob that anyone from his program could call me and I would be honest. The NCAA turned down Dorial's request to play immediately that fall. He never played another college game, and he entered the 2015 NFL draft and became a second-round draft pick.

We would experience a similar situation with another prominent player in 2015.

• • •

We felt really good about Maty Mauk taking over at quarterback after the glimpses we saw in 2013. He was talented. He played a big role in our 12-win season. He was an electrifying playmaker. We figured we'd have another three great seasons with him running the offense. He was next in line. Brad, Chase, Blaine, James, and now Maty.

Some of the national media and folks who had covered the SEC for a long time figured 2013 was a fluke. They must have thought our success couldn't be real. Meanwhile, we stayed humble. In 2013, we won 12 games and made it to Atlanta with wins over Georgia, Tennessee, Florida, Vanderbilt, Kentucky, Ole Miss, and Texas A&M. We beat five nationally ranked teams. And we were picked fourth in the East in 2014.

I didn't care. I barely knew about those preseason rankings. Our players were aware of those things, and it became an obvious motivator for them. We had great players that were hungry to prove we could sustain that success.

We played at Toledo in the second game of the season. That was a very odd day, my first game coaching at the Glass Bowl since I left there after the 2000 season. We put that game on the schedule as a favor to Toledo, but it was a scary situation. I told our players the history of Toledo's program and their tradition of beating power conference teams. Before my time at Toledo and after my time at Toledo, the Rockets knocked off teams they were never supposed to beat. We had to be ready. The fans there were very kind to me that week—but they would have loved nothing more than a big upset over an SEC team. We survived 49–24 with Maty throwing five touchdowns.

We cruised through our first three games, giving us 15 wins in our last 17 games. It reminded me of 2008 when we started hot and had things rolling over a two-year period. I don't think I did a very good job making sure our players kept that edge this time. We lost that edge when we played Indiana at home. We had beaten the Hoosiers in Bloomington the year before, so maybe our players assumed we'd easily handle them at home the next year. If so, that's my fault. They got after us and scored a touchdown in the final minute to win by four. Our defense played much better the rest of the season, but that was a difficult loss to overcome.

The next week we went to South Carolina where our struggles continued. But we made just enough plays down the stretch to erase a 13-point deficit and win 21–20.

I told our team after that game, "We've got to do more. We're the hunted now. We used to be the hunters. There's no more sneaking up on anybody."

Any momentum we captured didn't last. We turned over the ball five times against Georgia the next week in a 34–0 loss, just the second time we'd been shut out in 14 years. I'd never been part of a game like that. We just gave the ball away on a few of those turnovers. Our defense played okay, but it's hard to overcome five turnovers.

I went home after that game and said a prayer. "God, why isn't my team ever on the right side of a five-turnover game?" I'd never had a game handed to me like we handed that one to Georgia. Just once it would have been nice.

We went to Florida the next week with a 4–2 record. My prayers were answered. Kickoff return, touchdown. Punt return, touchdown. Interception return, touchdown. Fumble return, touchdown. You can't make this up. We went from getting pummeled at home against Georgia with five turnovers to building a 42–0 lead at Florida midway through the third quarter. I looked up at the sky and wondered, *Am I in Coaches Heaven?* That's the place where everything works out for coaches all the time. And on that day, it did. Once we got into the third quarter and had that big lead, I wanted to go conservative. I told Josh Henson and our offensive staff to slow down the tempo and run the ball. I wanted this game over as fast as possible. We didn't need flashy offensive numbers—just a win. We won 42–13 and passed for only 20 yards.

We won the next two games at home over Vanderbilt and Kentucky to clinch another bowl trip and, suddenly, we were in the hunt for the SEC East again.

We always put a big emphasis on the month of November. "Those who win in November will be remembered." It sounds corny but it's absolutely true. And our teams developed a reputation for winning in November starting in 2007.

2007: 4–0 in November.

2008: 3–1 in November.

2009: 3–1 in November.

2010: 3–1 in November.

2011: 3–1 in November.

2013: 4–0 in November.

At 7–2, we went to Texas A&M and won by a touchdown with a great second half. We took care of Tennessee the following week in Knoxville. That set up another home finale for the SEC East crown. If we beat Arkansas at home, that would be it. We would be SEC

East champions and would head back to Atlanta. It was the first time we would play Arkansas as our new cross-division rivals. On the Friday after Thanksgiving, a sold-out crowd watched us struggle to move the ball. We trailed 14–6 headed into the fourth quarter but quickly tied it on a touchdown pass and two-point conversion. From there, our defense made stand after stand. Marcus Murphy ran in the winning touchdown and our defense did the rest with Markus Golden recovering a late fumble to preserve a 21–14 win. We were back-to-back SEC East champs, again in a season when nobody outside of our locker room expected us to challenge for the division.

Our reward? Top-ranked Alabama and my old teammate Nick Saban, who had his team on a mission that fall.

As a player, Nick was a great competitor, and as a young coach on Coach James' Kent State staff, Nick's sincerity always stood out to me. I was still a senior during his first year as a graduate assistant. I'd watch him coach the other guys and he was a natural, just very genuine with the players. Nick bounced around college football and coached at five different schools, then the NFL's Houston Oilers before landing his first head-coaching job at Toledo. After one year back in the Mid-American Conference, Nick spent four years on Bill Belichick's staff with the Cleveland Browns then returned to college as the head coach at Michigan State and later LSU, where he won a national championship in 2003. Nick spent two years coaching the Miami Dolphins, then he returned to the college game in 2007 at Alabama and continued a career I believe is unparalleled in college football. He's won five national championships, including four at Alabama in a seven-year span.

Not since scholarships were reduced to 85 per team in 1992 has anyone come close to matching Nick's success. I would suggest it might not ever happen again in college football. His APR rankings are very good. His kids graduate. It's not just a football factory in Tuscaloosa. If he's not the best coach in college football, who is?

His two influences were Don James and Bill Belichick. That's a pretty good tandem. Nick runs a structured, disciplined program. He believes in the process and preaches a strong infrastructure. He does things the right way for the right reasons. He should go down as the greatest coach in college football. And that's based on results, not because he's my friend.

• • •

Nick's Crimson Tide were just too good for us that day in Atlanta. Shane Ray, our All-American defensive end, was ejected in the first half on a targeting call. We never quite recovered and lost 42–13.

Of course, we were disappointed with the outcome. That made me 0–4 in conference championship games at Missouri—and 0–6 overall as a head coach going back to Toledo. But this team had reasons to be proud. We had two difficult losses early in the season but recovered to win the division and earn an invitation to another good bowl game. The Citrus Bowl chose us to play Minnesota in Orlando on New Year's Day. This was the first year of the College Football Playoff and the entire bowl selection process changed. The Citrus Bowl had the first selection of SEC teams that weren't chosen for the playoff bowls. That was a strong statement for our program.

Shane Ray and Markus Golden played that game like they had all season and dominated from the edges of our defense. In his final college game, Markus earned MVP honors with one of his finest games: 10 tackles, 1.5 sacks, and a forced fumble. We recruited Markus out of Affton High School in St. Louis, but he needed some time at junior college before he joined us in 2012. When he first got to campus, he walked into my office, got about three feet from my face, and said, "Anything you ask me to do, Coach, anything academically, socially, in the weight room, on the field, anything you ask me to do, I'm going to do it." I thought that was so cool. This kid, for some reason, felt this program was really going to help him. He was already invested before ever playing a game. Now with the Arizona Cardinals, Markus is already one of the great young defensive players in the NFL.

Shane was one of several great defensive players we had at Mizzou, one of several NFL first-round draft picks, and one of several All-Americans. But he was unrivaled as a competitor. I put him in an elite category of competitors, right there with Jack Lambert, my former teammate at Kent State, and Steve Emtman, the great defensive lineman at Washington. Shane needed to grow up a lot in our program before he could become a great player. He had an attitude—and not the good kind. We didn't want grumpy guys around the program, but sometime after his second year in the program, he changed dramatically. You'd see him in the practice facility and he'd have a smile on his face. He'd give you a hug. He lost that scowl that he'd worn for two years. Life's better when you have a great attitude. It was no coincidence he became a great player when his attitude changed. Like Markus in Arizona, Shane has become an important part of the Denver Broncos' defense.

For me, personally, my football life had come full circle. Way back in 1972, our Kent State team played in its first Division I bowl game at the Citrus Bowl. Here I was 42 years later going back to Orlando for another bowl game. It was my 23rd bowl game as a player or coach. Little did I know it would be my last.

• • •

Before that 2014 season, I made a decision that changed the course of my life. But first, let's rewind a couple years. We played a day game at Tennessee in 2012. I had plans that night in Columbia, my first date with Missy Martinette, a magazine publisher from the Lake of the Ozarks who I had known socially through mutual friends. Her magazine had done a cover story on me a few years earlier. I later found out I was her most difficult interview. We planned to meet at a sushi restaurant in Columbia, but of course, the game went into overtime. Then double overtime. Then triple overtime. Then quadruple overtime. Missy was back home watching every second and would later say she stopped thinking about the dang date. She just wanted the Tigers to win!

We'd have to push back our date, but that was okay. We needed every win we could get that year, and that was a huge emotional victory for our program.

Eventually, after our four-hour game, I got back to Columbia and Missy drove up from the Lake to meet for a late dinner. I had been separated for almost a year, but it was odd being on a date. I was nervous. Obviously, I'm a public figure in Columbia—and all around the state—so I'm under a microscope in any social setting. I was aware of that, but it didn't stop me from having a life.

Over the next year or so, our relationship just evolved. There was no magical moment when I decided it was time to take things to another level. But over time we grew closer and more serious.

Missy was born in Columbia and grew up in Kansas City. Mizzou was her team. She graduated from MU, just like both of her parents. The basement in her family's home was decorated in black and gold with all kinds of Mizzou memorabilia. She was seven years old the first time she tailgated at Memorial Stadium. Naturally, we were a great match.

Missy has two children, Mira and Jace, who were in elementary and middle school when we started dating and just a bit older than some of my grandchildren, so this was obviously a different experience for me. She's done a remarkable job raising them. As we got more serious and her kids grew into teenagers, it took some adjustment on my part. Missy could have moved to Columbia to run her magazine from there, but her kids were in school at the Lake. Back at Toledo, my goal was to make sure all three of my kids graduated from the same high school. This situation was similar. The last thing I wanted to do was make Missy's kids move to Columbia, change schools, and disrupt their lives. It was on the adults, Missy and I, to adjust, not the kids. So I'd travel back and forth between Columbia and the Lake. I'd use that drive from Columbia to make my recruiting calls.

In July 2014, Missy and I flew to New York City for a quick getaway. We made dinner plans and got a rooftop table at a restaurant in the city. A DJ was playing music for the dinner guests, but I pulled out my phone and ear buds to listen to another song. I popped one bud into my ear, handed Missy the other one. She looked at me a little confused. I then played the song "Marry Me" by Train. I pulled out a ring and asked her to be my wife. Thankfully, she said yes. Life was about to change, a lot.

Mizzou vs. Texas A&M

November 30, 2013

Columbia, Missouri

Beat Texas A&M in the regular-season finale and we clinch the SEC Eastern Division and book a trip to Atlanta for the SEC championship game.

Team Meeting,
Thursday, November 28, 3:30 PM

"I know how badly you want this. On Sunday, December 9, 2012, at last year's team banquet, this is the last thing I said to the players who would be returning for 2013. Before I sat down I told all of you, 'This was the most adversity I've experienced in 35 years of coaching. I'm very sorry that our season didn't finish the way we wanted to. It's hard to win. But the challenge to all the returning players and coaches is to compete next year for an SEC championship and to get right back to our winning ways.'

"Then we started the countdown. On January 23, we had our first workout in the Winning Edge program. There were 220 days until our first game when you walked in that locker room. On March 12, there were 173 days until our first game when the seniors decided on our 2013 slogan: 'Leave nothing, take everything.' On May 28, there were 96 days until our first game when summer ball began. You busted your ass as a football team. On July 31, there were 32 days until the season's first kickoff when we began fall camp. Our seniors established our goals and created our vision for the season. On August 31, we opened the season against Murray State. The rest is history.

"Finally, you should be very confident because you know how to care. You know how to grind. You believe in each other. You trust your teammates and coaches. We're going to play our best game of the 2013 season Saturday night at 6:45. About a month ago we started this November grind. We won three pressure-packed games. There is one game left in November. Texas A&M is in our way...and we have to take them out!"

Final: Missouri 28, Texas A&M 21

Henry Josey's 57-yard touchdown gallop was the difference as we celebrated our first SEC East championship. Our fans rushed the field to celebrate our fourth win over a ranked team and our fourth straight November victory.

9

2015: Season of Change

After our second straight division championship, I agreed to a new contract in March 2015 with an extension through 2021 that put my new salary in the top half of the SEC. We had been negotiating terms for months and had to work past some major changes the university wanted to make to my guaranteed salary and incentive clauses. We were able to work out the terms and announced the deal in April, just before my 63rd birthday.

That same week, I noticed a lump on the right side of my neck.

I've always been very health conscious. I think that probably has to do with my brother and sister. I had a swollen lymph node. Missy thought maybe it was the sign of an oncoming cold. I went to my doctor to get it checked out, and he thought I could wait a few weeks to see if the swelling went down.

If I ever sensed anything wrong with me, I usually went to Rex Sharp, our team trainer. I showed it to Rex and told him what the doctor said. I didn't have to say anything more. "You want me to get you an appointment," Rex said. Yes, I did.

So I scheduled a visit at Ellis Fischel Cancer Center in Columbia and saw Dr. Robert Zitsch. He said we could wait three weeks to see if the swelling went away or take a look right then and find out what was going on. I wanted to find out. So they ordered a biopsy and took a draw of fluid from the lump. They called me the next day and said I'd have to come back for the full pathology report. I asked if they saw anything that would indicate what this might be. They told me the draw initially showed signs of lymphoma.

Wow. Lymphoma.

Dr. Zitsch didn't give us any percentage of probability but laid it out there as a possibility.

The next day we went back to Ellis Fischel and he gave us the bad news. "You've got lymphoma," he said. It was a type of non-Hodgkin lymphoma.

Happy birthday, Coach. You've got cancer.

Missy was sitting next to me. I could sense her eyes watering up. I held on to her while we absorbed the doctor's words. "You mean I have cancer?" I asked.

It's such a helpless feeling. I had been so blessed my whole life to stay healthy. There was no explanation for how I got cancer, but that was the diagnosis. Going into the meeting I braced myself, knowing what he had already said over the phone. I knew this was a possibility. But when he said, "You've got cancer," the words slammed into me like a truck. That feeling lasted for about two weeks.

Initially, I told a few close friends and my kids, but I had to be careful because I didn't want many people in our football facility to know about the diagnosis. I told four people at Mizzou: my secretary, Ann Hatcher; my director of football operations, Dan Hopkins; my media relations director, Chad Moller; and my athletic director, Mack Rhoades. He had just been hired to replace Mike Alden, who retired after 17 years on the job. I wasn't ready to tell my coaching staff. My plan was to keep coaching, so they didn't need to worry about their futures being tied to mine.

When friends asked me what was wrong with my neck, I just said I had something small that had to be removed. Nothing serious.

I wanted to keep my cancer quiet because I didn't want it to affect our recruiting. I hoped coaches at other schools wouldn't use it against us—but you never know. Some just might. "Are you aware Coach Pinkel has cancer? Have you wondered if he might be there next year?" I didn't want our recruits to hear those things. Slowly, my diagnosis began to sink in. I'd catch myself driving around and looking at my face in the rearview mirror. "I've got cancer?" I'd say. "Are you kidding?"

I wanted to keep coaching as long as I could, but I didn't want to undergo any treatment locally at Ellis Fischel. It was important for me to keep this under wraps. I didn't want to be spotted getting treated in St. Louis or Kansas City either.

Wes Stricker, an allergist in Columbia and good friend, had done his residency at the Mayo Clinic in Rochester, Minnesota. We hadn't started discussing treatment options yet, but he recommended I get a second opinion before launching into treatment plans. He set me up with Dr. Thomas Habermann, a renowned lymphoma specialist at Mayo. Starting in May, we scheduled three visits to Mayo for monotherapy and they treated me with a drug called Rituximab. One of the nurses there told me they called the drug "Liquid Gold." Why? Because that's how well it worked. On each visit they injected me with the drug over five hours, with Missy always right by my side.

During my first visit to Mayo, while I was in the waiting room, another man waiting there must have recognized me. He looked at me and said, "M-I-Z..."

Oh, no. I was trying to do this as inconspicuously as possible. The last thing I wanted was for the public back in Missouri to find out I was getting cancer treatment in Minnesota. One of the nurses referred to me as "Coach Pinkel" while she was doing my blood work. Of course, I'm not listed as Coach on my paperwork—just Gary. She said to me, "Coach, my mom lives in Columbia." But I didn't have to worry about her telling anyone. Confidentiality is sacred to the staff there, which made me feel better.

I was fortunate to not have any strong reactions to the treatment. After my final treatment in June, I got up the next morning back home and worked out harder than I've ever worked out. I was trying to make myself healthier, even though I knew that didn't make any sense. I would live with lymphoma for the rest of my life. That night I paid the price. I jarred my system and gave myself cold sweats all night. I called Dr. Habermann and he set me straight. "Gary, it's fine to work out, but you can't overdo it." Otherwise, I felt fine physically.

So then we waited. In six months we'd find out if the treatment had worked.

I started to do a lot of soul-searching that spring and summer. I never felt sorry for myself. Those thoughts never crossed my mind for one reason: my sister. Kathy fought through her unfortunate challenges without ever feeling sorry for herself. I didn't allow myself to ask, "Why me?" Instead, I just prayed for the strength to fight this disease as best I could.

Just as my treatments ended in mid June, Missy and I got married in Naples, Florida, a week later on June 27. We were so blessed to have our entire family in Florida for the wedding along with close friends who made the long trip, most of whom didn't know about my cancer. Most importantly, all of our children and my grandchildren were part of the ceremony. We honeymooned in France and Monte Carlo. It was my first time in Europe, and it was amazing to be part of the culture and soak in all the history. We stayed at the Four Seasons Hotel George V, then flew to Nice and stayed at the Hôtel Hermitage in Monte-Carlo. We were going through customs in Paris and someone shouted, "Coach Pinkel!" It was a guy who played for me at Washington. Otherwise, I was undercover the whole time, which was kind of nice for a change. It was just an amazing experience that I treasured spending with my new bride and best friend.

That summer, thoughts began to bounce around in my mind. How much longer did I want to coach? When July came around I really started to wonder. How much longer can I live this lifestyle? Later in the fall, I knew I'd be getting an update on the drug treatment. They might give me a clean bill of health, or I might need to restart treatment. If I needed treatment, it would have to take place during the season. I started to ask myself a lot of questions. At the time I didn't discuss any of these thoughts with Missy. I wasn't ready for that.

By August, we were back on the practice field and the questions didn't go away. Is this how I wanted to spend my time for the next few years? I kept coming back to the same thought—*Am I doing the right thing?*

For the first time in my life I felt vulnerable. I always battled when things got tough. Any adversity that came up, I fought through it. You learn to persevere and get through the week so you can coach another week...and then another season, and another season. You overcome the hard times and keep coaching.

But this was different.

Football coaches aren't supposed to feel this vulnerability. This was certainly a new feeling for me.

I was getting ready for my 25th season as a head coach, but questions started to evolve in my mind. How did I want to spend my time? It became an internal battle, a personal discussion. Did I want to keep up with the grind of coaching and recruiting? At my age, with my family—a new family with Missy and her children—did I want to keep going? Those thoughts really consumed me through July and August, right up to the start of the season.

I kept coming back to time. For 40 years, my time and my family's time had revolved around my job and the college football calendar. Cancer made me realize my time wasn't endless. I continued to pray. Was I using what time I had left the right way? And it wasn't all about me either. I've got a new wife. I've got my kids and grandkids.

On top of the question of time was the matter of stress. I'm not sure there's a more stressful job than being the head coach of a major college football program. Yes, we're well-compensated, but the pressure to win and the pressure to recruit creates remarkable stress, not just for coaches but their families. You combine those pressures with the demanding lifestyle that keeps you away from home and constantly invested with work and it was enough to make me re-evaluate my future. I wasn't just 63 years old—I was 63 and diagnosed with cancer. I felt the need to de-stress my life so I could fight my cancer.

These thoughts and concerns were on my mind throughout the weeks leading up to the season. If I thought my job was stressful before, the 2015 season introduced me to another level of stress.

• • •

The adversity came fast. On the first series of our first game of the season against Southeast Missouri State, our starting running back Russell Hansbrough and starting center Evan Boehm both limped off the field with sprained ankles. They both struggled with their injuries all season. Maybe it was a sign of things to come. We were fortunate to beat Arkansas State and Connecticut the next two weeks, but it was obvious our offense was not nearly as explosive as we expected. In the offseason, Dave Steckel, our defensive coordinator, had left the staff to become the head coach at Missouri State. I replaced him with Barry Odom, one of our former assistants who had spent the last three years running the defense at the University of Memphis. Under Barry, our defense was again one of the best in the SEC. We just couldn't score. The UConn game embodied our team that season; we won 9–6.

A week later we went to Kentucky, and for the first time since joining the SEC, we lost to the Wildcats 21–13. By then, we had a quarterback problem. That would turn out to be the last game Maty Mauk played for Mizzou.

Maty was dealing with some personal problems away from football, and it reached the point that we had to address them. After the Kentucky game, we suspended him indefinitely. This was a new experience for me, having to suspend a starting quarterback. Never in my career did I have discipline problems with a starting quarterback. You can't afford to have your leader be someone who's not living up to the team standards. Maty did some great things for our team, and he made some changes in his life after he left our program, but that position is unlike any other on the team. Coach James taught me many years ago you can't have problems with your quarterback. None. Zero. The position is too vital.

On the field, Maty wasn't making progress like we usually saw with our quarterbacks. He did some great things as a redshirt freshman when he started four games in relief of James Franklin. As a sophomore in 2014, he helped lead us to 11 wins and made some progress as the full-time starter. But I kept wondering why he wasn't following the typical trajectory for a quarterback. Why isn't he taking off? That's when we realized he had some personal problems. I wish I had known sooner because we could have done more to help him earlier in his career. I was extremely disappointed in him for what he did to the team. It created distractions. He was the quarterback. He was expected to carry himself to a certain standard. That's the nature of the position. But I still cared about him. I still loved him. You still have to think of these players as your own kids.

Later in the year we reinstated Maty, and he apologized to the team. But he got into more trouble and spent the rest of the season on suspension. Eventually, he was dismissed from the program and transferred for his final season.

As for our team, we failed to overcome the problems we had at quarterback. Drew Lock, a true freshman, took over for Maty and made his first start at home against South Carolina. Drew is wonderfully talented and had some success early but ultimately struggled. He was put in a really difficult situation. Drew had never been a full-time football player like some quarterbacks. He was an outstanding high school basketball player in Lee's Summit, Missouri, so he didn't have the complete football background that would help him handle the transition as a freshman. He had to absorb a lot that season, and it wasn't necessarily fair for him because he wasn't ready for that role. Quarterback problems get magnified more than anything else that goes wrong, but that's the responsibility you have as coaches. And we didn't do enough. We were coming off two division championships, and sometimes after you experience success you have to coach harder to avoid complacency. No excuses. I should have done more.

We beat South Carolina in a game that I thought would help build Drew's confidence. But our offense never got going. We went three straight games without scoring a touchdown, each game ending in losses, to Florida, Georgia, and Vanderbilt, respectively. I wasn't accustomed to these kinds of problems on offense. Nothing we tried seemed to work.

. . .

Once the 2015 season started I was able to focus on football and not get too occupied with my health. I had been trained for decades how to manage the structure of the season. The great Coach James lesson—when things get tough, just focus on your job—applied to that season more than ever. We weren't winning like we expected, but that wasn't a season where I was facing a lot of outside scrutiny. My pressure came from within, from the secret that I was carrying about my health. But I knew how to focus. There wasn't enough free time during the season to mope around about cancer. I was too busy. At the time I would get on the phone with recruits, players who had committed to us, and I talked to them about their future. In a matter of weeks I'd have to tell them about my plans to retire. But not yet.

After our eighth game of the season we had a bye week. We were 4–4. In June, I had scheduled my checkup at Mayo for the Monday of that bye week, on October 26.

Around that time I met my daughter Erin for coffee one day and talked about these thoughts I was having. She could tell I was wavering. She knew how analytical I am with big decisions, but she could sense I wasn't committed to coaching much longer.

I didn't want to coach three more years then have my tests come back and have the doctors tell me I needed more intense treatment. Because then I would have looked back on those three years I spent coaching and wondered about all the time I could have spent with Missy and the kids. I would have regretted that decision every day for the rest of my life. I was concerned, too, about my body handling the stress of the lifestyle that I had experienced for the last 40 years in coaching.

I was ready to walk away.

I gave the decision a lot of thought and prayer. I talked a lot with Missy. There were many tears. But I made up my mind before we boarded the plane for Minnesota.

I once heard the Hall of Fame coach Bobby Bowden talk about the prospect of retiring. "Do I want to die on the practice fields or die on the beach?" he said. He wanted to die on the field. Not me. I want to die on a beach. I love coaching. I had a great run. I coached great players on great teams. But I never saw myself coaching forever.

The Monday of our bye week, October 26, we went to Mayo for my scheduled PET scan. It stands for positron emission tomography. They inject you with a dye that runs through your body and shows every spot where the cancer resides. On a computer screen Dr. Habermann showed me an image of my body before the drug treatment and another image from the PET scan. The Rituximab was working. My body had reacted well. That was great news. But it wasn't going to change my mind. I told myself before we went to Minnesota that my decision was never going to hinge on the results of that test. The scan wasn't going to impact my decision. This decision was about stress and time—not test results.

We hadn't been home 24 hours when I told Missy my final decision.

"I don't know how much time I have with you," I said. "I might have 20 years. I might have four. Do I want to spend those years being gone all the time coaching and recruiting?"

Missy understood, but she didn't want me to regret any sudden decisions. She challenged me. I was 10 wins away from 200 for my career. She wanted to make sure I was absolutely sure I was ready to quit coaching. She didn't want me to walk away and by February start kicking myself.

I had so much more life ahead of me, but I didn't want to spend those years on a field away from family.

Money was never a factor in my decision. Coaching was never about money for me. But I had just signed a new contract in the spring, and by retiring I would pass on a lot of guaranteed money. My new deal paid me more than $4 million a year—and I had six years left on my contract. I had my closest friends question me, "Are you sure you want to give up a $24 million contract?" My mind was made up. The money didn't matter.

On Wednesday of that week, October 28, I scheduled a meeting to talk to Mack Rhoades, our athletic director. I needed to tell him my decision. I had told him about my diagnosis back in the spring, but he was surprised by my latest decision. "Gary," he said, "since I've known you I know you're not the kind of person I can talk out of this. But are you sure you really want to do this? Is there anything I can say to make you stay?"

I went through all the reasons, none of which had anything to do with our record through eight games. We were 4–4 and I expected to get to a bowl game. We could have been 8–0. I had already made up my mind.

"The reason I'm telling you today and not three weeks from now is I want you to have some time to work on hiring my replacement," I said.

I didn't want to surprise him at the end of the season and push back the hiring process any longer. I didn't want to wait until the first of December, after the Arkansas game, and say, "Oh, by the way, I'm leaving." I couldn't do that to him. I had worked too hard at Missouri. We had worked too hard. He would need time to find the right candidate, and the next coach needed significant time to recruit based on the circumstances. I was concerned about the program having every opportunity to continue successfully.

I planned to tell my staff and the players either the Sunday before our final home game against Tennessee or the following Sunday, before our final game at Arkansas.

It was incredibly important that I tell my players and coaches on my terms.

That's why I told Mack I wanted to keep my plans confidential. Mack had to tell our chancellor, R. Bowen Loftin. The chancellor would probably have to tell the university system president. They would also have to tell the university board of curators. If Mack had to start looking for a new head coach, they needed to be aware that he was about to launch a search. Also, I hoped I could work out some kind of position with the university once I retired. I loved Mizzou and wanted fans and players to know I would still be on hand to help with fundraising and facilities. To begin those conversations, the curators had to be aware of my retirement plan. They were professionals. I could trust my decision would stay confidential. Or so I thought.

From that point, I just wanted to finish the season strong and get to a bowl game. It was important to me that we end the season the right way.

• • •

After our bye week we played Mississippi State at home on a Thursday night, November 5. Our offense finally scored some points, but our defense had an off night. Dak Prescott, Mississippi State's outstanding senior quarterback, was too much for us to stop. A year later he'd lead to the Dallas Cowboys to the NFL playoffs. We lost 31–13.

With that Thursday night game, we didn't play on Saturday. I was at our house at the Lake of the Ozarks in the evening watching a James Bond movie with Missy when I got a phone call. It was Ian Simon, a senior safety and co-captain on our team. He was with a group of teammates gathered on campus. I could tell this was not going to be a normal phone call, though it was not a normal time on our campus.

During the fall semester there were some racially charged incidents on campus that had sparked a protest by a group of African American students that called themselves Concerned Student 1950, which was a reference to the year Mizzou admitted its first black student. I was aware that there were some rallies on campus, but I didn't know many details. Once the season has started, our attention is focused on football. The protest group was upset about equality issues on campus and delivered a list of ideas and demands to Tim Wolfe, the university system president, one of which was his immediate removal from office. One of the group's leaders, a graduate student named Jonathan Butler, had started a hunger strike in connection with the list of demands.

Some of our African American players had learned about the protest group and spent some time with Jonathan Butler. They called me because they were scared. They were watching him go through this hunger strike and wanted to help him. Ian passed the phone around and let me talk to a few players. Charles Harris was there and Anthony Sherrils, too. They were all emotional. Some of them were crying. The players were on campus. More teammates joined them there. In their eyes, they had a kid starving and they wanted to save him.

It reached the point where they told me they were thinking about backing this guy by not playing our next game. We were scheduled to play Brigham Young in Kansas City at Arrowhead Stadium the following Saturday. The players wanted to announce a boycott of team activities—and they wanted to do it now so the situation would get resolved by the next day, Sunday, or Monday morning and they could play their game. They were genuinely afraid this guy was going to die. This was their sacrifice. They couldn't live with themselves if he died and they didn't do anything to help him.

That's a phone call I wasn't expecting.

I listened, but then I had to talk. "No, you guys can't do that," I said. "I get that you want to help this guy, but this isn't the solution." There was something else important I had to ask. "Are you sure you're not getting played here?" I was concerned they were being exploited because of their status on campus. But I knew these kids well. These weren't troublemakers. Ian and Charles were two leaders in our program. These kids didn't call me demanding that campus leaders address all these agenda items. When they talked to me, they were only concerned about the student eating and not dying. Was he really going to die in a matter of days if he didn't eat? Maybe not, but none of that mattered at the time to my players. This is what they believed.

My next impulse was to buy time. I had to talk to my boss, but I also needed the players to wait before they made any decision. I wanted to have a team meeting the next morning. It was important that we meet in person to discuss all of these issues and concerns. I told them, "Before you make any announcement, we have to meet tomorrow morning."

"We want to help this guy, Coach."

I had to talk to Mack Rhoades, and we agreed to talk later. I hung up with the players. I called Mack over and over again. He was in his office but had his phone turned off.

In all the years of being a head coach, there was a procedure I followed when we had a serious personnel problem on our team. I had to let the A.D. know what was happening and he'd immediately alert the chancellor and president. Then we'd discuss possible solutions and come up with a decision about how to handle the situation. My boss, the athletic director, made the final decision. I always followed the chain of command. This situation was no different.

Finally, I got in touch with Mack and told him what was happening. We were on the same page. Mack made his point clear. He didn't hesitate. He knew this was a tough call, but we had to address it right away.

"We have to support our players," Mack said. I don't know what I would have done if Mack said we couldn't support the players. I would like to think I would have still supported them, but it never reached that point.

Ian called me back and said they were going to announce a boycott.

"The reason why," he said, "is if this kid dies Tuesday, Coach, and we didn't do anything for him, then we couldn't live with ourselves. That's where we are with this."

We were hoping and praying this would get resolved in 48 hours. The players didn't want to miss the game. That's why they believed they had to act Saturday night and couldn't push off their decision. The sooner they acted, the sooner the hunger strike would end. That was their belief.

For me, it was a helpless feeling. But I loved my players. And I loved that they felt compassion and respect for others. I told them I still wanted to meet as a team the next morning.

After we spoke, the players took a photo of the group of 31 black players surrounding Jonathan Butler, some with their arms linked together. Several players along with the Legion of Black Collegians attached the photo to tweets with a message saying they would no longer participate in any football-related activities until President Wolfe resigned or was removed from office.

That's not what we talked about on the phone. That conversation was about the hunger strike. We would have to discuss it more the next day.

We met the next day at the team facility, almost all of our players and our staff along with Mack. We sat down in the dining hall for more than an hour. Mack asked the players to explain what led to the boycott. The players involved stood up and explained their reasons. They brought up some valid points about ways our campus could improve experiences for African American students. It was a positive, healthy dialogue. I told the players, "For us, this is about saving this kid. This isn't about agenda." Mack made our overall message very clear. He asked the players, "When is this over?" Charles Harris answered, "When he eats."

This boycott wasn't contingent on any demands placed on the university. The players agreed. The hunger strike was tied to the protest group's demands, so it's easy to make the connection that the boycott was tied to the agenda, but that's not what we talked about with the players. We were not making any political statements.

We didn't even discuss the president. We didn't discuss any other demands the protest group wanted the university to address. This was about ending the hunger strike and nothing else. Once we made that point clear, the rest of the players gave their support.

Our players signed multiple agreements in terms of compliance regulations, privacy rights, and other student-athlete provisions when they enrolled at Mizzou and joined the football program. They're not required to sign any agreement that says they're obligated to participate in team activities or they would risk losing their scholarship. If they had to sign a clause like that, maybe this would have unfolded differently. In the heat of the moment, we could have been able to say, "We can't do this, guys." During the meeting, one of the players asked if they were going to lose their scholarships over this. Mack said no. Right or wrong, there was no athletic department policy in place that could cost them their scholarship for boycotting games.

At the end of the meeting, the players who led the boycott wanted to take a team photograph to show we were united. Some people were resistant, but we took the photo. We posted the photo from my Twitter account along with the message, "The Mizzou Family stands as one. We are united. We are behind our players." But that wasn't all. The media assistant who handled my social media accounts was an outstanding staff member who did a remarkable job for us for several years, but a mistake was made this one time. The hashtag #ConcernedStudent1950 was added to the end of my tweet. Nobody noticed initially. Then everybody noticed. The hashtag connected me and our team to the protest group and its list of demands. That's exactly what we were trying to avoid. I didn't think it would have the impact it did, but I could understand how it would upset people. There was some symbolism there—unintended symbolism. We made the point as a team that we weren't invested in the agenda. But then the tweet came out and the protest group's name was right there on my account. We didn't make many mistakes like that publicly, but that was a big one. Once it was tweeted, there was nothing we could do. We could have deleted the tweet, but the damage was already done. I'm not sure what we could have done differently. Mack was extremely upset.

I anticipated negative reaction. Whenever you're dealing with issues of race, there's a very polarizing reaction. When things like this happen, it brings out the very best in people and often the very worst. A lot of the worst came climbing out of the rocks in swarms to criticize me and our program. But I knew we had to support our kids, who in their hearts believed they were doing the right thing.

We canceled our Sunday practice. For our players, Mondays were always an off day other than meetings and media obligations. If the issue on campus wasn't resolved by Tuesday, we thought our players might try to work out something and return to practice by Tuesday.

As a staff we discussed contingencies. How many players do we need to have a practice? How many would we need for a game? We tossed a lot of ideas back and forth without knowing when the boycott would end. If we don't practice Tuesday, when's the latest we can make a decision on the game? Can we play if we only practice on Wednesday and Thursday? The school would also be responsible for a costly buyout to BYU if we had to cancel the game.

On Monday morning, President Wolfe stepped down. The hunger strike ended and our players canceled the boycott.

We had to activate our plan. We didn't have meetings that Monday afternoon but instead had a press conference, just Mack and me, which was attended by the local media and outlets from around the country. National media showed up in droves that week and thought our campus was going to riot. Nothing like that ever happened. The satellite trucks and cable programs eventually went home.

On Tuesday, we held our regular 7:00 AM meeting and got back to work. We had to focus as best we could. Once we reached Tuesday, everything was completely back to normal. For a few days, at least.

If I had to do it all over again, I'm not sure what I could have done differently. The football staff and other Mizzou athletic programs would surely struggle recruiting African American players had this unfolded differently. At that point I had already decided to retire at the end of the season, but I still cared about the future of the program. I didn't want to see what we built left in ruins.

We were 4–5 when the players announced the boycott with three games to play. The season wasn't lost, but by our standards it was already a disappointing year. If we were 8–1 or 7–2 and in the hunt for the SEC East, would the players have still staged the boycott? I would like to think so. It wasn't about our team having a bad season. We still had chances to become bowl eligible.

• • •

On Tuesday morning I called Chad Moller, our media relations director, and told him I planned to step down at the end of the season. I needed to start telling the people within the program who were closest to me. It was already such a crazy week, and it was only Tuesday. "I hate to throw this on your plate, Chad," I told him. Initially we thought about making the announcement Sunday, November 15, leading up to our final home game. We also could have done it the following Sunday. Either way, Chad needed to start working on the press release. He was one of the few people I had told about my cancer diagnosis.

I just didn't want my decision to become a distraction. I'd tell the team on Sunday, the news would come out, and we'd settle down in time for our next game. I planned to tell the staff first, then call in my seniors and explain my diagnosis and my reasons for retiring. I would have needed their support to help me with the rest of the team.

On Friday afternoon I got back from lunch and my secretary, Ann, had some troubling news. Her husband had heard a report on the radio that I was going to retire because of illness. My plans had leaked. We thought it first surfaced on an online message board. I was distraught. We quickly huddled in my office. Chad was there, along with Bryan Maggard, our assistant AD. Missy arrived. So did my daughter Erin. Mack Rhoades was already on the way to Kansas City. We had to get him on the phone. Chad convinced me we couldn't ignore the leak. We had to act fast.

My mind was blown. This was the last thing I wanted to happen, especially after everything my team had been through that week. For someone who wants to control everything, suddenly everything was out of my control, and my players and staff would have to pay the price. We called a team meeting for 2:35 PM. We were scheduled to leave on busses to Kansas City right after the meeting.

I sat at my desk in tears. I was just an emotional wreck. "They don't deserve this," I kept saying. "They don't deserve this."

First, I wanted to tell my coaches, but we ran out of time for a staff meeting because we had to leave Columbia for Kansas City. I tell my staff everything, but my cancer diagnosis and my plans for the end of the season were things I had to keep from them. I wanted to tell them on my terms. Not like this. We had to gather the players for an unscheduled team meeting.

I jotted down a few notes on a legal pad because I knew I'd have trouble getting the words out. Chad helped along with my wife and daughter. Tears poured out as I wrote words then scratched them out and started over. I needed time to think. How do I say this? The team meeting lasted no more than five minutes. I told them about my cancer. I told them how I needed to prioritize my time. You could hear some loud gasps in the room. Then there was silence. We filed out of the room and climbed on busses to Kansas City.

I knew the staff was scared. When you worked for me, you had security in a remarkably insecure business. But I unhinged their world with this news. Some of those coaches had worked for me for more than 20 years. I felt a great sense of guilt for the uncertainties they were feeling. It was going to happen in a matter of weeks when I told them my plans, but it wasn't supposed to happen like this, not 24 hours before a game after the most turbulent week of our careers. We had the Maty Mauk issues already that year, which were unprecedented for our program at the quarterback position. Then we had the boycott. Now I was throwing cancer and retirement at them.

I had strong suspicions about the source of the leak and traced it back to the top of the university leadership. I had reason to believe someone in a position of power didn't approve of how I handled the boycott. Maybe they would take credit for pressuring me to step down, which is absurd. It had been 16 days since I told Mack my plans to retire after this season. And, I would have made a lot more money from my buyout had I been fired. By retiring, I left millions of dollars on the table. My athletic director made the final decision on how we would handle the boycott. He was my boss, and I agreed with him.

I never feared the news of my diagnosis and retirement plans would leak. This was confidential information about an employee's health. There were very few people who were privy to my health and my plans. To leak that information goes against the code and honor of being a university leader and showed a remarkable lack of character.

I was livid. I was hurt. But we had a game to play and a season to salvage. I had a job to do.

• • •

We had to refocus in a hurry. Heading into that game our staff had heard rumors about BYU players taunting opponents with racial slurs. I didn't know if that was true, but we heard it from other coaches who played BYU. We called the BYU head coach, Bronco Mendenhall, to make sure nothing like that would happen in our game. After everything that had just happened on our campus, we couldn't have anything like that in this game. We weren't accusing BYU of anything, but it's just what we were told. Thankfully, we didn't have any issues in the game. That would have been the last thing we needed.

Our whole world is focus. That's what you learn to do no matter the conditions in a game or the distractions outside the game. Our guys deserved better than this, but we still had to play the game.

We got off the bus at Arrowhead Stadium for our Friday night walk-through. The players went to the center of the field, gathered in a circle, held hands, and prayed. It was an emotional moment that my wife and I appreciated.

The odds were against us to beat BYU, but I had never gone into a game thinking we couldn't win. That night we found a way.

We fell behind but went ahead in the fourth quarter on a Drew Lock touchdown pass to J'Mon Moore. We hung on for a 20–16 victory. It was such an emotional night. I was just happy for our players and staff. While the ESPN crew tried to interview me on the field, my players surrounded me after the game and chanted my name. Hugs came from all directions. That was a surreal experience I will never forget.

Now we had to keep everyone focused. That was a challenge with two games left in the season. Reality set in after the big win. We were doing the right things, but it was hard for everyone to stay on task. The kids didn't know what was going to happen after the season. The staff had to be wondering what the future held. They had never been through something like this.

After the BYU game, we needed to win one of the next two against Tennessee or Arkansas to make a bowl game. But just looking at the team and talking to the guys around the facility, I realized the reality had set in. They all had questions that I couldn't answer. What does this mean for Mizzou's future? Will they hire someone from the staff? Will they keep the whole staff? They weren't focused on the games, and I didn't do enough to keep them focused. There were a lot of closed office doors around the building that week.

We lost our final home game, my final home game, to Tennessee 19–8. After the game, our two senior offensive linemen Evan Boehm and Connor McGovern carried me off the field. It was so nice of them to do that. It was for all the right reasons. But I was miserable. We lost the game and there was nothing to celebrate. But that was such a wonderful gesture from those guys on a night that was their final home game, too.

We ended the season at Arkansas. Sunday, Monday, and Tuesday of that week I could see it in the team's body language. They were so worried about the future. We didn't give ourselves a chance in the game, a 28–3 loss. It was a good time to play Missouri those last two weeks. Tennessee and Arkansas were good teams, too.

It was an awful way to finish a season. The BYU game was, "Win one for the Gipper," but that euphoria wore off the next week. The players didn't have time to process what happened before the BYU game. But they had plenty of time after the game. Things peaked emotionally against BYU, and from there they didn't have much left in the tank.

We had a staff meeting leading up to the Tennessee game and I looked around the room at my coaches. I told them, "You guys look like you want to kick my ass right now." They looked angry. Their lives were in total disarray, and that wasn't supposed to happen when you worked for me.

We ended the season 5–7, a year stuffed with more challenges and adversity than any season I had experienced as a head coach. It wasn't the way I wanted to end my career, but I was ready to step away.

I was aware people were angry that I had supported our players during the boycott. I didn't pay attention to the media coverage, but I always wanted to be aware of what my players were reading and hearing. In Jefferson City, state legislators threatened to cut funding for the university because of the boycott. Other legislators proposed a bill stripping college athletes of their scholarship if they protested social issues. Others made comments about me and Mack and disapproved of how we had handled the situation in the fall. One state senator threatened to launch an investigation into my actions and said I discredited the university. They were making judgments about what happened when they simply had no idea. That was disappointing. But I couldn't worry about those things. We had to do the right thing, and I believe we did. Sometimes things happen and you make tough decisions that some people don't like.

• • •

Back to the BYU game. I received a bunch of calls and texts from former players on the bus ride to Kansas City. They were all very touching.

We got to the hotel and I went to my room. Andy Hill, one of our assistant coaches, called me from the lobby to say someone was there to see me. I got in the elevator, the doors opened, and there was Jeremy Maclin, who was then playing for the Chiefs. He had a game in Denver that weekend, but he came to see me before leaving town. J-Mac wrapped his arms around me and said he loved me. It started to hit me what I was going to miss most about this job.

Mizzou vs. Arkansas

November 28, 2014

Columbia, Missouri

The start of the Mizzou-Arkansas rivalry game came with an extra incentive. If we win, we capture the SEC East and punch our ticket to Atlanta for the conference championship game. We played the game the Friday after Thanksgiving, so I delivered my Thursday speech on Wednesday.

Team Meeting
Wednesday, November 26, 3:30 PM

"We must understand that this is the beginning of the Arkansas SEC rivalry. This game will be played the last game every season on Friday or Saturday after Thanksgiving forever. There is a responsibility you and I have. You will have your personal record against Arkansas on your stay here as a Missouri Tiger. I hope you understand that responsibility.

"Seniors, I know this is not your last game, but it's your last game at the ZOU, the tradition you helped to continue and build. How can I thank you? Thank you for all that you have done for Mizzou football, the University of Missouri and the state of Missouri.

You should be proud of your efforts. I am proud of you. You've made your mark for greatness, examples of leadership and determination that will always be remembered in Mizzou history. Your sacrifice has been incredible. You have helped Mizzou persevere through the ups and downs of competition and have propelled us into one of the winningest programs in the country. Seniors, you will remember your experiences here at Mizzou, but none more than your last game in the ZOU!"

Final: Mizzou 21, Arkansas 14

A tight game broke Mizzou's way when Markus Golden corralled a fumble late and we clinched a second straight SEC East championship and another trip to Atlanta to play for the SEC championship.

10

Retirement: A New Direction

I QUICKLY REALIZED once I officially became a former college football coach that my life was missing two things: a plan and a desk.

I was so busy with the football season that I hadn't given much thought to my retirement. I didn't have a plan for what I should do next. Once reality set in that I was done coaching, there was nothing for me to do. And that was scary.

After the season, I signed a three-year contract to serve as an ambassador to the university. I would essentially be on call to help the athletic director and campus leaders for fundraising events and public relations. It was a less time-consuming role than coaching football, but it's something I wanted to fulfill, to help the department raise money so our program and the university could grow.

Otherwise, I had no plan and little purpose.

For 25 years I had an enormous responsibility to lead 127 players and all my staff in a job that never stopped. As a head coach, my calendar was filled with precise tasks every single day. I never had 30 minutes just to chill out in my office. Something was always happening.

Then, suddenly, I retired and I had...time, so much time. I wasn't sure what to do with it all. That was a very hollow feeling. I was used to solving problems and making decisions. I was used to constantly evaluating people and praising people to make sure the daily operations functioned the right way. Then, all of a sudden, my schedule was blank. I loved running the program, but now I wasn't running anything. For the first time in 25 years, I wasn't the boss. That was difficult to process.

For 40 years, and especially the last 25 as a head coach, my routine was predictable and my mind was focused on my job during the season. In the morning, I would meet my coffee group at Lakota for 10 minutes or so before heading to the office. These were friends who knew my demeanor. The closer we got to the season, my friends could tell my mind was elsewhere, locked in for those crucial months during the season. I was physically present, having a few chuckles over coffee with my friends, but my mind was on the season because every year, those months decided my future. That's why coaches wake up at three in the morning thinking about players and plays and schemes. As a young head coach at Toledo, I had to learn how to manage all those thoughts and concerns. By the time we got to game day, I was too wired. I had to chill out so I could just focus on my job. Being a head coach at this level is like running a major corporation but with more public scrutiny and less certainty from year to year. Not every coach in the business can handle that stress.

Once I retired, I learned quickly that it was important to have a plan every day before I went to bed at night. People who had retired warned me against waking up without knowing how to spend the day. I'm so detailed-oriented, but I had to learn how to use email and the calendar on my iPhone. That was one of the biggest adjustments for me, mastering all of the technology. I didn't have my secretary, Ann, or director of operations, Dan. Now I was a staff of one.

And my staff of one didn't have a desk. In my Columbia home, I have a den where I hung pictures from my Mizzou office, but there was something missing. I didn't have a desk. As a coach, my office in the team facility was my personal headquarters, my home base. I had a desk my whole life and had everything meticulously organized on my desk and inside my desk. I knew exactly where everything was located in every drawer. Things were placed precisely where I knew they would be. My desk gave me a sense of order and calm.

It sounds crazy, but when I retired and began spending more time at home, I really struggled without a desk. So I went and bought one, and I organized my new desk with everything I needed to recapture that sense of organization and calm. I bought filing cabinets, too. My home office needed that same structure I had in the football office. Once those were in place, I felt much better. I had an office. I had my desk. I could work on writing letters and other projects that would keep me busy. I dressed the room with photos and plaques that reminded me of the blessings I had enjoyed during my career.

I received so many thoughtful letters from fans when I announced my retirement. I was a little overwhelmed by the response. I received probably a dozen letters from Kansas fans wishing me well. Kansas fans! Among the countless letters was a handwritten note that came from Colorado, dated November 18, the week before we played Tennessee for my final home game. It was from the most famous Tennessee Vol of all time.

"Coach Pinkel, I just want you to know you and your health are in my thoughts," the letter began. It was from Peyton Manning, who I'd met a few years earlier at an NFL awards banquet where one of my former players was honored. Peyton, in the middle of Denver's stretch drive toward his second NFL championship season, took time out of his day to send me a handwritten letter. That was so touching.

Gradually, I found ways to occupy my time.

My first responsibility was to the university. I'm on call for any events or speaking engagements they need me to attend. I was thrilled that Mizzou decided to move forward on a new football team facility in the south end zone of Memorial Stadium, a concept that I initially urged our leadership to pursue. This is critical to continuing the program's growth.

For the first few months of retirement, I did some broadcast work with ESPN and SEC Network, which I really enjoyed. I thought about pursuing it further, but I wasn't ready to make that kind of time commitment. That would have defeated the purpose behind my plans for retiring, to de-stress my life and spend more time with family.

I gave leadership talks to corporations and student groups. I didn't play much golf my first year in retirement. Golf helped Don James once he retired from the University of Washington because he could compete on the course. He didn't want to lose that competitive edge that came with coaching, and golf became his outlet.

Missy and I attended some big NFL and college games as fans, something I could never do while still coaching. We watched Washington play Alabama in the Peach Bowl, my former school against an SEC team led by my former teammate and friend Nick Saban. We went to Tampa for the national championship game when Clemson beat Alabama. We visited some former players at their NFL games. We went to the Super Bowl, and we watched the Patriots pull off the biggest comeback in Super Bowl history—and got to see Lady Gaga's remarkable halftime show.

My favorite part about being retired is putting my grandchildren in my schedule. I now have the convenience of hopping in my Jeep to visit Kansas City to see my son Blake, his wife, Jenny, and their two kids, Bradley and Grant. And then I can swing through Sedalia and visit my son Geoff, his wife, Jen, and their three kids, Taylor, Kellan, and Chace. My daughter Erin, her husband, Josh, and their three daughters, Madison, Ella, and Gracy, live in Columbia, so I'm fortunate that I can see them all the time, too. And my dear sister Kathy and her husband, Greg, who relocated from Ohio to Columbia in 2015, live just three miles from my home after we lived in separate cities for more than 50 years. I enjoy catching up on old times with frequent lunch visits.

That's the great reward of being retired. There's so much more family time, something that wasn't always possible for a college coach.

Once I settled into retirement, I spent more time around Missy's two children, Mira and Jace, and began to realize just how seldom I was home when my kids were growing up, first in Seattle and then Toledo. It's been a huge eye-opener to see them go through stages of teenage life and experience things that I sometimes missed with my kids. College coaching is an amazing profession. Schools pay us a lot of money to coach the sport. But the calendar demands so much of our time and energy at the expense of being home with family.

My first year out of coaching I had a sort of awakening. I looked back on my calendar from a recent season and found it staggering. I was consumed by the job and the lifestyle. And that comes at a price.

That's what propelled me to pick up the phone about six months after I retired. I called all three kids and apologized for being gone so much. My kids were great, so understanding. All three of them had similar responses. "Dad, you always came home when you weren't coaching. You weren't out drinking beers with your buddies or out playing golf all the time."

All three children had great benefits from my career. For the most part we stayed in the same place for long periods of time. I didn't pack them up and make them move schools and find new friends every other year. My wife did a great job raising the children when I couldn't be there to help.

I always knew what was going on with the kids, but I missed a lot of the day-to-day activities from August to February. I was almost always gone on the weekends, especially during the fall. Recruiting dominated my schedule in December, January, and February. You've got 104 weekend days a year, and I probably had 20 of them free. That's it. I was fortunate that our kids understood the routine. Bowl games became our vacations, and our kids appreciated those trips. We went to 11 bowls in 12 years at Washington. We went to 10 bowls at Missouri. It was a great reward for all the coaches' families.

Erin, my oldest, was very competitive in sports, and I tried my best to make it to her games. I was always very protective of her. When she started dating, I was incredibly strict, especially with curfews. She was supposed to be home at 11, but one night she walked in at about 11:02. I lost my mind. Another time, a guy called the house and asked for Erin. She wasn't there, so he asked if she could call him back. I unloaded on the poor guy. "My daughter does not call boys back!" She talked to her mom and her mom told me I had to lighten up. I think I did, eventually. Erin attended Toledo when I was coaching there, and there came a time when I caught a player saying her name in front of me. Big mistake. It never happened again. No player ever had the guts to date her, much less mention her name in my presence. I was probably overly protective. She sometimes called me Mr. L, because I liked to lecture at home.

When we were in Toledo, Erin could sense when I was going through rough times. Her solution was she would print out motivational Bible verses and tape them to the stairs in our home. That way, when I'd come home from work, I'd see those messages as I climbed the stairs. She has such a big heart. Here I was working ridiculous hours away from home and spending almost all my time with other parents' kids—and it was Erin, my daughter, helping me get through the hard days.

I prayed often that she would find the right guy. Her husband, Josh, is the right guy. I used to kid around that he was on probation for 10 years.

Now, as adults, Erin and I can confide in each other. That's developed over time as she's grown up. We can talk about a lot of personal things. She trusts me and I trust her. For a father, it's the greatest feeling you can ever have, to develop that kind of relationship with your kids. It's so different now that she's got her own family and she's an adult. You want to become friends with your kids when they're adults. You help prepare them to become responsible people so that when you push them out the door into the real world they can deal with what's out there. You throw some tough love in there, too.

My oldest son, Geoff, played sports growing up in Seattle and Toledo and became a really good golfer. He graduated from Toledo and now lives in Sedalia, Missouri. He married Jen, his high school sweetheart. I'm so proud of him. He has obtained a position in a prestigious energy company, which has catapulted him into an executive level that requires great responsibility and trust. As his father, I could always count on Geoff for his insight. His savvy knowledge of college football would offer me a perspective with details that I might not otherwise have known.

Blake, my youngest, graduated from high school in Toledo after I took the Missouri job then enrolled at Mizzou and got his degree there. He's a great father and loving husband to Jenny, also a graduate of Missouri. Blake reminds me more and more of my father. Like my dad, Blake can fix most anything. He is a problem-solver and is persistent in all things he sets his mind to. Even though he has a somewhat calm demeanor, his aggressiveness in sales and business management has made him a professional in his field. Once I retired, I made an effort to talk to my boys more regularly on the phone and visit them as much as possible.

As a father, I can't be prouder of their accomplishments and the people they have become growing up in this crazy family life of coaching. They endured reading news articles that were critical of their dad and fans in the stands yelling obscenities. They also witnessed the love and commitment that fans displayed over the years. I want to believe it gave them a broad perspective of life. You want your kids to be responsible people, considerate and self-sustaining. You hope they develop that work ethic. All three kids have done just that.

When I see my boys and how they've grown up and become parents, I see myself in them. I'm just so proud of what my kids have accomplished. Now that I'm retired we can establish set holiday traditions that in the past were always dictated by football and my busy schedule.

Missy's children, Mira and Jace, have introduced me to a whole new world of activities that I get to watch and experience up close, from dance competitions to track meets, basketball games, and band concerts. When I decided to retire, Missy was afraid I wouldn't be ready for this new kind of active lifestyle with her and her children. But it's been a blessing as I've gotten adjusted to my new pace of life. One day, not long after I retired, we were watching one of Mira's dance recital rehearsals. I'm pretty sure the former football coach was the only male in the entire building. Life moves pretty fast, right?

• • •

Before I made my retirement plans public, I visited with Mack Rhoades a couple times to talk about Mizzou's next head coach. Barry Odom was my guy. Publicly, I didn't back any potential candidates for the job. Privately, I pushed hard for Barry, who had been my defensive coordinator. Mack didn't know much about Barry, but I told him he was the right guy for the job. There would be some transition, but even though we were coming off a tough season, he had been part of the program when we were winning at a high level. I was thrilled when he got the job. Nobody wants Barry to win more than me. I want to see him take the program that we built and guide it to another level and win the championships that we didn't.

The team's first game in 2016 was a strange day for me. The Tigers were playing at West Virginia. I was back home with a house full of company to watch the game. Missy joked that she wanted to get me a headset to wear while watching the game to avoid having withdrawal. That was a surreal experience to watch the Missouri Tigers on a sofa.

The next week, Mizzou's first home game, was remarkably uncomfortable for me. Before the game I met some Mizzou alumni and longtime supporters at their tailgate outside Memorial Stadium. I had never tailgated before. Missy called a bunch of my friends and had them all meet at one tailgate so I didn't have to wander around the parking lots. I felt uneasy by the scene. This wasn't what I was supposed to be doing hours before kickoff. I was able to kid my friends a little. "My life's on the line every Saturday and you guys are out here drinking and having a good time?" I kept thinking I was supposed to be on the field, not having a glass of wine while hanging out with my friends. I went around that day and visited with so many people around the stadium. I don't think I was ready for that. I adjusted my game day routine as the season went on and usually watched the game from a private suite. I had to sit down and lock into the game. I still watched it unfold like I was coaching. Later in the year, we went to road games at LSU and Florida, and those were fun experiences. I was able to relax more on the road.

But back to the 2016 home opener. It was September 10 against Eastern Michigan. Before the game I got to see something I'd never witnessed in 15 years at Memorial Stadium—the national anthem. The teams are always kept in the locker room during the pregame ritual. On this day, as the sun started to set over the west side of the stadium, I stood up and turned toward the flag waving in the wind, just as Mike Alden stood, too, alongside me. He put his arm around me as we looked over the field, the program's future in new hands.

• • •

So how do I want to be remembered? When you walk off the field for the last time and pack up your office of memories, you're supposed to think about your legacy, but that's not something that crossed my mind. I'm proud of what we did at Toledo and Missouri. Mizzou had two winning seasons in 17 years before I took over. Back then, you weren't supposed to win at Missouri. If by chance you did, it would be nearly impossible to sustain. We built a respected program that became nationally relevant over time.

We came to Missouri with a structured player development program that had its roots in the system I learned under Don James. Over time, we gave it a name: Mizzou Made. We defined Mizzou Made as our program's approach to developing student-athletes academically, athletically, and socially better than any program in the country. It was how our staff shaped the lives of our players, on and off the field. We had four core values in our program.

1. Honesty
2. Treat women with respect
3. No drugs
4. Respect cultural differences

On the field, becoming Mizzou Made started with work ethic and discipline. Pat Ivey, our esteemed strength and conditioning coach, set the tone for our principles in our summer workouts and offseason Winning Edge program, our five-week session of winter morning agility drills.

We taught our players how to compete and how to avoid distractions. We taught them the values of teamwork, commitment, and accountability. We worked in a no-excuses environment and developed players into self-starters.

Kenji Jackson, a safety on our team from 2008 to 2011, came up with the term Mizzou Made when he worked on our staff as a graduate assistant. It became our philosophy, our brand, our catch-all term for the way we developed players, students, and people in our program.

Our Mizzou Made program is how we developed the less-heralded prospects into productive playmakers, many of whom embraced our system and earned all-conference honors and reached the NFL. Many of these players arrived on campus with little fanfare but left as cornerstone players in our program. To name just a few: Sean Weatherspoon, Ziggy Hood, Danario Alexander, Andrew Gachkar, Justin Britt, Michael Sam, and, most recently, Charles Harris, a player who came to Mizzou with only one scholarship offer from a major conference school and left as a 2017 first-round draft choice by the Miami Dolphins. Overall, 37 players who came through our program during my time as head coach were chosen in the NFL draft, including eight in the first round.

I'm never comfortable talking about individual honors, but I was fortunate to earn some recognition over my career, getting inducted into the hall of fames at Kenmore High, Kent State, Toledo, the Mid-American Conference, and the state of Missouri Sports Hall of Fame. I was so touched and honored by all of those acknowledgments. I was also voted coach of the year in three different conferences: the MAC (1995), the Big 12 (2007), and the SEC (2014). Those awards were a reflection of the coaches around me. I left Toledo and Missouri as the career wins leader at both schools. Only two other coaches in major college football history also own the wins record at two schools: Bear Bryant (Kentucky, Alabama) and Steve Spurrier (Florida, South Carolina). For me, that kind of distinction is a statement of consistency—and also reflects that I didn't move around much, maybe to a fault.

I'm too much of a homebody to hop from job to job. I like my friends. I like going to the same gas station or same coffee shop day after day and saying hi to the staff there. At Washington, I got my hair cut at the same place for 12 years. I'd go into the same 7–Eleven all the time for a Big Gulp and I knew the guy behind the counter. It's the same in Columbia, Missouri. I like the familiarity. It's difficult for me to think about picking up and moving all the time—even more so when you're raising a family.

From the day we got to Missouri to the day I stepped down, the program went through radical changes. But it took five years to create the right kind of environment for the players. It was hard, but it was rewarding to see it develop and finally take hold. The first glimpse was beating Nebraska in 2003. That was the sign of good things to come. I knew it was going to be difficult. Most people in coaching knew that. Time will tell for the future at Mizzou, and I hope Barry can do it, too.

When I became a head coach, I always wanted to go to bowl games every year with no setback seasons. Maybe we could have kept the streak going had we stayed in the Big 12, but in the SEC, the margin for error is slimmer. In both 2012 and 2015, we needed to win just one more game to be bowl eligible. It was disappointing that I couldn't find a way to get that done both years. But what I'm proud of is after the 2002 season, we responded to our few difficult years and improved the following season and always reached a bowl game. That's a true test of how strong our program became. In 2003 we had a winning season. We struggled in 2004, but we came right back in 2005. In 2012, we didn't overcome our injuries and had another tough season. We recovered quickly and won the division the next two years. We always responded by staying loyal to the process. On top of all that, our graduation rate was consistently recognized for being among the best in our league. We did the right things for kids. We helped the university grow.

Obviously, I wished we could have won a conference championship. I coached in two conference championship games at Toledo and four at Missouri, two in the Big 12 and two in the SEC. I was so proud that we won enough games to be in position for those championships, but we still came up short. That's disappointing. I don't dwell on those losses, but as a competitor I wanted to win championships. Twice in seven years we were one win away from playing for the national championship. One win away. Whenever I hear someone say you can't win big at Missouri, I point to those seasons. Don't tell me you can't compete for a national championship at Mizzou. We were right there.

Our fans matured so much over the years, too. We started winning more in the Big 12 and our fans stopped rushing the field after big victories. That was okay at first, because fans hadn't experienced much winning. But over time they had to make the same adjustments our team made when we joined the Southeastern Conference. SEC fans are just different. There's more enthusiasm for football in the SEC and a deeper commitment at most schools. Our fans understood that and helped elevate Mizzou's program.

• • •

In 2000 it was Mike Alden who had the vision and faith to hire a head coach from the Mid-American Conference and give my staff a chance to build our program at Missouri. I warned Mike when he hired me that there was going to come a time when I needed his support, when there would be pressure to continue the Mizzou tradition of cycling through coaches when adversity strikes. Mike was incredibly loyal and supportive during our 14-year run working together. During my first year we lost at Colorado, and outside the locker room at Folsom Field I told him I wish we could just fast forward to a day when the program was fully installed and we were competing for championships. Fortunately, he was patient. He'd later say he was struck by my passion and commitment that day, but it was Mike's commitment to my plan, my process, that helped us reach 10 bowls in 14 years and win five division titles.

So many people work within a football program, but I owe special gratitude to Chad Moller, our media relations director, for the bulk of my time at Mizzou. Chad and I shared many late-night phone calls when we had to tackle difficult incidents, but he also played a vital role in promoting all the positive things that happened within our program. His loyalty is greatly appreciated. There are countless others who made our organization run at a high level. Rex Sharp, our trainer. Pat Smith, our team surgeon. Pat Ivey, our strength and conditioning coach. Dan Hopkins, our director of operations. Bryan Maggard, our assistant AD. Tami Chievous, our academic coordinator. Don Barnes, our equipment manager. Ann Hatcher, my secretary.

Most importantly, I had a great staff of assistant coaches working around me. It took a group of hard-working and loyal assistants to change the culture at Mizzou, to recruit players that met our standards, and to develop players who would win big games and compete for championships. A head coach can't run a program on his own, and I had lots of help from a diligent, sharp staff that stayed true to our core philosophies but also stayed on the cutting edge of change. We preached relentless evaluation, and when the team would have setbacks we always found ways to recover through hard work and innovation. I used to joke that maybe I wasn't mean enough when the media or fans asked about our unparalleled continuity, but truthfully, our loyalty went both ways. I valued their commitment to our program.

You can't have a team without players, and at Toledo and Missouri our success came down to players making plays. I'm so grateful to all the players who chose to play for me and my staff and the dedication they gave our program. I've named names in these pages, but it was difficult to single out a few when my 25 teams were built by thousands of young athletes who grew into men under our watch. We broke ground in many ways and experienced a lot of firsts together. All I ever wanted to accomplish was to impact their lives in a positive way, the same way Coach Fortner and Coach James had changed mine forever.

I've truly been blessed. MIZ!

Appendix

GARY PINKEL

1974–75: Kent State, graduate assistant

1976: Washington, graduate assistant

1977–78: Bowling Green, receivers coach

1979–83: Washington, receivers coach

1984–90: Washington, offensive coordinator/quarterbacks coach

1991–00: Toledo, head coach

2001–15: Missouri, head coach

RECORDS

Toledo: 73–37–3

Missouri: 118–73

Total: 191–110–3

CHAMPIONSHIPS

Mid-American Conference: 1995

MAC West: 1997, 1998, 2000

Big 12 North: 2007, 2008, 2010

SEC East: 2013, 2014

BOWL GAMES

Player
Tangerine Bowl: 1972

Assistant Coach
Sun Bowl: 1979, 1986

Rose Bowl: 1980, 1981, 1990

Aloha Bowl: 1982, 1983

Orange Bowl: 1984

Freedom Bowl: 1985, 1989

Independence Bowl: 1987

Head Coach: Toledo
Las Vegas: 1995

Head Coach: Missouri
Independence Bowl: 2003, 2005, 2011

Sun Bowl: 2006

Cotton Bowl: 2007, 2013

Alamo Bowl: 2008

Texas Bowl: 2009

Insight Bowl: 2010

Citrus Bowl: 2014

HEAD COACHING SEASONS

1991 Toledo: 5–5–1

1992 Toledo: 8–3

1993 Toledo: 4–7

1994 Toledo: 6–4–1

1995 Toledo: 11–0–1, MAC champion

1996 Toledo: 7–4

1997 Toledo: 9–3, MAC West champion

1998 Toledo: 7–5, MAC West champion

1999 Toledo: 6–5

2000 Toledo: 10–1, MAC West co-champion

2001 Missouri: 4–7

2002 Missouri: 5–7

2003 Missouri: 8–5

2004 Missouri: 5–6

2005 Missouri: 7–5

2006 Missouri: 8–5

2007 Missouri: 12–2, Big 12 North champion

2008 Missouri: 10–4, Big 12 North champion

2009 Missouri: 8–5

2010 Missouri: 10–3, Big 12 North co-champion

2011 Missouri: 8–5

2012 Missouri: 5–7

2013 Missouri: 12–2, SEC East champion

2014 Missouri: 11–3, SEC East champion

2015 Missouri: 5–7

COACHING HONORS

1995 Mid-American Conference Coach of the Year

2007 Big 12 Coach of the Year

2014 SEC Coach of the Year

HALL OF FAME HONORS

Kenmore High School Hall of Fame

Kent State University Athletics Hall of Fame

University of Toledo Athletics Hall of Fame

Mid-American Conference Hall of Fame

St. Louis Sports Hall of Fame 2014 Sportsman of the Year

Missouri Sports Hall of Fame

Acknowledgments

This process began with an interview at Lakota Coffee where Gary Pinkel shared his experience of watching Mizzou's first game of the 2016 season from the uncomfortable comfort of his couch at home. As he settled into retirement, we began to discuss working together to tell the story of his life and career. From there, the process took off quickly. I'd like to thank John Capinagro for believing in our idea and helping turn a concept into a project. We tell the story through Gary's eyes and voice, but I needed others to share memories and perspective and provide color and detail. Three women were especially valuable with that process: Kathy Grinch, Gary's sister; Erin Hendershott, Gary's daughter; and Missy Pinkel, Gary's wife. I can't thank them enough for their time and candor. Mike Alden and Chad Moller, two colleagues who worked closely with Gary at Mizzou, were incredibly generous with their insight. I'm indebted to my wife, Molly, twin boys, Jackson and Connor, and infant son, Will, for their patience and understanding with my chaotic sportswriter schedule, but they sacrificed even more during this project. I'm forever grateful for their love and inspiration.

Lastly, I was thrilled that Gary Pinkel agreed to let me help tell his story. Having covered his time at Mizzou for the Columbia *Daily Tribune* and the St. Louis *Post-Dispatch*, I was intimately familiar with the highlights of his career, but for this project we had to tackle other points along the way and travel roads he's rarely uncovered for others. Gary won more games than any head coach at Toledo and Missouri, but his story transcends wins and losses and championships. His 15 years at Mizzou touched on compelling issues and pivotal moments that shaped his career and legacy. I'm forever thankful to be able to tell those stories in these pages.

—*Dave Matter*

A FEW WEEKS AFTER I OFFICIALLY RETIRED, I had many people ask me if I was going to write a book.

I smiled and said, "I don't think so." Yet, Chad Moller, University of Missouri athletics media director, and I always joked about the journey of my career. "You can't make this stuff up. Save it for the book." Honestly though, I really never had intentions. I'm a football coach.

It got serious a few months later when a few writers and publishers began asking if I was interested. My first move, as it was in any career-related decisions, was to call my friend, attorney, and agent for the last 25 years, John Caponigro. John and I developed a great friendship over the years, and I am thankful for his wisdom and advice throughout my career. So now writing a book got serious.

Dave Matter, writer for the St. Louis *Post-Dispatch*, was the first person who came to mind. I've known Dave for many years as a part of the avid sports media crew that followed the Tigers throughout the years. I always admire his professionalism, talent, and integrity.

Dave and I would meet weekly for almost seven months. He took me down memory lane of game history as I shared my most personal thoughts and feelings. He met a side of me that wasn't the usual press conference disposition of Head Coach Gary Pinkel. My sincerest appreciation and heartfelt thanks goes out to him for taking on this challenge while spending enormous amounts of time dealing with an old football coach.

There have been so many people who have touched my life, career, and heart. From the greatest mentors, coaches, support staff, and bosses to the many special friends who stood with me on and off the field, and those who never failed to send me an encouraging message win or lose.

And finally, a special love and appreciation to my entire family. From my parents, sister, and brother to my family and extended family, your support and dedication has allowed me to be on the playing field for more than 57 years. I will forever be grateful. Your sacrifices and commitment to Team Pinkel has been instrumental in making my dream to coach football come true. Thank you for sharing and being a part of each and every day of My 100 Yard Journey. You are my blessings and forever my greatest W.

—*Gary Pinkel*